In the spring of 1962 the Chaminade senior class gathered
on the football field for this photograph.

Before middle age do not fear.
After middle age do not regret.

— Jim Turcott

Acclaim for
THE PERFECT SEASON:
The Untold Story of Chaminade High School's
First Undefeated and Untied Varsity Football Team
By Tom Kiley and Chuck Mansfield

Angela M. Biasi, widow of the team's outstanding halfback, Frank Biasi, has communicated, "I am delighted that you have chosen such an inspirational story of how faith, persistence, desire and brotherhood can make great things happen. I know Frank would be so pleased, as I am, knowing the past of those wonderfully spirited men and men of values from the early '60s."

Lucine Marous has emailed, "A group of septuagenarians reminiscing about a formative time in their lives together has become the foundation for this memoir. To read *The Perfect Season* is to be invited to vicariously share in a series of recollections that the contributors all agree molded their lives while at the same time adding a valued quality of life for each of them. The strength of the testimonials will make the reader glad to have had the opportunity to share a bit of their history."

According to Chaminade varsity football head coach **Kevin J. Dolan**, "I am very excited to get a chance to read *The Perfect Season*. Over the years I have written many letters of recommendation for students to the various military academies. In those letters I *crow* about Chaminade High School as a microcosm of the academy experience. Although we are not an academy, we *are* forged in the spirit of love and friendship through common struggles, achievements, picking each other up through failure, the outstanding role models and of course our common faith. Teams like this are another expression of the Chaminade journey; a perfect journey."

Dr. Dennis C. Golden, President Emeritus of Fontbonne University, former Marine Corps officer and All New England, All East and All American (Honorable Mention) College of the Holy Cross football co-captain, has texted, "This book is a sterling and fascinating must-read. A core commitment of Chaminade High School is to provide students with numerous educational, spiritual, leadership and holistic developmental opportunities. In 1961 their legendary head football coach, Mr. Joe Thomas, his staff and players committed themselves to actualizing their once-in-a-lifetime core value of becoming the first untied and undefeated team in Chaminade history. The fall of 2021 will mark the 60th anniversary of this quintessential achievement. Co-authors Tom Kiley and Chuck Mansfield have prepared the way for this grand celebration via publication of *The Perfect Season*."

Retired CEO **G. Michael Hostage** has written, "I spent a couple of very enjoyable hours with *The Perfect Season* this week and it's a winner if ever I saw one. I laughed or chuckled all the way through, and envy the warm relationships Mansfield and his teammates have maintained over the years. A long time ago I was asked to reminisce, for a book, about my own athletic experiences at Cornell and, because of that, can appreciate better than most the pure joy in reliving such a unique experience of one's youth. I highly recommend the book."

According to **Kevin R. Loughlin, M.D., M.B.A.,** "I mean this seriously, *The Perfect Season* would make a great movie. The story of young men coming of age in the sixties and how they continued the relationships throughout their lifetimes. Some producer should make the book into a screenplay. I think it would resonate with multiple constituencies. The list of movies like *Hoosiers*, *Hoop Dreams*, *Friday Night Lights*, just to name a few, were compelling narratives about young men and athletic teams. Don't dismiss my suggestion out of hand – it would make a great movie."

According to **Anthony Mercogliano**, "This book contains recollections of over half of the living 1961 Chaminade High School varsity team members. The one theme that is repeated in the great majority of these submissions is the respect, admiration and, may I say, love all had for our coaches, Joe Thomas and Charlie McGuckin. There is a common thread of the success of Chaminade football in the 1940s, 1950s and 1960s – Coach Joe Thomas. Most if not all of the men who succeeded him as head coach at Chaminade were either his student athletes or worked for him while he was head coach/athletic director at Chaminade. Other than his parents, Coach Thomas' formation as Catholic Christian man was due to his education and the example he received in high school and college staffed by the Marianist priests, brothers and lay teachers. I can honestly say the same about myself. When I first read Kevin Loughlin's comment on the first page of the book – that someone should write a screen play about this story I thought it was a bit of hyperbole – but after reading the entire book and thinking about it, believe it, he is right on target."

Retired CEO **James C. Norwood, Jr.** has emailed, "As a member of the Holy Cross High football team I remember the games we played against each other from freshman, junior varsity and varsity. I was among the first class to complete four consecutive years at Holy Cross. Our school was founded in 1955 and we had played just a couple of varsity seasons when we played Chaminade in 1961.

Chaminade was founded in 1930 so 16 to 0 wasn't so bad! For sure the Kiley-Mansfield team will be the real winners with this wonderful work."

Retired airline pilot, former real estate executive and once star Navy wide-receiver **Edward A. "Skip" Orr, Jr.** has written, "In *The Perfect Season* Chuck tells the story of how the bond among his teammates began and how it has grown over the years. This riveting story is told through the eyes and words of those who lived it – Tom Kiley, Chuck and their teammates. Their remembrances are interesting, humorous and emotional. Chuck is a great story-teller as evidenced in the variety of topics and scope of his previous books. I would highly recommend this book for not only sports fans but for anyone interested in a feel-good story."

Of the book former U.S. Air Force pilot, Vietnam War veteran and business executive **Valentine W. Riordan II** has commented, "What a great idea! I remember that season well. It was electric! What an accomplishment. I remember going back for our 50th [reunion] and your team picture still proudly displayed over the west entrance to the main floor lobby. When one of my classmates asked if any other team would have their team picture displayed in such a way, [Chaminade president] Brother [Thomas Cleary] pronounced, 'Yes, when they go undefeated and untied.' BOOM! Drop the mike!"

Former Marine Corps combat helicopter pilot and Vietnam War veteran **Bain D. Slack** has written, "A perfect season? It hardly ever, ever happens. It is one of the rarest achievements in sports or in any endeavor. I applaud Chuck Mansfield and Tom Kiley both for their being part of such a great team and for their great book recounting this fantastic story. Bravo, Flyers!!"

Retired CEO **Raymond P. Zambuto** has emailed, "Thanks for the opportunity to preview your book with Tom Kiley, *The Perfect Season*. My relationship to football has always been as an observer. I fondly remember those heady days of 1961 at Chaminade, which your manuscript brought back to life from the unique perspective of the men on the field. I found it hard to put down and was left wanting more when I was finished."

THE
PERFECT
SEASON

THE UNTOLD STORY
OF CHAMINADE
HIGH SCHOOL'S FIRST
UNDEFEATED AND
UNTIED VARSITY
FOOTBALL TEAM

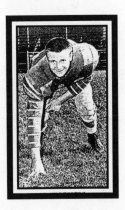

Tom Kiley and Chuck Mansfield
With Foreword by Dr. Kevin R. Loughlin

Library of Congress Control Number: 2021905963
ISBN: Hardcover   978-1-6641-6460-4
               Softcover   978-1-6641-6461-1
               eBook   978-1-6641-6459-8

Print information available on the last page.

Rev. date: 04/09/2021

To order additional copies of this book, contact:
Xlibris
844-714-8691
www.Xlibris.com
Orders@Xlibris.com
823533

CONTENTS

Foreword xiii

Preface xix

Other Writings by Tom Kiley xxv

Other Writings by Chuck Mansfield xxvii

Acknowledgements xxxi

Where the Hell Did Our Picture Go?
By Tom Kiley 1

The 1961 Chaminade Flyers Varsity Football Team Photograph
    and Roster 5

'61 Season Marks 30 Years of Chaminade Grid History
By Bob Knoll 8

Flyers Shoot for First Perfect Record
By George Vecsey 10

Well, You Could Look at the Record
By George Vecsey 14

Let's Look at the Record
By Chuck Mansfield 18

Which Team Was Mr. Thomas's Best?
By Chuck Mansfield 23

"A Football Team That Teems with Team."
By Earl P. Kirmser, Jr. 33

Secrets of Our Success
By Tom Kiley 35

Joe's Ace in the Hole
By Tom Kiley 43

"We Truly Were a Team."
By George Ackerson 47

Of Quarterbacks and Scout Teams
By Roderick T. Dwyer 50

Chute Strings
By Spunklo 53

Undefeated Flyer Eleven Look to Mount St. Michael
By Charles Raubicheck 55

The Defense Never Rests
By Chuck Mansfield 58

"For The Rest of Your Life, Nobody Can Ever Say that You Couldn't
    Do It."
By Albert M. Groh...66

Two Plays That Shook Our World..80

A Song of Triumph by "The Valve"
By Tom Kiley and Chuck Mansfield..96

Coach Joe Thomas: Exhortations to Excellence
By Chuck Mansfield 99

The Master Motivator
By Clifford F. Molloy..108

Chaminade Holds Memorial for Former Football Coach
By Geoffrey Walter... 111

Flyer Football: What Priority?
By Chuck Mansfield 116

A Tribute to Coach Charlie McGuckin
By Tom Kiley and Chuck Mansfield..119

In Praise of Charlie McGuckin
By Tom Kiley..122

"I Always Wanted to be Like Mr. McGuckin and Still Do."
By Carl T. LoGalbo...127

Teacher, Coach, Friend: Charlie McGuckin
By Cyril J. Rottkamp 130

A Letter of Condolences to the McGuckin Family
By Chuck Mansfield 133

"Talent Was Just the Beginning."
By Francis X. Biasi, Jr. 135

Frank Biasi: A Teammate Remembers
By Tom Kiley 137

A Letter of Condolences to Angela Biasi
By Chuck Mansfield 139

"We Could Play Ball."
By J. Michael Reisert 141

"Thanks, Tiny!"
By Kevin M. Walters 145

My Journey to an Undefeated and Untied Championship Season
By William E. Sellerberg 148

The Enigmatic Irishman: Ed Flynn
By Tom Kiley 156

My Close Encounter of the Coach Flynn Kind
By Chuck Mansfield 162

Thoughts and Memories: Our '61 Team
By Raymond F. Condon 166

"I Stood on the Sidelines Praying the *Memorare*"
By George C. Valva 174

"Dreams of Playing at Chaminade"
By Paul A. Lombardi 176

Happy Birthday, Mr. Thomas
By Chuck Mansfield 178

Thoughts of a Quarterback
By John T. Zimmermann 185

1961: Chaminade's First Perfect Football Season
By William J. McGovern 190

Chaminade Undefeated Varsity Football 1961
By Philip J. Pignataro 194

Chaminade High School: 1959-1963
By Cyril J. Rottkamp 197

Views From the Bench: A Junior Scout Player's Perspective
By Lawrence P. Grassini 199

Memories of a Chaminade Lineman
By Tom Kiley 202

Random Thoughts from an Offensive Right Tackle (#75)
By Richard W. Darby 206

"Singing Chaminade Songs"
By David J. Tuohy, Sr. 211

Flyer Gridmen Win 21 Positions on New York All Star Teams
By Charles Raubicheck 215

The Boys of Summer
By Tom Kiley 217

Sheer Talent or True Grit?
By Chuck Mansfield 220

A CHSFL Super Bowl: 1961 Versus 1962 Flyers
By Chuck Mansfield 225

Shoes Make the Man
By Tom Kiley 234

The Night I Met "The Boiler"
By Chuck Mansfield 238

Managers
By George E. Meng...241

The Perfect Season
By Anthony Mercogliano...243

The Year of Champions (1961-62)
By Edward J. Christie, Jr...249

A Troubling Dream: Chaminade vs. Holy Cross 1961
By Tom Kiley...255

Congratulations to Bruce Salerno!
By Chuck Mansfield 257

Chaminade Varsity Football Best Team Records.........................259

Chaminade Varsity Football Team Records By Decades
(1931-2019) 261

Chaminade Varsity Football All-Time Series Records 264

"Brother, You Owe Me!"
By Patricia Mansfield Phelan...265

My Mother Mary, Non-Football Fan
By Chuck Mansfield 267

Do You Remember?
By Chuck Mansfield 271

Defending Against Orr, Mansfield Intercepts Staubach and Scores!
By Chuck Mansfield 274

Criteria for the Chaminade Man Award
By Chuck Mansfield 279

The Chaminade Flyer Fight Song 281

"Life Takes Us to Many Places, but Love Always Brings Us Home
Again."
By Tom Kiley...283

Ode to Chaminade, Cornerstone and Classic
By Chuck Mansfield 287

In Memoriam...290

"We Played as One."
By Tom Kiley..292

Epilogue
By Tom Kiley..295

About the Authors..297

FOREWORD

PAIDEIA: A TRIBUTE TO THE
PERFECT SEASON
By Kevin R. Loughlin

Kevin is a 1967 Chaminade graduate who served as Student Council president and valedictorian. He received an A.B. in 1971 from Princeton University where he majored in biology. He was awarded an M.D. from New York Medical College in 1975, an honorary M.A. from Harvard University in 1999 and an M.B.A. from Boston University in 2000.

He is currently retired from active practice at Brigham and Women's Hospital where he served for 35 years. He is a faculty scholar at BWH and a professor emeritus *(urology) at Harvard Medical School. During his career he won the faculty teaching award on several occasions and was named to multiple "best doctor" lists.*

A member of the American Urological Association board of directors from 2011 to 2017, he received the AUA Distinguished Service Award in May 2019.

During his long career Kevin has authored over 230 papers and has been the author or editor of 13 books. He has designed several surgical instruments and holds two patents. According to Kevin, his education regarding leadership, like so many other things, started at Chaminade.

We are proud and grateful that Kevin, an extraordinarily ardent fan of our 1961 team, has agreed to write the following outstanding foreword to our book.

Thank you, Kevin.

It was a different time – a different era. When the class of 1962 began their senior year in September of 1961, one can argue that it was the end of the age of innocence for our nation. Earlier that year,

John F. Kennedy, the first Catholic president, took the oath of office and exhorted us, "Ask not what your country can do for you, ask what you can do for your country." That exhortation for sacrifice, for unselfishness, would serve as the underpinning for successful endeavors in life and for successful football teams.

It was the end of the age of innocence. Soon the country would witness assassinations, protests and a divisive war, but the friendships and values forged in the autumn of 1961 would endure and now continue almost six decades later. When I reflect on the team members whom it has been my privilege to know, I think their collective spirit is best captured by the words of F. Scott Fitzgerald in *This Side of Paradise*, "I don't want to repeat my innocence, I want the pleasure of losing it again."

Chaminade was then and continues to be a very special place. This bond that has persisted for almost sixty years was galvanized both in the classroom as well as on the athletic fields. The classical, arduous classroom education at Chaminade provided the foundation of teamwork and accountability that translated so well to the gridiron. For some, the Chaminade curriculum included Greek instruction. *Paideia* (Παιδεία) is the Greek word for perfection. The Greek quest for perfection was idealized in their sculptures of the male body and through athletics. It is the word that captures the quiddity of the 1961 Chaminade team.

It is important to put perfection of any type in the proper perspective. Army and Navy have long, enviable football traditions. Navy, since the inception of its football program in 1891, has never had a perfect season. Undefeated on several occasions, but perfection always marred by ties. Likewise, West Point since 1891 has had only three perfect seasons, 1944 and 1945 (the Blanchard and Davis teams) and 1949. Perfection has not returned to the banks of the Hudson for the past seventy-one years.

The football tradition at Chaminade has been similar – many outstanding teams, many championships, but perfect seasons – oh so elusive. The 1961 team achieved the first perfect Chaminade football season, only to be since duplicated by the 1977 and '78 teams with records of, respectively, 8-0-0 and 10-0-0, a Catholic High School Football League (CHSFL) record. Ninety years and only three perfect seasons and none for almost the past half century.

Coach Joe Thomas lives through this book and his spirit and values continue to permeate the hallways and fields of Chaminade. It is clear from the remembrances in this book that Coach Thomas was not just respected, he was beloved. To put his record in its proper context, recall that even Vince Lombardi during his nine years with the Green Bay Packers only compiled a .754 winning percentage. Coach Thomas during his twenty-two years as Chaminade's varsity football head coach, without a single football scholarship, achieved a winning percentage of .694.

When you drill down further into the perfect season of 1961, the accomplishment is even more impressive. In three of the eight games, the defensive effort was perfect – not a single point allowed. What made the 1961 team so special? Coach Thomas demurred when asked if you were his best team in terms of sheer athletic talent, but it was your sense of team, to share a common goal that made you *sui generis*. Jerry Kramer once said of Lombardi, "He made us better than we thought we could be." The same could be said of Coach Thomas and the 1961 team.

In September of 1962, the senior team members were off to college and again JFK issued a challenge to the country when he said at Rice University, "We choose to go to the moon and do the other things, not because they are easy, but because they are hard." His underlying message of the value of resolve and hard work had already been woven into the fabric of the team members on the chill autumn afternoons on the fields near Jericho Turnpike. You carried those values throughout your lives.

Paideia, perfection, that elusive goal, that is hard, not easy. The goal comes with the pursuit of excellence. The journey is, in many ways, more important than the destination. The relationships you formed together resulted in a perfect season. But the values of your team were far more durable than a single season, they served you all for a lifetime.

When I walked through those large doors on Jackson Avenue with my classmates in 1963, we were engulfed by the Chaminade tradition. The names of the honor roll students were the first thing you saw in the lobby. The team picture of the perfect season was the next thing you saw. The faculty told us to think big and aim high because much had been achieved by those who came before us. "The Year of Champions" was often recounted by the faculty and it referred not just to athletics, but to academics, behavior and character. You became our heroes, our avatars to be emulated. It is not hyperbole to state that every Chaminade class that has followed you has, in a palpable, tangible way, stood on your shoulders. Few have achieved your perfection, but your legacy of the pursuit of excellence continues to be the essence of the Chaminade tradition and remains to this day.

Res ipsa loquitur – the facts speak for themselves – serves as the exclamation point for the publication of this book. I used to tell surgical residents after a mistake or complication that, "Nobody goes through life undefeated." All of you, I am sure, have had some disappointments, some failures, some defeats. But the greater story is of your successes. "The Year of Champions" has evolved into the "Lives of Champions."

Let me close by recalling a quote by Ernest Hemingway who said, "As you get older it is harder to have heroes, but it is sort of necessary." On behalf of myself and the other members of the class of 1967, I want to tell you that you are still our heroes. This September, the next group of freshmen will walk through those doors on Jackson Avenue. They will see the names of the honor roll students on the wall. They will look to the left and see the team picture of the perfect 1961 season, they will look to the right and see the team pictures of the perfect 1977 and 1978 seasons. Their mission will be clear – to achieve the next "Year of Champions" before they graduate. They will inherit the special Chaminade tradition and you will become their heroes too. Your legacy endures, the tradition continues, you have inspired all of us to be better than we thought we could be.

The team of 1961 has completed its second undefeated season. It didn't last for just another eight games, it lasted a lifetime.

The key takeaway for me from the '61 season and one that stayed with me during my senior year at Chaminade and subsequent four years of football at The Citadel was winning is an "attitude." Anything less is an unacceptable performance! Your class and the '61 team epitomized that attitude and I learned it well.

— Ken Darby

PREFACE

The gratifying feeling that our duty has been done.

— Sir William Schwenck Gilbert
From *His Excellency: The
Played-Out Humorist [1894]*

Chaminade is an all-boys high school in Mineola, New York. It has been teaching traditional values to Catholic young men since 1930, and is generally regarded as the top Catholic high school on Long Island. It was founded and remains currently staffed by the Society of Mary (Marianist) teaching order of brothers and priests, as well as lay personnel.

The origin of this book is a 2018 telephone call from former New York Jets head coach Al Groh to his teammate Chuck Mansfield during which Al spoke passionately of the necessity for Chaminade's 1961 varsity football team to hold a reunion in 2021 to commemorate the sixtieth anniversary of the Flyers' first undefeated and untied season and its second consecutive CHSFL championship.

Within a short time it became clear that Al's instinct was not only correct but also widely shared among our teammates.

Subsequently, the following email was sent by Chuck to the team's manager, Bob Lewand '62, and all teammates for whom email addresses were then available:

"The autumn of 2021 will mark 60 years since we were all part of Chaminade's first undefeated and untied varsity football season and, once more, CHSFL champions. For many of us it was the thrill of a lifetime. Indeed, Al Groh showcases all together in his home one

Super Bowl Trophy, one AFC championship trophy and two CHSFL championship trophies.

"We are planning a reunion of our great team for a weekend in the fall of 2021 when a Chaminade varsity home game is scheduled. Early inquiries have yielded something of a consensus that such a reunion should be held on Long Island within easy striking distance of Chaminade. I have requested home game dates from the coaching staff but don't expect that the 2021 schedule will be set anytime soon. So I will just ask for your patience for the time being.

"When our team last gathered in the fall of 2011, we attended football practice on Friday afternoon, had an informal dinner on Friday evening and a more formal dinner on Saturday at a fine local restaurant. On Sunday some of us met for an outdoor pre-game brunch at Chaminade and then attended a football game in the early afternoon. Wives, of course, were included, as I presume would be the case in 2021.

"Since we have plenty of time to plan, I ask for your suggestions regarding a program of events/activities.

Fortes,

Chuck"

On March 10, 2020, Al emailed Chuck concerning when to have the reunion: "The key issue is to bring together the teammates who are forever bound together by their collaborative achievement. It was not Latin class, homeroom, or student assemblies that created these bonds, it was Flyers football and the shared common goal of striving to be our very best and winning CHSFL championships. Our team picture continues to hang in the hall; there is no picture of a geometry class! The year we do it is secondary. However, if there is no compelling reason to celebrate 59 years, 60 is what stands out, plus allowing max time for the very best in arrangements.

"In any case, it will be a special event to gather with our teammates to celebrate what we accomplished and how what we learned in doing that led to adult successes."

Al Spitzer, a sports columnist for the *Long Island Press* for more than forty years, wrote in the 1961 post-season that "Arguments probably will rage into the winter in an effort to determine how the current edition of the Chaminade High School football team compares with powerhouses of another era, but the rare achievement of an unbeaten and untied campaign is a distinction that belongs only to the 1961 squad."

Dr. Kevin Loughlin of the Chaminade class of 1967, who wrote the fine foreword to this book, gets credit for its title and suggesting that the book be written.

Chuck and Tom Kiley agreed to write and edit it on condition that all or at least several team members and others connected with that '61 season commit to writing down their thoughts and feelings about the team and its success. The intent was that this would not require a major commitment of time or effort. All that was requested was a paragraph, a page or a chapter. It was agreed that, if sufficient material were received, the book would be published.

One of the remarkable aspects of Kevin and his knowledge of and enthusiasm for our 1961 team is that, although he was only in the seventh grade at the time of our unprecedented championship, he has become perhaps the principal expert on and historian of our football team.

Deo gratias!

The foregoing is the story of how this reunion and this book came to be. With luck, each will prove a special memory in the lives of those who were part of *The Perfect Season.*

At least two players from our '61 title team – Paul Lombardi and I – actually still have dreams about playing Chaminade football that season.

— Chuck Mansfield

For our esteemed predecessors on Chaminade
Flyers' varsity football teams;
the forty-six young men who played
Chaminade varsity football in 1961;
their moderators, Brother Carmine Annunziata, S.M.,
Brother Raymond B. Gohring, S.M. and
Brother Peter A. Pontolillo, S.M.;
their managers, Ray Hess, Bob Lewand,
George Meng and Bob Pacifico;
their athletic director, Edward J. Flynn; and
their epic coaches, Joseph F. Thomas and Charles G. McGuckin.

Even old men were children once.

— Tom Kiley

OTHER WRITINGS BY TOM KILEY

A Soldier's Story

*"Life Takes Us to Many Places, But Love
Always Brings Us Home Again"*

Vietnam from a Distance

OTHER WRITINGS BY CHUCK MANSFIELD

Books

NO KIDS, NO MONEY AND A CHEVY: A
Politically Incorrect Memoir (2003)
BITS AND PIECES: Stories to Soothe the
Soul or Raise the Hackles (2017)
VIETNAM: Remembrances of a War (2018)
LEADERSHIP: In Action, Thought and Word (2019)

With Mary Ann Mansfield
KEVIN COURAGEOUS: A Journey of Faith, Hope and Love (2020)

Poems

Ode to Chaminade, Cornerstone and Classic
Ode to Joy, Also Known As Mame
Ode to the World of Light
Time Cannot Kill
Vietnam Valentine: Reflections on Leaving You and Coming Home

Articles, Essays, Letters and Thesis

A Comment on Al Gore
A Few Choice Words about Jimmy Breslin
A Footnote on the Simpson-Bowles Commission
A Letter to a Fellow Marine
A Letter to a Liberal
A Letter to a Misguided Classmate
A Letter to a Very Young Chaminade Alumnus
A Letter to Another Very Young Chaminade Alumnus
A Letter to My Holy Cross Classmates
A Letter to the Chief Justice

A Letter to the Not-So-Holy College of the Holy Cross
American Culture in Extremis
A Message to a Friend in Doubt
A Message to the Mother of a Fine Young Student-Athlete
An Approach to Evaluating Foreign Bank Credit Risk
Another Obama-Generated Disgrace
Another Vote for Export Trading Firms
A Would-be Cantor Who Can't
Biography of G. Michael Hostage
Captain Cancer
Connection: The Mansfields
Contemporary Commercial Bank Credit Policy:
Economic Rationale and Ramifications
Credit Policy and Risk Acceptability for
International Financial Institutions
Crisis and the Five Fs
Do You Know the Mustard Man?
Fail to the Chief
Fannie and Freddie's Chickens Come Home to Roost
Fidel in Hell: A Message for Pope Francis
First Lieutenant Ronald Winchester, USMC
Frank Teague, Marine
Giving the Best Its Due
How I Came to Know and Love the iPad
In Memory of John F. Donahue
It Wasn't Mere Flaw That Led to Tragedy
Jack Lenz – In Memoriam
Joe Altman: A Reflection
Legislators and Regulators Failed in 2007
Lessons from a Legend
Letters of Credit: Promises to Keep
Marines as "Extremists"
My Fellow Marines React to Trump Election Victory
Of Valor, Victory, Virtue and Vietnam
On Tom Brokaw and Vietnam Veterans

Please Go Home, Ms. Tierney
Roman Catholicism and Socialism
Stuprate Mesopotamiam
The Bane and the Pain of Bain D. Slack
The Function of Credit Analysis in a U.S. Commercial Bank
The GCGC
The Kaepernick Caper
The Rise, Fall and Rise (?) of a Middle-Aged Executive
Things That Paid Off for Me in My Life
Too Many Hats
Vietnam Memory: Acts of Good Faith
Vocations: Our Urgent Need
What Does the Tet Offensive Have to Teach Us 40 Years Later?
You People are Disgraceful

ACKNOWLEDGEMENTS

The authors' gratitude is owed and offered to the following, whose willingness to share their writings and/or otherwise help in the production of this work is deeply appreciated.

Peter Accardi
George Ackerson, B.S., M.B.A.
Bro. Carmine Annunziata, S.M.
Matthew Arnold
Bro. Stephen V. Balletta, S.M.
William J. Basel, B.S., M.A.
Angela M. Biasi
Francis X. Biasi, Jr.
Earl Blaik
Ryan Bonner
Book of Ecclesiastes
Stephen G. Boyd, B.S.
Mel Brooks
Frank Broyles
Paul "Bear" Bryant
Joseph Campbell
Dougal M. Casey, B.A., M.C. & R.P., J.D.
Major General Matthew P. Caulfield, USMC (Ret.)
Chaminade *Crimson and Gold* Yearbook
Maurice Chevalier

Edward J. Christie, Jr., B.S., C.P.A.
Bro. Thomas J. Cleary, S.M.
Ben Cohen
Raymond F. Condon, B.A., M.B.A.
Thomas G. Condon
Confucius
Meghan Cybriwsky
Kenneth M. Darby
Richard W. Darby, Esq.
Duffy Daugherty
Brian Dennehy
Paul Dietzel
Kevin J. Dolan
Roderick T. Dwyer, Esq.
Peter Eisenhauer, B.S.
Ralph Waldo Emerson
Robert Paul Evans, B.A., M.Ed.
Angelo Ferdinando
Louis E. Ferrari, B.S.
Edward J. Flynn
Jake Gaither
Captain A. Norman Gandia, USN (Ret.)
Sir William Schwenck Gilbert

Dennis C. Golden, Ed.D.
Gospel of John
Cary Grant
Lawrence P. Grassini, Esq.
Albert M. Groh, B.S.C.
Bro. Richard H. Hartz, S.M.
Minnie Louise Haskins
Woody Hayes
John Heisman
William Ernest Henley
King Henry VIII
Lou Holtz
Bob Hope
G. Michael Hostage
Ed Hurley
Deborah Kendric
Barbara Ramsey Kiley
Earl P. Kirmser, Jr., B.S., M.A.
Robert F. Knoll
Bro. Albert J. Kozar, S.M.
Bro. Robert Lahey, S.M.
Mark LaMonica
Frank Leahy
Carl T. LoGalbo

Paul A. Lombardi,
B.S., M.A. Ed.,
C.B.I.
Vince Lombardi
Look Magazine
Kevin R. Loughlin,
M.D., M.B.A., M.A.
Thomas Lynch
General Douglas
MacArthur, USA
(Ret.)
Bro. George
MacKenzie, S.M.
Colonel Lawrence P.
Magilligan, USMCR
(Ret.), B.A.
James J. Manion
Laura Mann
Charles F. Mansfield,
Sr.
Charles F. Mansfield
III, B.S., C.F.A.,
M.B.A.
Mary Ann Mansfield,
B.A., M.A.T.
David Maraniss
Lucine Marous
George P. McCabe, Jr.,
B.S., Ph.D.
John F. McFeely, B.S.
William J. McGovern,
B.S.B.A., M.B.A.
Mary McGuckin
George E. Meng, Esq.
Anthony Mercogliano
Elena Metzler
Clifford F. Molloy,
B.A.

Theresa Morra
Thurman Munson
Newsday Media Group
James C. Norwood, Jr.,
B.A.
Dallin H. Oaks
Edward A. Orr, Jr.,
B.S.
Dominic Papagno
Kevin R. Parente, B.S.,
M.S.
Pheidippides
Patricia Mansfield
Phelan
Lieutenant Colonel
Philip J. Pignataro,
USAF (Ret.)
Charles J. Raubicheck,
Esq.
J. Michael Reisert,
B.B.A.
Grantland Rice
Ronald A. Riescher,
B.S.
Lieutenant Colonel
Valentine W.
Riordan II, USAF
(Ret.)
Philip Rivers
Knute Rockne
Daniel M. Rooney
Cyril J. Rottkamp,
B.S., M.A., M.S.
Darrell Royal
Roger Rubin, *Newsday*
Bro. Patrick H.
Sarsfield, S.M
William E. Sellerberg

William Shakespeare
Bain D. Slack, B.A.
Andy Slawson
Al Spitzer
Spunklo
Sun Tzu
TARMAC
Francis J. Teague, Esq.
Tim Tebow
Joseph F. Thomas
Joseph F. Thomas, Jr.
Marlo Thomas
David J. Tuohy, Sr.,
B.B.A., M.B.A.
Jim Turcott
Michael F. Vaccaro, Jr.,
New York Post Lead
Sports Columnist
George C. Valva
Kenny Vance
General A.A. Vandegrift,
USMC (Ret.)
Peter Vanderberg
George Vecsey
Cory Vega
Dick Vermeil
Herschel Walker
Shea Walker
Geoffrey Walter
Kevin M. Walters,
B.A.
John E. Wehrum, Jr.,
Esq.
Mackenzie Wehrum
Corinna Vecsey
Wilson, Esq.
The Honorable
Woodrow Wilson

Father John A.
  Worthley, A.B.,
  M.A., Ph.D., M.Div.
www.almanac.com
www.cottonbowl.com
www.en.wikipedia.com
www.lawyers.
  findlaw.com
www.patch.com
www.pixabay.com
www.silive.com
www.tailgatesports-
  entertainment.com
Bowden Wyatt
Steve Young
Francis J. Zaino
Raymond Peter
  Zambuto
Paul Zimmerman
John T. Zimmermann,
  B.B.A., M.B.A.

WHERE THE HELL DID OUR PICTURE GO?

By Tom Kiley

Our strength is that we don't have any weaknesses.

— Frank Broyles
University of Arkansas

It is a bright, blustery, unseasonably warm December afternoon, a few days before Pearl Harbor Day. It is the biggest game played at Chaminade since the Saint Francis game in 1961. Saint William the Abbot, Seaford, is challenging perennial basketball power Saint Anne, Garden City. My twin granddaughters are playing for Saint William. My son is coaching, smartly donating precious time before that time is lost forever. I shrug off a familiar guilt I've felt many times before. Forget about it. For me there is excitement mixed with consternation this day.

But wait a minute, the gym doors are locked, keeping everyone waiting in the hallway. Ah ha! Only I know another way in, an ancient way, like an old Indian trail, via the back door I know so well. Perforce a parent drives me around back. I cannot walk around in my current condition. I take a quick glance at the old field and see us running from the locker room, down through the stands and a thousand cheering fans. Eight times in '61 my teammates and I have entered that familiar portal victorious. Of course, I let them enter first, then I follow at a safe distance.

I open a familiar door and veer to the left as if to enter our old locker room. I think I can hear laughter and the sound of pads and helmets and cleats falling on a cement floor. I try to enter but a voice from behind the old cage mocks me, "What the hell are you doing in here, old man?" As in a dream I try to form words to answer but

1

cannot, so instead I lean right and climb the old stairs that lead to a darkened, familiar gymnasium. I enter as I have done so many times before, perhaps looking for some long lost three-on-three basketball game. Why not, I think? You never leave the court until you are beaten.

Though it will soon be filled with the cries of younger competitors, the old gym is quiet now, nothing exacting. I walk around remembering and sometimes trying not to, but apparently it does not work that way. "Donnelly, you're supposed to be an all-star but you just let a fat man like Kiley steal the ball from you?" Often our coaches were not child psychologists. I walk around a little more but I cannot hear my own footsteps.

To my utter confusion this ancient space looks exactly as it did 55 years before, only newer! In the quiet darkness I hear prescient marching orders barked out by our gym teacher, "right face, left face, about face," and boot-camp-like drills on ropes and parallel bars. Marine-standard sit-ups and push-ups are standard indeed. Far away, I think I hear a steady drummer calling to war.

Some considerate hand just then turns on the lights. Yes, the stands are shinier now, bathed in thick coats of fresh stain and varnish, preserved for all eternity it appears. I remember well our '61 team practicing here when the weather would not cooperate and a game is near. I leap and intercept a bullet pass by Zim [Flyers' '61 and '62 championship quarterback John Zimmermann] and run off the floor holding the ball like a running back. I smile remembering those times. And yet life goes by so fast. How did I get here? It seems one day I woke up and I was old.

Remembering, finally, my true purpose, I open the gym doors from the inside and two teams of tweens pour in. As they enter I walk out into the hallway. Now, where the hell is that picture I was looking for?

I have not been back to Chaminade in quite a while and I want to know what happened to our '61 team picture that had hung in the main hall for so many years. I have been told or thought I had heard that our ancient photo was removed from its former place of honor to a much less conspicuous place in the building. Perhaps in the basement, I thought, next to the Rifle Team's photo. They were undefeated during their never to be forgotten '56 season. Ten wins, no losses, no ties, no wounds. That was a pretty good season.

I whirl around, look up and assume my old linebacker stance, except for the bending part, ready to be outraged. But no, to my happy surprise there it is, right where it always was! I smile broadly, happy to see it once again after so many years. My son comes back out into the hall with his daughters and starts showing them my '61 teammates, all in their youth and prime. A good deal of excitement ensues as a few players and their parents look up at our still undefeated squad. I notice a couple of parents looking sideways at me, thinking, at least as I thought, "How can this antique figure ever have been that vigorous?"

Then those bygone autumn struggles on fields of friendly strife, long forgotten by all but a few, come to mind once again. As feeling becomes stronger than thought, memories come flooding back, memories I will never forget as long as I live. I remember the sheer joy of a kid from Elmont getting a chance to play ball and "fight for dear ol' Chaminade." Then, sadly, I think of Bobby Bowman, who made "The Catch," and my old pal, Frank Biasi, flying around left end, both gone now, along with several others of our band of brothers, each of whom did all he could to help make our team the championship outfit we became. Smart lads they were, perhaps, to slip away betimes, leaving us to mourn and celebrate without them.

Then sentimentality is interrupted once and for all by the loud and victorious Abbots as they burst through the front doors and bound excitedly down the long stairway toward Jackson Avenue below, while my rebellious limbs head for the rail and slowly follow. How can these triumphant tweens know or care that, as they rush into the fading sunlight, victorious, they pass within a few feet of our '61 team photo, where pictured are all those players who gave every ounce of effort they had in order to ensure that our team might succeed. They cannot realize that those of us who remain and those of us who are gone were once young and active boys, cheered on by thousands, both home and away.

The day changes into a nice, soft winter night, the blustering wind quieted. I call out to my granddaughters, lest in their excitement they forget their Old Pa and leave him behind. But they cannot hear. I have something important to tell them, but how can they ever understand that of all losses the most irretrievable is time? It can never be redeemed. Even the young can do nothing about that.

Tom Kiley
#54

*Your '61 team was swift and sure and will
be rightfully honored forevermore.*

— Dennis C. Golden

THE 1961 CHAMINADE FLYERS VARSITY FOOTBALL TEAM PHOTOGRAPH AND ROSTER

The most talented players don't always make the best team, but the best T-E-A-M always wins.

— Al Groh

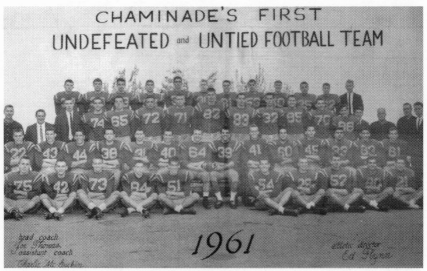

First row seated left to right: Rick Darby, George Ackerson, Jack Kernaghan, Pete Eisenhauer, Cliff Molloy, Tom Kiley, Dick Edgar, Bruce Salerno, Bill DeMeo and Kevin Walters. *Second row:* Guy Faillace, Rod Dwyer, Skip Rottkamp, Bob Gabriele, Frank Biasi, Ray Condon, Bill Sellerberg, Earl Kirmser, Dave Tuohy, George Valva, Tommy Liesegang, Carl LoGalbo, Chuck Mansfield and Kemp Hannon. *Third row:* Coach Joe Thomas, Manager George Meng, JV Manager Mike Brady, Paul Lombardi, Joe Nanna, Joe Mauro, Mike Reisert, Barry O'Connor, Skip Sullivan, Bob Swanson, Al Groh, Len Friedel, Paul Swanson, Manager Bob Pacifico, Athletic Director Ed Flynn, Coach Charlie McGuckin and Manager Ray Hess. *Fourth row:* Greg Hughes, Bobby Bowman, Phil Pignataro, Billy Keahon, Don McDonough, Tom Higgins, Bill McGovern, Ken Darby, John Zimmermann, John Pellegrini, Larry Grassini and Manager Bob Lewand. *Absent:* Mike Maher.

(Photograph courtesy of Peter Accardi and used with permission.)

Authors' note: The photograph above is the iconic one that has been hanging in the corridor of Chaminade's main school building for sixty years and that for which Tom Kiley successfully searched in the preceding chapter.

Player's Name, Year, Number and Position

George Ackerson '62	42	HB		Carl LoGalbo '62	33	FB
Francis Biasi '62	31	HB		Paul Lombardi '62	74	T
Robert Bowman '63	20	HB		Michael Maher '63	NA	HB
Raymond Condon '62	40	HB		Charles Mansfield '62	63	G
Kenneth Darby '63	53	G		Joseph Mauro '62	72	T
Richard Darby '62	75	T		Donald McDonough '63	36	E
William DeMeo '62	80	TE		William McGovern '63	81	E
Roderick Dwyer '62	43	QB		Clifford Molloy '62	51	G
Richard Edgar '63	29	G		Joseph Nanna '63	65	T
Peter Eisenhauer '63	84	E		Barry O'Connor '62	82	E
Guy Faillace '62	22	HB		John Pellegrini '63	35	T
Leonard Friedel '63	70	T		Philip Pignataro '63	23	LB
Robert Gabriele '63	38	T		Michael Reisert '62	71	T
Lawrence Grassini '63	62	G		Cyril Rottkamp '63	44	HB
Albert Groh '62	85	TE		Bruce Salerno '63	52	C
Kemp Hannon '63	61	C		William Sellerberg '62	64	G
Thomas Higgins '63	30	FB		William Sullivan '62	83	E
Gregory Hughes '63	37	G		Paul Swanson '64	86	HB
William Keahon '63	34	HB		Robert Swanson '64	32	E
John Kernaghan '62	73	DE		David Tuohy '62	41	HB
Thomas Kiley '62	54	LB		George Valva '62	60	G
Earl Kirmser '62	39	FB		Kevin Walters '62	21	DB
Thomas Liesegang '63	45	QB		John Zimmermann '63	50	QB

Authors' note: Players' jersey numbers shown on the roster above may not jibe with those worn during the season, and we do not fully know why. Accordingly, we have listed the numbers that they wore for the team photograph shown above. Nonetheless, Tom has since shared this recollection: "I now rather believe we changed jerseys mid-season owing to the rather decrepit condition of our game jerseys. Even on JT's limited budget, he probably felt it a necessity."

Or you got it or you ain't. We had it!

— Mel Brooks and Tom Kiley

'61 SEASON MARKS 30 YEARS OF CHAMINADE GRID HISTORY

By Bob Knoll

[The 1956] squad together with the '58 and '60 teams gave the Flyers their three latest crown teams... with more to come.

— Bob Knoll

Bob is a 1962 Chaminade alumnus, a member of Tom's Kingsmen homeroom and a fellow 1966 graduate with Tom and Chuck of the College of the Holy Cross.

His essay below was written and published in TARMAC, *Chaminade's student newspaper, in the fall of 1961. The last four words of his piece hint at yet another championship season for the Flyers.*

Thank you, Bob.

Football was brought to America by the early colonists and was played on village greens and school campuses, reaching the playing fields of the colleges in the early part of the nineteenth century. As in England, the game was strictly intramural, but it became exceedingly rough. For this reason football was banned at both Yale and Harvard at about the middle of the nineteenth century, but this proved only temporary.

The first American collegiate football game resembled soccer. This contest was played at New Brunswick, N.J. on November 6, 1869. Rutgers won by a score of 6-1, under its own rules, but Princeton evened the score a week later at Princeton, by winning 8-0 under Princeton rules.

Later the Rugby Code, used in England, was adopted with the exception that the American colleges gave the touchdown more importance than the English gave the try. The basic change was the introduction of the forward pass in 1906.

Chaminade saw some of its finest teams in the early thirties. The 1933 team distinguished itself by being the highest scoring team on Long Island. The captain that year, Bob Callaghan, highest individual scorer on the Island, led his team to its first victory, over Sewanhaka, setting a 6-2 record. The Flyers first won the Nassau Conference title in 1935, staging a surprise 1 point victory over Baldwin. These were the lean rough years when Chaminade's teams were fashioned by the legendary coach, Frank "Boiler" Burns. In 1938, Chaminade had its first game under the lights. That year Bill Johnson became the first Flyer to be named All-Scholastic in the *Long Island Daily Press*.

Consecutive years proved dismal for the Flyers mainly due to the war effort. In the late Forties, however, the Flyers revived and in 1954 the Silver Anniversary game was played to a capacity crowd of 8,000. The 1956 team was one of Chaminade's greatest due to the efforts of [Larry] Eisenhauer,* [Joe] Tucker, [Charlie] Vachris and [Ken] Wessels. That squad together with the '58 and '60 teams gave the Flyers their three latest crown teams . . . with more to come.

* *The late Larry Eisenhauer's younger brother Peter of the Chaminade class of 1963 is a member of the 1961 Flyers' first undefeated and untied varsity football team, and went on to play at the U.S. Naval Academy in Annapolis, Md.*

You guys are so out of shape, you should report to the sock hop!

— Coach Joe Thomas
after the '62 Flyers' 14-0
loss to St. Francis Prep
per Pete Eisenhauer

FLYERS SHOOT FOR FIRST PERFECT RECORD

By George Vecsey

Don't get me wrong; we have some football players here. But they're just not coming along. I don't know why.

— Coach Joe Thomas
in an interview with
George Vecsey

According to www.en.wikipedia.com, "George Spencer Vecsey (born July 4, 1939) is an American non-fiction author and sports columnist for The New York Times. *Vecsey is best known for his work in sports, but has co-written several autobiographies with non-sports figures. He is also the older brother of fellow sports journalist, columnist, and former NBATV and NBA on NBC color commentator Peter Vecsey." He began his extraordinary career at* Newsday *in 1961.*

The following article by Mr. Vecsey was published in Newsday *on November 11, 1961.*

Thank you, George.

Mineola – No Chaminade High School football team has won all its games in a season since the school opened in 1931 [*sic*]. This year's team can do it by beating Holy Cross at Flushing tomorrow. Does that make this year's team the best Chaminade ever produced?

"Maybe we're not," said co-captain Bill Sellerberg. "Mr. (Joe) Thomas hasn't said we are and maybe we aren't. But we're a good solid ball club. We try awfully hard."

Titans two: Coaches Joe Thomas (left) and Charlie McGuckin.

Authors' note: Of our great coaches Tom Condon '65 (younger brother of '61 teammate Ray Condon), who played halfback for the Flyers in 1963 and '64, has written: "My reward was having Coaches Thomas and McGuckin as an inspiration for my 48-year career in high school athletics as a football and track coach and Athletic Director. Their character, dedication and work ethic most certainly set the standard for me."

There is reason to believe that Thomas does not regard this as the best team he has coached in 14 seasons here. He hedged when asked which team was the best. He alludes to the 1955 team (won two, lost four, tied one): "I always thought that team had the best material I've had here." Then there was the 1951 team that won seven and tied one.

But if this is the best team Thomas has coached, Sellerberg doesn't expect to be told. "Mr. Thomas wouldn't tell us outright," he said. "That's his method. He's been bugging us all season to do better. That's why he's such a good coach. He doesn't baby us. He drives us to our limit. He makes us players. We're not players when we come here."

Thomas was not happy with his team early in the season. "It isn't measuring up to previous teams," he said. "Don't get me wrong; we have some football players here. But they're just not coming along. I don't know why."

The team did come along. It defeated Hicksville and St. John's Prep in non-league games and swept through its first five league games to win its second straight Metropolitan Catholic League championship. "There's a lot of pride on this team," Thomas said after a recent victory. "They've worked very hard. They've showed me a lot." Are they the best team he ever had? "I've had a lot of good teams. There was the 1955 team…"

But it's all right with the players. They're happy. "Mr. Thomas is a good coach," said Mike Reisert recently. "He pushes us hard in practice. We're in great shape because of him."

"Mr. Thomas is the best coach I ever had," Sellerberg said after Sunday's victory over Hayes, "although, I guess, he's the only coach I ever had…No, he is a good coach. I've seen other coaches. Mr. Thomas is the best."

Sellerberg is not a lineman in the tradition of Bernie Larkin, Larry Eisenhauer and Dick Kennedy. He weighs 169 pounds. The others weighed over 200 pounds. Reisert is 225 right now and still growing.

It would seem that Sellerberg might look for a small football college. But he isn't. "I want to go to Notre Dame," he said. "If I get in I'll go there. Sure, I'd go out for the team. Maybe I could put on weight. But I'd go to Notre Dame even if I couldn't play football there. It's a good school for engineering."

Reisert is considering some of the bigger schools. "I've always liked big things," he said, staring down at the six-foot, 190-pound reporter. Then he turned and bent his knees to look in the mirror while he brushed his crew cut into shape.

He drives us to our limit. He makes us players.
I've seen other coaches. Mr. Thomas is the best.

— Bill Sellerberg

WELL, YOU COULD LOOK
AT THE RECORD

By George Vecsey

It was Thomas' first undefeated, untied team in 14 years at the Mineola school. No team had been undefeated in the 17 years before Thomas. A coach might be expected to go overboard with praise for his undefeated team. Not Thomas.

— George Vecsey

The following piece by Mr. Vecsey was published in Newsday *under his All-Scholastic byline on November 16, 1961.*

His article "Flyers Shoot for First Perfect Record" appears previously.

Thanks again, George.

The season is over now. Joe Thomas, if he were wearing one, could rip off the mask and show his true feelings for his Chaminade team. But, then again. Maybe he is.

Thomas' football team went undefeated this year. It was Thomas' first undefeated, untied team in 14 years at the Mineola school. No team had been undefeated in the 17 years before Thomas. A coach might be expected to go overboard with praise for his undefeated team. Not Thomas.

"I said it before and I'll say it again," Thomas said. "I don't know if this is the best team I ever coached. I wouldn't say it is. It's all relative. These are good kids. They try hard. But are they the best team I ever had?

"Well, they certainly have the best record."

Thomas doesn't necessarily think he will remember this team any more than he remembers any other team. "Every group you graduate you remember," he said. "I can remember every team I ever had. I remember names, not years. There's the Charlie McGuckin era, for instance. Now Charlie's coaching here for seven years. But you see what I mean."

Just whose name will be attached to this "era" is not easily determined. There were so many outstanding players on this year's team that Thomas might be pressed to select an individual to remember above the others. His problem in selecting all-star teams will illustrate that.

"A newspaper sent me a ballot the other day. I couldn't name my own kids to the team. But I could say at the bottom which player I would name from my own team if I was allowed to. I was stuck. I didn't know what to do."

Movies of the league games were consulted so that Thomas could select an all-league team. If Thomas was honest to the way he felt after watching the movies he would have named an all-Chaminade line. He isn't saying whether he did or didn't. But he could have. The line of Bill DeMeo, Mike Reisert, Tom Kiley, Rick Darby, Charlie Mansfield, Bill Sellerberg and Al Groh was that outstanding. Then there was Earl Kirmser, the best fullback in the league, and Zimmermann, maybe the best quarterback.

"Not only that," Thomas reminded. "They played tremendously as a team. They were always working together. If one of them was down the others would pick him up. They were always out [on the practice field] at 2:40 every day, ready to work. Any coach on the Island would try to work his players as hard as I did. But these players wanted to work."

High School All American fullback, Flyer co-captain and Terzi
Award recipient Earl Kirmser closes in on another score.

The next project for Thomas will be the placement of his seniors in colleges. The problem is compounded by the fact that there are boys on Chaminade's bench who can play football at college. They may have attracted little attention as substitutes at Chaminade but they could help a small-college team somewhere. Thomas knows this and works hard for them. Then there are the stars.

Reisert is being chased by many of the good eastern football colleges. "He has potential," Thomas said. "He's 225 right now and he's gonna be 250 before he stops. He's tall enough to be 250. There's room for him to grow. He's strong and he's rough. Is he the best lineman I've ever had? Well, Reese wanted to find out. He went and watched our movies of Skip Clements five years ago. He didn't say anything when he came out. But he's a good boy and a good prospect."

Five Chaminade players have taken examinations for the service academies. They are Kiley, [Rick] Darby, Kevin Walters, Ray Condon and Rod Dwyer. Sellerberg, a good student, would like to study engineering at Notre Dame. But he has no illusions about a 170-pound guard at South Bend. One-hundred-and-seventy-pound engineering students there are. But 170-pound guards there aren't.

Thomas will be sad to see this group graduate, "but there's always the next year to think about." He likes working at Chaminade, finding the closeness of the students an asset. There are good points to coaching at a selective private school. The prospective players will be fairly bright. But Thomas could probably recite the names of good football players who couldn't qualify to enter Chaminade or who couldn't stick.

In his 14 years at Chaminade, Thomas has won 78 games, tied four and lost 28. It is one of the better records among Nassau coaches. Thomas looks back to the first three years when he was .500 "as things took a while to straighten out."

Maybe this wasn't his best team. Maybe he has had better material. But as he points out, "they certainly have the best record."

●

If winning isn't everything, why do they keep score?

— Vince Lombardi

●

LET'S LOOK AT THE RECORD

By Chuck Mansfield

The way that a bunch of teenagers come together as a team at such a formative time can be a powerful force that shapes the rest of their lives.

— Ben Cohen
The Wall Street Journal

Chaminade's 1961 varsity football team was the school's first to go undefeated and untied. Ten years earlier, the Flyers, under Coach Joe Thomas, went undefeated but tied Cardinal Hayes 0-0.

In a November 1961 *Newsday* column, which appears earlier herein, George Vecsey quoted Coach Thomas: "They played tremendously as a team. They were always out [on the practice field] at 2:40 every day, ready to work." Wrote Vecsey, "A coach might be expected to go overboard with praise for his undefeated team. Not Thomas."

"I said it before and I'll say it again. I don't know if this is the best team I ever coached. I wouldn't say it is. …But are they the best team I ever had? Well, they certainly have the best record."

Here is that record:

Chaminade 28 - Hicksville 7
Chaminade 14 - Archbishop Stepinac 6
Chaminade 6 - Saint Francis 0
Chaminade 27 - Saint John 6
Chaminade 28 - Iona 0
Chaminade 34 - Mount Saint Michael 6
Chaminade 12 - Cardinal Hayes 8
Chaminade 16 - Holy Cross 0

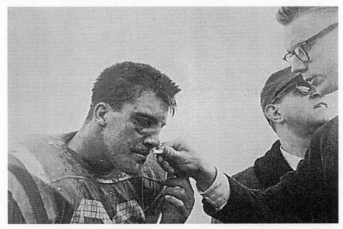

Manager Bob Lewand administers much-needed smelling salts to Flyer fullback Earl Kirmser during a well-deserved break on a hot day.

Here are several facts and statistics that provide additional perspective on our team's unprecedented championship season:

➤ We scored 165 points in eight games, an average of 20.6 per game.

➤ Only 33 points were scored against us, an average of 4.1 per game.

➤ The ratio of Flyer points scored to those of our opponents was 5:1.

➤ Only 25 points were scored against our defense, an average of 3.1 per game.

➤ The ratio of Flyer points scored to those scored against our defense was more than 6.6:1.

➤ We rushed for 1,925 yards in eight games or just over 240 per game.

➤ We scored 21 touchdowns or 2.6 per game, and 21 points after touchdown.

➤ We produced 102 first downs or nearly 13 per game.

➤ Assuming our time of possession was 30 minutes per game, we made a first down every 2.35 minutes.

➤ Our top scorer was Earl Kirmser with 66 points. Bill McGovern, George Ackerson and Dave Tuohy followed with 18, 12 and 12, respectively. These four players accounted for more than 65% of our offensive output.

➤ Three touchdowns were scored by linemen: Bill McGovern (two) and George Valva.

➤ Our largest margins of victory were 28 points (twice), 21 (twice) and 16.

➤ No team scored more than eight points against us. That team, Cardinal Hayes, gave us our closest game, which we won by only four points, 12-8.

➤ We shut out three of our eight opponents.

➤ We were never behind in the score in any of our eight games. In two, Saint Francis and Holy Cross, we were in scoreless ties at half time but emerged victorious with shutouts, 6-0 and 16-0, respectively.

While we do not have similar numbers for our 1960 CHSFL championship team, here is how the 1961 Flyers stacked up against Chaminade's 1958 and 1962 CHSFL champs:

	1958	1961	1962
Rushing yardage	1,828	1,925	1,563
Passing yardage	419	500	598
Total yardage	2,247	2,425	2,161
First downs	71	102	85

Accordingly, it is clear that the 1961 Flyers had all the offensive and defensive tools they needed to win the championship.

Pictured above, the Catholic High School Football League championship trophy was presented to Chaminade for the third consecutive year in 1962, then retired.

Of our perfect season Tom Kiley has recorded the following personal remembrances:

"I remember each of those eight games very well, but two incidents in particular still make me smile:

"I scored only one touchdown in my eight seasons of playing football, which included four at Chaminade and four for the College of the Holy Cross. My sole TD occurred during our JV year. George Valva blocked a punt in our opponent's end zone and I fell on it.

"In 1961 I blocked a quick kick/punt by Mount Saint Michael quarterback Mike Cunnion in their end zone, and I went to fall on it, but George got there first. No TD for me, but who cared? It broke open a close game.

"Against Cardinal Hayes on the last play of the game, with the result still in the balance, I intercepted a desperation pass on their 20 and ran for the goal line ... 20, 15, 10, 5 and ... as I crossed the five their halfback tripped me up from behind and I fell down with my nose on their one. Just then the final gun sounded. Nobody cared about the interception. I sheepishly handed the ball to the ref as we celebrated a close win. For some reason I was a little embarrassed. And I never came as close to scoring a TD again. Never."

Show class, have pride, and display character. If you do, winning takes care of itself.

— Bear Bryant
Alabama

WHICH TEAM WAS MR. THOMAS'S BEST?

By Chuck Mansfield

You play this game with your power. You do what you do best—and you do it again and again.

— Vince Lombardi

Newsday *sports columnist George Vecsey quotes Coach Thomas early in the preceding chapter accordingly: "I don't know if this is the best team I ever coached. I wouldn't say it is. It's all relative." He ends the chapter with these words: "Maybe this wasn't his best team. Maybe he has had better material. But as he points out, 'they certainly have the best record.'"*

Later in this work another prominent sports columnist, Al Spitzer, is quoted as follows: "Thomas doesn't think it is fair to go out on the limb to compare teams of different years." Several people I've spoken with have belatedly and posthumously complimented Mr. Thomas on his non-comparison policy. Still others, including members of the '61 team, have wondered about it considerably.

I have decided to perform some research mostly on what Mr. Spitzer once called Flyer "powerhouses of another era," and they are impressive. Readers may find themselves challenged to judge which team is best.

My findings about mostly earlier fine Thomas-era (1948-1969) Chaminade varsity football teams were instructive not only for those units' talent and performances but also because they provide insight into Coach Thomas's initial reticence to acknowledge which team was his best. Seven of the eight squads cited below – 1951, '53, '56,

'57, '58, '60, '61 and '62 – were champions, and had a combined record of 55-7-2 for a winning percentage of .859.

On the occasion of his retirement from Chaminade in 1962 Coach Ed Flynn, who succeeded Frank "Boiler" Burns as Flyer varsity football head coach until Coach Thomas took over, observed, "Chaminade has built up a football dynasty that will not be dethroned for years to come if ever." I am confident that the aforementioned eight teams constitute the dynasty to which Mr. Flynn referred.

Therefore let the record show that the members of the 1961 and 1962 squads played during a golden age of Chaminade football, a time never to be repeated.

— Tom Kiley

The 1951 Flyers were champions and Chaminade's first undefeated (8-0-1) varsity football team. Cardinal Hayes High School spoiled its otherwise perfect record by holding the Flyers to a 0-0 tie. This Flyer squad included great players such as All Met, All Nassau and Terzi Award recipient and end Pete Cassidy, co-captains All Met and All Nassau tackle Ollie DeJesu and fullback Roy McQuillan, quarterback Carl Ehmann, All Met halfback and MVP Jack Kraus and quarterback Jim Saville. Fiercely proud of his team's championship, my friend Jack has never forgiven the '61 team for besting '51's outstanding record.

The 1953 championship team had an impressive 7-1 record and boasted such great players as ends Paul Butler and Jack McFeely, Terzi Award recipient; guard Norm Gandia, later a Navy Captain, Top Gun fighter pilot, Vietnam combat veteran and a Blue Angel (lead solo no. 5), who passed away on March 20, 2021; tackle Paul Boguski; quarterback Jack Dalton; halfback Jed Dioguardi and others. Of his team's sole loss Norm writes: "Freeport was the culprit in the person of a little [halfback] by the name of Fred Waddlington [who] literally ran circles around us. Final score was 31-2! Ugh. Little Fred was aided by some meathead plays by us; the only excuse was it was the first game, night, and in their stadium. Coach T. was so pissed off that he had parents directing their car headlights on our CHS field while we ran wind sprints forever!"

Jack McFeely adds that it was a "sad night. I think the one second-guess of mine, is [that] our great man and coach, Joe Thomas, stayed with a 5-4 defense, which was not working. Our ends would drive toward their QB, who would lateral to the great Fred W., who would scoot around the outside defensive linebackers. It was time to switch to 6-2 defense and see if our ends could do a better job."

Parenthetically, wind sprints were the bane and the pain of every Thomas football team, and are referenced several times herein. On this topic, I love Tom Kiley's recollection: "We ran sprints on darkling autumn evenings in tandem, often on the big field – two young men of more or less equal speed – in relative quiet, the only sound that of equipment and the hard breathing of in-shape young men. Indeed, we were encouraged, exhorted by our coach to give our all every time. Via this crucible we got in shape and knew what our duty was."

I laugh when I think that we ran wind sprints together because we were just about the same speed, as I put it somewhere, "so nobody could dog it." I know we were not the fastest guys but we pretty much gave everything we had as did so many others. That was the secret and cornerstone of our team's success.

— Tom Kiley
in an email to
Rick Darby

In connection with getting in shape and knowing our duty, here is an excerpt from Vince Lombardi's letter to his Green Bay Packers after their 1962 NFL championship victory (16-7, a game I attended in frigid weather at Yankee Stadium) over the New York Giants, who had tried to intimidate the Pack physically but failed because "in the final analysis, we were mentally tougher than they were and that same mental toughness made them crack. Character is the perfectly disciplined will, and you are men of character." Coach Lombardi's words echo in these pages through our teammates Ray Condon, Rick Darby, Pete Eisenhauer, Larry Grassini, Al Groh, Tom Kiley, Bill McGovern, Cliff Molloy, Phil Pignataro, Mike Reisert, Skip Rottkamp, Bill Sellerberg, John Zimmermann and others. To be sure, Coaches Thomas and McGuckin are proud of and smiling at our teammates' acknowledgement and appreciation of their lessons well taught, well learned and well executed to produce a perfect season.

Permission granted to a guy who, like myself, knows what it's like to look down field at twilight and see Joe Thomas and Charlie McGuckin with their arms folded, knowing if you're dogging it in wind sprints.

— Jim Manion
in an email to
Chuck Mansfield

Although the 1954 Flyer varsity (5-2-0) was not a championship team, I will mention its guard, linebacker and Terzi and Lou Gehrig Award recipient, the late Bill Fowkes, who was an outstanding varsity player, even as a sophomore. Of him the aforementioned Norm Gandia has written, "he was GOOD and quiet. His plaudits were many and well deserved." Indeed, Bill may well have been the most highly acclaimed Chaminade varsity football player ever with All Star recognition from several NYC and two Long Island newspapers.

As my Chaminade 1959 assistant JV football coach and my 1960 JV baseball coach, he always kept in touch with Coach Thomas about whom he cared deeply. Indeed, after visiting Mr. Thomas at his Syosset home in his declining years, Bill was distressed at the condition of Coach's easy chair. He then called me and another Thomas-coached player, whose name escapes me, and together we bought Coach a fine state-of-the-art electric recliner, which he greatly enjoyed thereafter. Thank you, Bill.

Chaminade's outstanding 1956 title squad included such luminaries as tackle Gerry Clements, Terzi Award winner and Army football standout; end Larry Eisenhauer, a four-time Boston Patriot American Football League All-Star and Chaminade's only All Pro; quarterback Charlie Vachris and halfbacks Gene Laborne, Lou Ferrari and Ken Wessels. This team won the CHSFL championship with an overall 6-2 record and may have had the edge in pure talent over our team, but their record fell shy of the '61 Flyers'.

Despite their impressive 7-1 season record, the 1957 Flyers did *not* win the League title. Still, that team had outstanding players such as quarterback Bill Basel; guard and Terzi Award recipient Tim Gannon; halfback Joe Tucker and other greats, clearly another talent-laden unit. Their team lost to St. Francis (18-12) in the final game of the season before 8,000 people at Chaminade. Both teams had entered the game with 7-0 records. What a heartbreaker for our Flyers.

The 1958 team, CHSFL champs with another 7-1 record, boasted All Scholastic co-captains halfback Dave Johnston, Terzi Award winner, and guard Jim McLain, as well as All Scholastic and All Catholic tackle Paul Mayhew, quarterback Ron Riescher, halfback Geoff Tobey, halfback Lou Gerstner, later IBM CEO, and end Terry

Kosens, who made Little All America, was MVP at Hofstra University and went on to play for the Minnesota Vikings, the Philadelphia Eagles and the Hamilton Tiger Cats of the Canadian Football League.

Similarly, the 1960 Flyers, who won the League title with a 6-1-1 record, had star players such as halfback Steve Colucci and end Ed Finegan; Lou Gehrig Award recipient tackle Lou England; MVP tackle Pat Higgins, who went on to play for the College of the Holy Cross and the Quantico Marines; Most Outstanding Player quarterback Skip Orr, a star Navy wide receiver; co-captains halfback Greg Shorten and center Jack Wehrum, Terzi Award recipient; and All League fullback Earl Kirmser, the '61 unit's Terzi Award winner, who also went on to a fine career at the College of the Holy Cross where he served again as co-captain. It was an honor to have been their teammate.

Fullback Earl Kirmser charges toward oncoming tacklers.
Quarterback John Zimmermann leads the way.

The 1962 squad became the only varsity football team in Chaminade history to "threepeat," that is, to win a third consecutive CHSFL championship. Our teammates from the '61 title season compiled an excellent 7-1 record but, alas, St. Francis again played the spoiler, beating Chaminade 14-0, a "big revenge game, I'm sure," as quarterback and co-captain John Zimmermann remembers. Four of these Flyers' seven victories were shutouts, eclipsing the '61 squad's three.

Moreover, Coach McGuckin has recalled that there would have been a fourth consecutive championship in 1963 but the Flyers couldn't put together any substantial offense and lost a must-win game to Holy Cross late in that season by a field goal. Post season, Zimmy received the Terzi Award; center Bruce Salerno made High School All American and All League, was named Most Outstanding Player and was designated All-Long Island by *Newsday*; tackle Ken Darby was named MVP and later played at The Citadel where he earned All South Carolina and All Southern Conference honors; co-captain and All League defensive end Pete Eisenhauer went on to play at the Naval Academy; other outstanding performances were turned in by fullback Tom Higgins, halfback Skip Rottkamp and linebacker Phil Pignataro, who subsequently played football at the Air Force Academy Prep School, was an All-Rocky Mountain League lacrosse player at the Academy and played for the victorious North in the 1968 North-South All Star game. In several stellar performances, Tommy Liesegang took over at QB for the injured Zimmy and led the Flyers to a 4-1 record and a third consecutive League title.

When queried about achievements in life, I say, "God was good to me – He let me play football for Joe Thomas and Charlie McGuckin at Chaminade High School."

— Jim Manion

The 1962 football season may well have been the most extraordinary in Chaminade's history. To wit: The Flyers' JV team went 8-0 while the freshman squad had a 7-0 record with six shutouts. Thus, all three '62 Chaminade football teams compiled a 22-1 record, a .957 winning percentage, with 12 shutouts. The three

League titles that year were quite rightly called the "Triple Crown." Furthermore, these champions outscored their opponents 490-100. Talk about impressive!

Also impressive, only the 1961 Flyers had *two* High School All Americans: co-captain, fullback and Terzi Award winner Earl Kirmser and tackle Mike Reisert. Other outstanding players included co-captain, MVP and Lou Gehrig Award winner guard Bill Sellerberg and Most Outstanding Player linebacker Tom Kiley, who was later a starter and three-year letterman at the College of the Holy Cross, as well as their All League teammates, end Bill DeMeo and halfback Dave Tuohy.

This photo was taken at Earl Kirmser's home on April 8, 2000, to celebrate Al Groh's being named head coach of the New York Jets. Pictured above (standing) are Earl, Carl LoGalbo, Tom Kiley and Al. Seated are Chuck Mansfield (left) and Coach Thomas.

(Photograph courtesy of Chuck Mansfield and used with permission.)

The following paragraph, which I wrote prior to our team's 50-year reunion in 2011, provides an answer to Coach Thomas's perhaps rhetorical question that may have crossed the minds of some of us over the years, especially in light of George Vecsey's questions and Coach's answers in their November 1961 *Newsday* interview.

"Coach may have sounded a bit reluctant or diplomatically non-committal at that time but he was almost certainly thinking about his most talented team and believed – and rightly so – that we were not the most talented. However, on April 8, 2000, at a gathering at Earl's house to honor Al Groh on his ascendancy to the New York Jets' head coaching job, at which Carl LoGalbo, Tom Kiley, Mr. Thomas and I, as well as our wives (except the late Kay Thomas), were also present, Carl pressed Coach on the question of which was his best team. Happily, Coach smiled, acquiesced and told us that the '61 Flyers were his best. How gratifying."

The following table shows the offensive and defensive performances of several Thomas-era powerhouses.

Team Year	1958	1959	1960	1961	1962
Won-Lost-Tied record	7-1-0	6-2-0	6-1-1	8-0-0	7-1-0
Flyer points scored	211	171	141	165	136
Opponents' points scored	61	56	70	33	34
Ratio of Flyer points scored to opponents'	3.5:1	3.1:1	2:1	5:1	4:1
CHSFL Champions?	Yes	No	Yes	Yes	Yes

These five teams had a won-lost-tied record of 34-5-1 for a winning percentage of .850. They scored 824 points versus their opponents' 254, a ratio of 3.2:1. The '61 squad ranked only third of five in points scored but its defense was the strongest, with the '62 team's a close second, giving '61 the highest ratio of Flyer points scored to opponents', 5:1. Indeed, the average of points per game given up by the four non-'61 teams was 55.3, or 1.7 times the points the '61 team's opponents scored.

Footnote to a footnote: Only 25 points were scored against the '61 Flyer defense, or an average of 3.1 per game.

Far off I hear the rolling, roaring cheers.
They come to me from many yesterdays,
From record deeds that cross the fading years,
And light the landscape with their brilliant plays,
Great stars that knew their days in fame's bright sun.
I hear them tramping to oblivion.

— Grantland Rice
in his poem
The Long Road

"A FOOTBALL TEAM THAT TEEMS WITH TEAM."

By Earl P. Kirmser, Jr.

*The fullback position has grown to become a thankless position...
But one thing is for sure, we can all appreciate these men for what
they contributed to their teams.*

— Cory Vega
Tailgate Sports

*Earl was a three-year starter for Chaminade's varsity from 1959
to 1961. As a sophomore he started at linebacker. He was named All
League fullback in '60 and '61 and garnered many additional post-
season honors including High School All American. He is arguably
the greatest fullback in Flyer football history. After graduating from
Chaminade he started every game of his three-year varsity career
at the College of the Holy Cross and was named co-captain of its
1965 squad.*
Thank you, Earl.

T om and Chuck have written a book about a football team that
teems with team. Just the kind of book we need during a pandemic.
They take names, and give us a "You Are There" account.

Their play in the line, along with that of co-captain Bill Sellerberg,
George Valva, John Reisert and Al Groh (yes, that Al Groh) enabled
scoring jaunts by Frank Biasi, Dave "Sugarhips" Tuohy and me.
Among others. As baseball savant Casey Stengel once said: "Thanks,
I wouldn't have done it without the players."

And you are there!

Thanks, fellas.

Earl Kirmser #39
Fullback

Pictured above is Earl Kirmser (#38) at Alumni Stadium in Boston
in 1964 in the College of the Holy Cross starting line-up against
Boston College. Earl co-captained the Crusader squad in 1965.
His Flyer teammate Tom Kiley (#50) is also pictured.

(Photograph courtesy of Tom Kiley and used with permission.)

*After the snap, a hole opened to my left and I headed for it. I soon
saw our star fullback, Earl Kirmser, charging fast for the same
opening. I was pretty sure this was going to hurt – and it did. He
was low, so I got lower and I think my helmet collided with his knee.
Stars appeared everywhere and I remember looking up into Coach
McGuckin's face. When he quizzed me to assess my condition, I knew
my name but not much else.*

— Phil Pignataro

SECRETS OF OUR SUCCESS

By Tom Kiley

In my opinion, having a consistent system with intelligent, disciplined players was one of the secrets of our success.

— John Zimmermann

It has been a pleasure to read in these pages opinions about which team was Chaminade's best or most talented or greatest. Of course, it was my good fortune to be a member of a team, the '61 squad, that must be a part of any such discussion. If Bill Parcells was right that every team is "what your record says you are," then certainly the '61 squad is right up there with any in the history of Chaminade football.

For myself, I have never cared too much about the answers to those questions, but I do think Parcells had it about right. Rather, I have recently begun to consider two underlying reasons Chaminade had such tremendous football success for such a long period of time under the tutelage of Joe Thomas. Several reasons have been proposed herein and those writers have illuminated them in great and accurate detail. Nevertheless, I suggest here two reasons sometimes overlooked:

Our Raw Material: Mental and Physical Toughness

Coach Thomas, for most of his coaching career, had the good fortune to be provided with a steady supply of tough, smart kids to mold into the consistently hard-hitting, best-conditioned team in the League. Like an ancient alchemist, he added a coaching intensity, a love of precision and an unequaled ability to break the game down into its component parts, turning what we provided into football gold.

At Chaminade in those long ago days big-time talent was to be found only now and then among linemen and even less often among the skill positions. An exciting passing and receiving game was rarely if ever at the center of Coach Thomas's coaching success. For example, in '61 our ends recorded a grand total of one TD catch. Ours was a running game and a rush defense oriented team, first, last and always. On offense we were a lineman-dominated bunch, behind whom ran arguably the greatest fullback in Chaminade football history. Five yards and a cloud of dust sum it up pretty well. I suspect this was true of most Joe Thomas teams through the years.

Ron Riescher, quarterback of the championship '58 team, recently told me that he started every game with a 44 or 23 dive just to see what kind of day it was likely to be in the trenches. He knew that would be the key to victory. In '61 we opened the first and second half against Mount Saint Michael with the same 44 dive. Both resulted in long touchdown runs, which keyed an offensive explosion and victory against the previously undefeated Mounties.

Chaminade's 1958 championship quarterback Ron Riescher (left) launches a jump pass over a St. John Redmen defender before an overflow crowd at the Chaminade Bowl. The visitor's side is pictured above.

(Photograph courtesy of Tom Kiley and used with permission.)

Where this constant supply of toughness came from remains a bit of a mystery. Certainly, it was not geographical, as our players came from everywhere on Long Island. Tough South Shore towns like Elmont, Freeport and Hempstead supplied hard-nosed youths who joined equally tough young men from tonier climes like Garden City, Munsey Park and Sands Point. As for me, my grandfather had been a professional club fighter in Brooklyn and my father a Willoughby Settlement House boxing champ in his own right. He taught me very explicitly from an early age never to back up in the face of a bully or adversary. Perhaps a little of that had rubbed off on me by the time I met a ball carrier coming through the hole at Chaminade. In sentimental moments, I like to consider the degree of hostility our defensive front seven brought to bear against any back trying to make positive yardage against us. And should our opponent try to strike through the air, we blitzed, rushed and otherwise harassed their QB, generally nullifying his passing game.

I like my boys to be agile, mobile, and hostile.

— Jake Gaither
Florida A&M

Of course our guys had to be shaped over the course of four years by the extraordinary Coach Thomas and his coaching staff, as indeed we were. Curiously, he was a slight man, very neat and very precise. He had been a scholarship quarterback in college, but he would take the innate toughness we provided and mold it into a well-oiled hitting machine. Line play and tough linemen became his specialty. Perhaps we did not realize it back then, but after the ball was handed to an opposing back, we let loose with all the innate hostility that muscle memory can supply. For us this was the culmination of all our hours of sled work, tackling drills, Oklahomas and Chaminade Specials, fighting fatigue all the while. When an opposing back came through the hole in '61, he was likely to be met by a group of cranky, hostile athletes who were unwilling to give up even one positive play in ten. We just didn't like ball carriers very much that year and thought the best way to keep them out of our end zone was to keep them on their collective asses. This we did in a way and at a rate that must have alarmed our opponents. We played for keeps on every play, and the way four or five of us went to gang tackling an unlucky halfback was an indication of just how irritated we could become at the mere sight of an opposing ball carrier. As Tennessee Coach Bowden Wyatt once put it, "My advice to defensive players: Take the shortest route to the ball and arrive in a bad humor."

[Lombardi] provided the will and the way, pushing [his players] to levels of performance that he knew were possible for them but that he could never attain himself, closing the gap between the hugeness of his desire and the smallness of reality.

— David Maraniss in his book
*When Pride Still Mattered:
A Life of Vince Lombardi*

School Spirit/Respect for Those Who Came Before

A second and perhaps less obvious secret of Chaminade's football success was the admiration that underclassmen had for their varsity counterparts and the *esprit de corps* that developed in us Sunday after Sunday as we watched the varsity play. This in turn bred a comradeship and school spirit that have lasted for nearly 60 years. A desire and willingness to "fight the foe for dear ol' Chaminade" became our one desire, other than girls, of course! Moreover, we had great respect for those ballplayers who came before us, and we sought to emulate them. As a freshman guard in 1958, I can vividly remember watching our 160-lb. co-captain and All Scholastic guard, Jim McLain, block downfield on every play that did not directly involve him. I took mental note from the stands and tried to do the same thing in our freshman games, trying to upend an unsuspecting defensive back who was standing around the pile thinking the play was over before it was. Early on I learned that Chaminade played to the whistle on every play and we learned that from Coach Thomas and from what we saw from the stands as underclassmen on those splendid autumn Sunday afternoons when the Crimson and Gold took the field. We watched and absorbed what we saw and, when it was our turn, we did not forget.

My teammates in the fall of 1961 exuded desire and, because of that element, we couldn't lose.

— Frank Biasi

(Photograph courtesy of Tom Kiley and used with permission.)

On a Sunday morning in 1973, my wife Barbara and I and our three young children entered a breakfast place on Jericho Turnpike just west of Chaminade. As we walked in, none other than Jim McLain walked out. I had not seen him since 1959, and as far as I could remember, I had never spoken a word to him in my entire life. I hesitated and then, somewhat uncharacteristically, I ran after him. When I caught up, I breathlessly introduced myself, shook his hand and tried to tell him, briefly and awkwardly, just how much he had meant to me as a 14-year-old and how much I had admired him. He looked at me a little quizzically but thanked me. He had no idea who I was. I retreated somewhat sheepishly but was elated to have shaken the hand of one of my boyhood heroes.

Some of my teammates, including myself, began watching Chaminade football while we were still in grammar school. Some had older brothers who played ball or had friends or relatives who did. My cousin attended Saint Francis Prep – a high school I was seriously considering – and was a member of their marching band. One day in November 1957, he asked me if I wanted to go to a football game at Chaminade. He was going to march at halftime. He said it was an important game. Thus, quite fortuitously, I wandered into the most famous game in CHSFL history up to that time and maybe of all time. On that brisk autumn afternoon the 7-0 Flyers played 7-0 Saint Francis Prep in the last game of the season, a game that would decide the '57 League title. It was an amazing spectacle for a 13-year-old to behold. Thousands on both sides of the field roared on every play. Bands marched at halftime. During play a strange chant rose up from my side, the Francis side. "Beat the hicks, beat the hicks" was the refrain. That was a good one, I thought. Everyone on the visitors' side laughed loudly. Then from the home side of the field came a response led by strange young men dressed in white pants, white sweaters and white straw hats. "Beat the hoods good, beat the hoods good." That was even better, I had to admit.

Fans were everywhere that day, completely filling both stands. They ringed the entire field, stood along walkways and the track, and were lined up inside and outside the perimeter fences. Kids climbed trees in order to get a glimpse of a game that Coach Thomas later called "the game that put the CHSFL on the map." I became hooked on Chaminade that day, although I had not the slightest premonition that I could ever be a Flyer football player.

As a sophomore in 1959, I can still see in memory a thin-as-a-rail, begrimed junior center, Jack Wehrum, an eventual Terzi Award winner, covering a punt during a live scrimmage against Brooklyn Tech. He ran directly towards me standing on the track at the east end of the stadium. He looked right at me, eyes flashing, glowering balefully, looking for any punt returner unlucky enough to pick up the ball. I wondered then if I could ever match that kind of football intensity and ferocity, but by then I knew I was going to give it a try.

Of course, all of this clamor and cheering and intensity were part of our long vanished youth. Today, the back field is no more. Our seven- and two-man sleds and air dummies are gone. No longer can be heard the shouts of young men running over a pile of tires. Our great coaches are gone. Sadly, Jim McLain is gone too, as are so many former Chaminade football greats. All of this was once upon a time many years ago. Still, it is sweet to remember those days every now and then. Where did those days go? Who the hell knows? But back then we cared so much and tried so hard and admired so well those players who came before us and gave their all for Chaminade, as we did later on.

But, as we all now know, once upon a time never comes again.

Tom Kiley
Linebacker 1961

Selfless teamwork and collective pride...accumulate until they have made positive thinking and victory habitual.

— Vince Lombardi
in *When Pride Still Mattered:*
A Life of Vince Lombardi
by David Maraniss

JOE'S ACE IN THE HOLE

By Tom Kiley

Life gives us a limit as to how long we can play the game of football, or coach it for that matter, but it never puts a limit on our ability to remember with respect and affection coaches like Charles Gerard McGuckin and Joseph Francis Thomas.

— Tom Kiley

I have written elsewhere in these pages about the twin secrets of our 1961 team's success, i.e. the raw ingredients of toughness and intelligence that we supplied Coach Thomas. Here I will suggest that one of the secrets of Coach Thomas's success was the singular contribution of his able lieutenant, Charlie McGuckin. This was his ace in the hole. But let's begin at the beginning.

The CHSFL was founded in 1954. Now in existence for over 65 years, Chaminade has been crowned League champion 11 times, but only six times since 1968, the last year a Joe Thomas-coached team won the title. Long gone are the days when Chaminade and Saint Francis Prep dominated, trading titles in alternate years.

Today, the football landscape has changed utterly. A relative newcomer to the dance, Saint Anthony won an astounding 11 titles between 2002 and 2013, and at one point had defeated Chaminade 18 times in 20 opportunities. This fact is difficult for any late fifties or early sixties Flyer player to understand, much less digest.

Lately, the balance of power has shifted to the north where Westchester County Catholic Schools Stepinac and Cardinal Hayes have divided the last six League titles.

Coach Thomas (right) and his "Ace."

(Photograph courtesy of Tom Kiley and used with permission.)

Therefore let the record show that the members of the 1961 and 1962 squads played during a golden age of Chaminade football, a time never to be repeated. As we know, three straight League titles were won between 1960 and 1962, and another in 1958 when the senior members of our '61 squad were freshmen. Add to that mix Chaminade's championship in 1956 and you have an incredible five League titles in seven years, all under the extraordinary leadership of Joe Thomas. Had not Holy Cross kicked a winning field goal in the waning minutes of the 1963 title game, Coach Thomas would have had his fourth straight championship and sixth in eight years. That, by the way, is a four-year record (1960-1963) of 28-3-1. Then, with the loss to Holy Cross, this golden era abruptly ended. Shortly thereafter, and just as abruptly, Coach McGuckin's tenure at Chaminade also came to an end, when Holy Family High School made him an offer he could not refuse.

If we drill down on this remarkable era just a little, however, one will notice that in all but two of those Thomas-led championship seasons, he was ably assisted by Charlie McGuckin, quite a record of success by any standard. For about ten years, those two guys fit together like a fine watch tightly wound. However, after Coach Mac left Chaminade to become head football coach at Holy Family, Coach Thomas could manage only one more title (1968) before he retired as head coach in 1970.

As soon as Coach McGuckin arrived at Holy Family, he quickly built her from the ground up into a CHSFL football power, becoming a coaching legend in the process, winning two League titles and contending for several more, while collecting a Suffolk County Coach of the Year Award along the way.

Following his success at Holy Family, he served for several years as Suffolk County Section XI football chairman. Finally, and for many years thereafter, Charlie was still leading a football life as a well-regarded pro personnel scout for the New York Jets.

Therefore, it is fitting and proper altogether that we remember our late, beloved Coach McGuckin along with Coach Thomas during our 60th reunion weekend and pause for a moment to consider the impact Mr. McGuckin had on our '61 team and the critical contribution he made to our undefeated season, not to mention the indelible imprint he made on many of our players.

Life gives us a limit as to how long we can play the game of football, or coach it for that matter, but it never puts a limit on our ability to remember with respect and affection coaches like Charles Gerard McGuckin and Joseph Francis Thomas.

To sum it all up at 76 years of age: You can only grow up once and I am certain that every member of our championship squad is very happy that it happened at Chaminade High School, 60 years ago, playing football under the tutelage of coaches like Charlie McGuckin and Joe Thomas.

As long as we are alive, therefore, may the memories of our extraordinary coaches never die.

Tom Kiley
Linebacker
1961

It all adds up to a winning combination that many more talented than we have tried but have never accomplished.

— Ray Condon

"WE TRULY WERE A TEAM."

By George Ackerson

A true T-E-A-M is one that has built strong player-player and player-coach relationships. It was rigorous to be a four-year Chaminade football player. Only a total commitment to the entire process would work. Thus standards were set and not going to change for any individual.

— Al Groh

A 1966 Villanova University alumnus, George served four years as a Marine Corps officer and is a veteran of the Vietnam War. After his time in the Marines, he and his wife Doris received Master's Degrees from William and Mary. Following a successful career in the corporate business world, the Ackersons (three children in tow) moved to Plano, Tex., where they owned and operated their own business until his retirement in 2014. He and Doris have kept busy raising a special-needs grandson and travelling whenever possible. They spend their time between Plano, where the children are, and Marco Island, Fla., where they have a second home.

Thank you, George.

As I looked at our team picture, I realized that what made us a success was that we truly were a TEAM. We had our "stars" – Kirmser, Kiley, Sellerberg and Reisert – but if you look at the picture and think about how many of those played and made meaningful contributions to the season, it's truly amazing. Not trying to single out the stars or offend anyone but without this group of dedicated and hardworking individuals, we would not have become the TEAM we were. It was a wonderful experience to live through.

It would be difficult to overestimate the value of football as part of a soldier's training.

— President Woodrow Wilson,
former Wesleyan University
football coach, 1918

Authors' note: At least 19 or 41% of the 46 players on the 1961 Flyer football team served in the U.S. armed forces. Of them no fewer than nine are veterans of the Vietnam War. Their names and service branches follow:

Name	*Branch of Service*
George Ackerson	Marines/Vietnam
Frank Biasi	Air Force
Ken Darby	Army
Rick Darby	Army/Vietnam
Rod Dwyer	Army/Vietnam
Dick Edgar	Army
Pete Eisenhauer	Navy
Guy Faillace	Navy
Larry Grassini	Army
Al Groh	Army
Tom Liesegang	Navy
Chuck Mansfield	Marines/Vietnam
Bill McGovern	Navy
Cliff Molloy	Navy/Vietnam
Phil Pignataro	Air Force/Vietnam
Bill Sellerberg	Army/Vietnam
Bill Sullivan	Marines/Vietnam
Kevin Walters	Army/Vietnam
John Zimmermann	Army

Back in the day all Chaminade students studied a so called dead language. Today let's let Latin live a little in expressions familiar to all Americans.

E pluribus unum *means "Out of many, one" and is a traditional motto of the United States, appearing on the Great Seal along with* Annuit cœptis *(Latin for "He [God] has approved our undertakings."). It applies aptly to our 1961 Flyers varsity football team, which consisted of 46 eager young players, four dedicated managers, three committed moderators and two extraordinary coaches, who together produced alma mater's first undefeated and untied varsity football squad. And our undertakings have been widely approved.*

As all Flyers know, Fortes in unitate, *Latin for "Strength in unity," is Chaminade's motto. And as a group purposefully united and goal-oriented, our team was one, strong and invincible for ours was a perfect season.*

— Chuck Mansfield

OF QUARTERBACKS AND
SCOUT TEAMS

By Roderick T. Dwyer

Truly 1961 was a wonderful season! It was hard work but I wouldn't change it or trade it for anything.

— Rod Dwyer

A lifelong friend and an attorney, Rod is a 1962 Chaminade classmate and a fellow member of our first undefeated and untied varsity football team. He also played varsity baseball at Chaminade.

After Chaminade, Rod earned a B.A. in History and an Army lieutenant's commission at Boston College and an M.A. in American History at Binghamton. Following infantry and intelligence training, he served three years on active duty, including tours in Germany and South Vietnam (advisor in Phoenix program). He earned his J.D. from Catholic University in 1977.

Rod and his wife Shari married in 1974. They have two sons and three young granddaughters. For 35 years Rod and Shari lived in Silver Spring, Md. He retired as Deputy General Counsel, National Mining Association. For the last 20 years, Rod has umpired, principally for high-school fast-pitch softball. Rod and Shari now live in Tappahannock, Va.

His fine essay below provides interesting background to the start of our extraordinary 1961 season.

Many thanks, Rod.

At the end of the 1960 football season, it looked like junior Dan Connors was a lock to replace the graduating Skip Orr, later star wide receiver for quarterback and Pro Football Hall of Famer Roger Staubach at the Naval Academy, as the next starting quarterback.

Then Dan left Chaminade, leaving the starting QB position wide open. When practice started in August '61, there were four QB candidates – senior Kevin Walters, juniors Johnny Zimmermann and Tommy Liesegang and yours truly. Kevin quickly nailed down a starting safety slot. Zimmy and Tommy both had a lot of play-calling experience, but for a while at the start I was working with the first team.

It soon became clear that I "had a long way to go and a short time to get there." A change in QBs was needed but how and when was the change going to be made? That's when senior right halfback Dave Tuohy stepped forward—literally. During a pre-season scrimmage against Freeport, I dropped back to pass. Dave crossed in front of me to block, planted his foot squarely on my right foot and pivoted, cleanly removing my big toenail. The doc gave me a tetanus shot and forbade me to take part in any contact for at least two weeks.

Our timing was perfect! The way was wide open for Zimmy and Tommy to move up, which they did in splendid fashion. This QB change would have happened one way or another, but when Dave "put his best foot forward" and I "toed the line," we did a very good thing for the team—having Zimmy as the starting QB was a wonderful change!

Star senior halfbacks Dave Tuohy (left) and Frank Biasi, who insists, "No, Dave. You dropped way more passes than me!"

Playing on the kickoff and punting teams, I had plenty of chances to run down the field and hit somebody—which was a lot of fun. I also got to QB the scout team, which, contrary to what junior guard Larry Grassini, [owner of Grassini Family Vineyards and Winery in California's Santa Ynez Valley] — may his grapes never fail! — might remember, was not an all-junior squad. And, unlike the starting team, the scout team got to learn new plays and formations every week! We even got to run the single-wing the week before the Iona game. Coach McGuckin said single-wing plays were slow to develop but that the single-wing provided a cloud of blockers. We got it half right, but I don't recall ever seeing a cloud of blockers. (Oooh, that still smarts!)

Truly 1961 was a wonderful season! It was hard work but I wouldn't change it or trade it for anything. We did it together, first-teamers and scout teamers, and we did it right! God bless all you guys!

*Dreams of playing at Chaminade or in
games of that '61 season still occur.*

— Paul Lombardi

CHUTE STRINGS

By Spunklo

Judging from the large number of returning lettermen, this year's team again appears to be a top-notch ball club.

— Spunklo

The following article was submitted by Skip Rottkamp, whose essays "Teacher, Coach, Friend: Charlie McGuckin" and "Chaminade High School: 1959-1963" appear later in this work. The piece below was first published in TARMAC, Chaminade's student newspaper, on September 29, 1961. "Chute Strings," a reference to parachute cords or suspension lines, purportedly used by the Chaminade Flyers, was a byline of Spunklo, who is actually our '62 classmate and '61 teammate, Carl LoGalbo, whose nicknames include both "Spunky" and "The Lo." Spunklo's words actually proved prescient.

Many thanks to Skip and Carl for this hidden treasure.

Amid all the confusion and expense of the first few weeks of school, a deep anxiety settles upon the whole student body (even the freshy Frosh). Everyone's biting his nails and wondering where this year's edition of the Flyer Eleven will finish at the end of the 1961 football season. Last year Coach Thomas' gridiron men brought Chaminade its second League Championship in three years; can the Flyers retain that title this year?

Judging from the large number of returning lettermen, this year's team again appears to be a top-notch ball club. With a tough, spirited fullback like co-captain "Oil" Kirmser and a front wall consisting of co-captain Bill Sellerberg, "the Ankle" Tom Kiley," "Chuckle" Mansfield, "Tiny the Terrible" Reisert, "Dangerous" Dick Darby,

"Ability" Al Groh, and "Tiger" Bill DeMeo, I believe that the odds that we will top the league are in our favor. We mustn't, however, forget the powerful bench support the team carries into this year. Valva and Molloy will back up at the guard position, while big Bill Sullivan and Jack Kernaghan will fill the end slots.

Success for the Flyers not only requires long hours of hard work but also that special ingredient dubbed "Student Participation." All the ball players look for support from each and every individual in the school and expect all-out attendance at every game. This might seem trite to the upperclassmen, but you know as well as I do, it's the truth. Without the students' support, the Chaminade Flyers will have only half a team.

A school without football is in danger of
deteriorating into a medieval study hall.

— Frank Leahy
Notre Dame

UNDEFEATED FLYER ELEVEN LOOK TO MOUNT ST. MICHAEL

By Charles Raubicheck

If the team's performances in the next few weeks match their previous efforts, the '61 Flyers could well become one of the best football teams in the history of the school.

— Charles Raubicheck

According to www.lawyers.findlaw.com, "Charles J. Raubicheck, one of the country's foremost Food and Drug attorneys, is a partner at Frommer Lawrence & Haug and heads the firm's FDA/Regulatory practice.

"Mr. Raubicheck has been listed in the New York Super Lawyers, Metro Edition."

A 1964 Chaminade alumnus, he wrote the following article for TARMAC *in October 1961.*

Thank you, Charles.

Paced by two of the best backs in the CHSFL, the 1961 Flyer gridders are well on their way to copping their second consecutive league title, according to many who watched the team sweep undefeated through its first five games. On the shoulders of Earl Kirmser and John Zimmermann, the aforementioned duo, now rests the responsibility of carrying the squad through the next two contests with stalwarts Mt. St. Michael and Cardinal Hayes.

Last Sunday the so far undefeated Flyers put down Iona 28-0. Big Tiny Reisert kicked off right into their end zone. They started to use their trap plays but Kiley found holes and stopped them cold. Then the Flyers got the ball and Kirmser started with powerful short drives. Zimmermann then passed 25 yards to McGovern for the TD. Kirmser went over for the 2 points. Earl started the 2ⁿᵈ quarter with two drives for 25 yards. Kiley then intercepted a pass. Zimmermann ended the quarter by passing to Ackerson, who scored; then by running for the conversion. After a scoreless third quarter Zimmermann passed to Ackerson for a third TD. Kirmser then passed to Bowman for the final tally.

Spirit and drive enabled the boys from Mineola to top their earlier opponents. A solid running attack topped St. John's. Early in the next quarter Dave Tuohy slanted one yard off tackle for another score. The Redmen, behind 13-0 in the second half, took to the air and brought the ball to the 5 where John Ludwig carried it over on an end run. This, however, was not enough to stop the Flyers, two fourth period touchdowns by George Ackerson and Skip Rottkamp giving Chaminade a 27-6 victory.

The outlook is good. With a backfield of Kirmser, Tuohy and Biasi and a line of Groh, Kiley, DeMeo, Reisert, Darby, Mansfield and Sellerberg, the Flyers have a starting line-up with power and speed. This is a team to go places. The '61 team goal is, as always, an undefeated season, which has not been produced since 1956.*

— *TARMAC*
September 23, 1961

* With its many talented players, the 1956 championship Flyer varsity logged six wins and two losses. For the record, however, only the 1951 squad was undefeated prior to '61, although its otherwise perfect season was marred by a scoreless tie with Cardinal Hayes High School.

St. Francis was not so easily overcome. The pesky Terriers, supported by their speedy ball carriers, were deadlocked with the

Flyers in a scoreless duel until only ten seconds remained in the game. On 3rd down Zimmermann lofted a 52 yard desperation pass which Bob Bowman hauled in on the 2 before being pushed out of bounds. The Flyer QB then hit Bowman with a scoring pass in the far corner of the end zone as the 4600 fans in Chaminade Bowl poured out on the field to congratulate their fellow class men.

This enthusiastic spirit for the Flyer grid squad was evident even on opening day as several busloads of students traveled to Stepinac and saw the Crusaders stopped 14-6. Zimmermann led the attack with a 5 yard TD jaunt in the first period, and Kirmser, who scored three times in the non-league game at Hicksville, smashed 3 yards for the clinching touchdown in the third period. The solid Flyer line held Stepinac until the fourth quarter, Crusader Tom Conroy's scoring plunge spoiling Chaminade's shutout bid.

So, with the two big games (the Mount and Hayes) looming in the near future, the Flyers are striving to maintain their winning ways in a league which gets tougher each year. If the team's performances in the next few weeks match their previous efforts, the '61 Flyers could well become one of the best football teams in the history of the school.

The principle is competing against yourself. It's about self-improvement, about being better than you were the day before.

— Steve Young

THE DEFENSE NEVER RESTS

By Chuck Mansfield

The axiom that "defense wins championships" still applies and clearly was a major factor in '61.

— Al Groh

On Sunday, October 29, 1961, the Flyers traveled to McGovern Field in the Bronx to face archrival Mount Saint Michael. At stake were first place in the CHSFL and the undefeated seasons both teams enjoyed up to that point. For Chaminade it proved to be its top two-way performance of the season. It was not only a great victory over an extremely tough opponent but also our highest-scoring game. Vanquishing the Mount gave us our sixth consecutive victory and a renewed confidence that we could win the League championship for a second consecutive year. Undoubtedly, it was our team's finest performance of our perfect season.

A headline from *The New York Times* sports pages on October 30, 1961, the day after the Mount game, read: "CHAMINADE POSTS 34-TO-6 VICTORY; FLYERS TOP MT. ST. MICHAEL IN LEAGUE CONTEST." Of that victory and his pivotal role in it, the game's MVP Dave Tuohy has written, "I will forever remember those two touchdowns versus the Mount. Scored by you, Rick Darby, Al Groh and myself. It was a wonderful day during a glorious season. [It] lives in my soul – those days on those fields that began and ended in Flushing, led by the best there was to offer – Mr. Thomas, Mr. McGuckin and Mr. Flynn.* God bless. Dave #41"

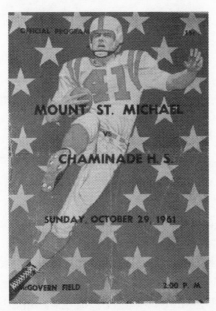

This is the cover of the program from the 1961 Flyers vs. Mount game. Perhaps prophetically, the player's jersey bears the number 41 – Dave Tuohy's!

(Photograph courtesy of Tom Kiley and used with permission.)

Dave is being overly generous to Rick, Al and me. Although some described the hole we opened as "big enough to drive a truck through," it was unmistakably Dave's performance that was the blockbuster, not those of his right-side linemen. Many of you will remember the play. Chaminade received the Mount's opening kickoff and brought it back to roughly midfield. Then, on the first play from scrimmage, junior quarterback John Zimmermann handed off to Dave, who galloped like a thoroughbred 44 yards to the end zone. And that was only his first touchdown of the day. Dave's second romp to pay dirt – on Chaminade's first play from scrimmage in the second half – was 54 yards and a back-breaker for the Mount. As Al has observed, "The blocking and running combined for two long touchdown runs, a wonderful example of the teamwork that made this team special."

They played tremendously as a team. They
were always working together.

— Coach Joe Thomas
per George Vecsey

Prior to our team's 50-year reunion in 2011, I wrote the following reflection: "Dave Tuohy's first touchdown against the Mount...is still vivid. We Flyers received the opening kickoff and got the ball first-and-ten. Our first play from scrimmage was a '44 dive,' which meant that the right halfback, Dave, was to receive a handoff from John Zimmermann, our outstanding junior quarterback. Dave was then to carry the ball between the right guard, myself, and the right tackle, Rick Darby. The exchange between Zimmy and Dave was flawless, and Rick and I executed our blocks superbly, if I do say so myself, opening a huge hole through which Dave galloped 44 yards all the way for a touchdown, his first of two on the day. (Chaminade won 34-6.) To say it was an inauspicious beginning for Mount Saint Michael on our opponent's home field is an understatement. Indeed, those boys were downright sullen."

In a recent conversation with Tom Kiley about Dave's first touchdown, I added the comment that I recall Dave running on a perfectly straight line from the line of scrimmage into the end zone. No one impeded or touched him. It was simply beautiful.

In an article entitled "Chaminade's Title Outfit Rolls On" published in the wake of the Mount game, the New York *Journal American*'s Morrey Rokeach penned, "Howie Smith, the little old Notre Dame grad who coaches Mt. St. Michael, tried something new – the Shotgun Offense – attempting to slay Chaminade.

"It was about as effective as bringing down an elephant with a pop gun since the Long Islanders made it 10 straight, ... with a 34-6 romp before 7,500 at McGovern Field.

"Smity, an old shrewdie, would have been smarter trying a bazooka, howitzer, or some of that 50 megaton nuclear fire power. ...

"We came back after that first score," added Howie, "but then Tim [*sic*] Kiley killed us by blocking Mike Cunnion's punt and George Valva fell on it in the end zone for a touchdown."

In another account of our Mount game, Ed Hurley, a reporter for the *Daily News*, wrote "It was Chaminade's 10th straight win over a two-season span, and fourth loop triumph this fall."

A third newspaper article (with no name attributed) ran the headline "Chaminade Needs One to Capture Grid Title." Its first paragraph read, "Chaminade's powerful football machine rolled right over the biggest obstacle to a second straight Catholic High School Athletic Association title yesterday when the Flyers blasted Mt. St. Michael's, 34-6, at the loser's field."

The same piece continued, "The Flyers broke the game wide open in the third period, scoring two touchdowns, one on Dave Tuohy's 54-yard blast up the middle, his second long TD run of the day, and another on Earl Kirmser's one-yard plunge."

The Mount came close in the first quarter but that was their last hurrah. Here's the scoring in that game by quarter:

Chaminade	8	6	14	6 – 34
Mount	6	0	0	0 – 6

In a big game, don't be afraid. Make your mistakes but be sure to take your chances when they come. Above all keep giving 110 percent. That's how you become a big game player.

— Tom Kiley

A peculiar footnote to that first touchdown run by Dave Tuohy: One sports page credited Tom Kiley with the offensive block that opened the chasm through which Dave was to fly to his exciting first score. According to all our teammates, Tom was unquestionably a major factor in our team's championship and most deservedly named Most Outstanding Player at season's end. Still, it was a curious report because Tom was on the sidelines for both of Dave's electrifying runs that day. Of Tom's performance in that contest, Mr. Hurley declared that "Kiley, the league's outstanding linebacker, played havoc with the Mount's attack all day." Adds Al Groh: "Tom was a tackling machine vs. the Mount, as he was throughout the season…but the reality is that, while a lot of guys played key roles, the defense would not have been quite as overpowering without his performances." Indeed, on the day after the Mount game Dr. Z, aka Paul L. Zimmerman, who also wrote for *Sports Illustrated*, headlined his newspaper column with "Kiley Keeping Chaminade Alone At Top of CHSFL." High praise and well earned.

Parenthetically, I add here insights gleaned from emails I have received from Tom: "We chased Mount QB Mike Cunnion all over the field all day long and made him 'scramble' on nearly every pass play. One night, three years later, I was shooting pool with Mike at the College of the Holy Cross, where he had become a top quarterback, and he confided that that afternoon had been the worst of his football life.

"Indeed, our ends rushed him from the outside, our linebackers blitzed him from the inside. And, of course, the Mounties simply could not block us anywhere along our defensive line. In addition, our defense blocked a quick kick of his in his end zone, intercepted his late-game lateral and caused a fumble in the shadow of his goal line, each resulting in touchdowns. Moreover, our defensive backs were on their receivers like white on rice from start to finish.

"And yet, our defensive plan that day was a perfect example of Thomas-McGuckin creativity in pulling a little used defense out of their bag of tricks for one crucial game, confusing the hell out of the Mount. I remember Coach Thomas telling me on Tuesday that our base defense that week would be the 7 Diamond, a defense we never used in our junior year and never used before Mount or after. We had learned its individual responsibilities pre-season and our coaches put it in their back pockets until they felt it was the right time to use it. Coach gave me a couple of variations that would allow our end(s) to drop into coverage if we were getting hurt in the flat, but as it turned out, we just got after Cunnion from every angle on every play. We completely dominated defensively from start to finish.

"Finally, all credit to our coaches for unleashing the 7 Diamond on Cunnion. It destroyed him and the Mount. And it was risky: Eight guys in the box and only three pass defenders against the best pure passer in the League."

Every battle is won before it is ever fought.

— Sun Tzu
in *The Art of War*

Al continued that "For a team to only allow 33 total points, only 25 of them against the defense, is quite remarkable in any era. The axiom that 'defense wins championships' still applies and clearly was a major factor in '61." He also pointed out that 12 of the Flyers' 34 points versus the Mount were scored by the defense, which was potent testimony to the "full-game, full-team" approach we employed that day.

Here's the 1961 Chaminade defense in action. At left Bobby Bowman prepares to tackle a Hicksville ball carrier while Chuck Mansfield (center) and Mike Reisert follow in pursuit.

Speaking of defense and the central role that Tom played in forging its excellence, his modesty compelled him to enjoin me from calling him the heart of Chaminade's in 1961. After all, as Al has stated, "a lot of guys played key roles…and the 'heart' of a team is always a collective heart."

While this narrative has so far been very complimentary of our defense, it may have scanted the absolutely sensational year it had. Truth be told, our offense had some difficulty in four of our eight games. Although it always managed to score more than enough points to secure a victory, had the defense not shut out Saint Francis, our undefeated season would have gone a-glimmering. The same was true to a lesser degree against Holy Cross, as we were tied 0-0 well into the third quarter. Then Tom Higgins and Frank Biasi bailed us out with successive championship runs to pay dirt. Had our defense faltered even a little that day, we could have been in big trouble.

Finally, with the exception of Cardinal Hayes' long scoring drive in our 12-8 win, we rarely permitted sustained marches.

One last thought: Hicksville's only score was on a 68-yard run from scrimmage by all-star running back Chris Coletta. Teams rarely moved the ball against us on the ground or in the air that perfect season.

* Edward J. Flynn coached the senior members of our team on the JV level in 1959 and the juniors in 1960.

Coach Ed Flynn as JV football coach.

Football is not a contact sport — it is a collision sport. Dancing is a contact sport.

— Duffy Daugherty
Michigan State

"FOR THE REST OF YOUR LIFE, NOBODY CAN EVER SAY THAT YOU COULDN'T DO IT."

By Albert M. Groh

The sustained success of the Flyers was built on a foundation of a team culture that Mr. Thomas had created by forging a consistent set of standards and values for one common purpose – winning – and doing so by bringing out the very best in every player and team.

— Al Groh

A friend of almost sixty-three years, Al is a 1962 Chaminade alumnus who is also our classmate and '61 football teammate. In 1967 he was awarded a B.S. in Commerce from the University of Virginia and subsequently served two years as a second lieutenant in the U.S. Army.

Afterward, he spent 45 years as a college and National Football League coach (where strategy, tactics, planning, leadership and adaptability were essential), including 16 years as the head coach at Wake Forest, the University of Virginia and the New York Jets. Twice named ACC Coach of the Year, Al also served as defensive coordinator and offensive coordinator. Moreover, he twice coached in Super Bowls with the New York Giants and the New England Patriots. He currently serves as the analyst on college and NFL broadcasts for Westwood One radio and ESPN.

He is married to Anne, his wife of 51 years, with whom he has three children and five grandchildren.

Thank you, Al.

The legacy of Chaminade football was already strong as the Flyers prepared for the 1961 football season. However, a segment of its fans was beginning to believe that the League-wide strength of the CHSFL and the challenging public school opener that Chaminade annually played made the odds of an undefeated and untied season very long. Indeed, the 1960 Flyers were CHSFL champions with a 6-1-1 record. A spotless record is rare on any level and, of the NFL franchises that have won multiple Super Bowls, including the Patriots, Steelers, 49ers and Giants, only the 1972 17-0 Miami Dolphins have finished with an unblemished record.

The tradition of football excellence at Chaminade was started by Coach Frank "Boiler" Burns, whose early success was built upon and continued over the next thirteen years by our head coach, Mr. Joe Thomas, who led the Crimson and Gold to three CHSFL titles. But neither coach had ever achieved a perfect season. The sustained success of the Flyers was built on a foundation of a team culture that Mr. Thomas had created by forging a consistent set of standards and values for one common purpose – winning – and doing so by bringing out the very best in every player and team. A Joe Thomas-coached team was always well trained fundamentally, physically tough and rugged, and conditioned to outlast any opponent. There are four critical components that must be in full alignment before any team can have a superior season, and the '61 Flyers put them all together. They are:

THE COACH

Very few teams fail to win because their playbooks – the offensive and defensive schemes – are inadequate. Sure, some are more strategically advanced than others but just about every team has schemes that are good enough to win. So, then, why do some teams win often and other teams lose often, or at least don't win as much as they should? There are two main reasons and both are a direct reflection on the head coach: the first is talent, both the acquisition and the development of talented players. The second, and most distinguishing, is leadership.

There is a coaching axiom that "Coaches with schemes but without talent quickly become the coaches of unimportant teams," which Mr. Thomas instinctively understood and had a detailed blueprint for how to prepare players for varsity competition. With very few exceptions, all players spent their first season on the freshman team and their second on the JV. While the players were not under the direct, daily supervision and coaching of Mr. Thomas, everything done fit within his philosophy and master plan. These young players were learning the skills and attitudes they would use as juniors and seniors on the varsity. Primary to that plan was Coach's belief that the best way to learn how to play football was by playing games. Therefore each team would play a game against a CHSFL opponent on Saturday and a game against a public school opponent on Wednesday. Other days were devoted to competitive drills and fundamental techniques.

One of the best things about playing football under Joe Thomas at Chaminade was the continuity. From the first day of tryouts as a freshman to the last snap as a senior, the system was unchanged. I could run our offense from the early '60s right now, 60 years later.

— John Zimmermann

Thus the seniors on the '61 team played eleven freshman games (6-4-1) and twelve JV games (10-1-1). This ingenious plan had the juniors on the Chaminade varsity much more prepared for CHSFL competition than some of our opponents. This was a definite advantage for us. It also gave the coaches plenty of opportunities to evaluate players and the roles they might play as upperclassmen. A significant part of leadership is a clear vision of the objective to be achieved and a definite plan to accomplish it. Mr. Thomas certainly had just such a vision and plan.

Leadership can be tricky to recognize and define during its active phase because it can vary so much from individual to individual and from situation to situation. But, it is always quite clear in the results that it produces. Through his words and actions a leader makes clear what his vision for the team is. A dynamic leader touches human emotions and sets the standards for his organization, and, above all, demands compliance with them. A head football coach as a leader is skilled at creating a common purpose, a collective spirit, and a shared goal that every player's efforts are directed towards. The legendary coach Bear Bryant said that all his energies were aimed at creating "a team with one heart and one pulse." Coach Thomas epitomized all these characteristics of leadership. His will to win was evident every day, and his commitment to his process of maximizing performance was constantly on display. We got his very best every day and he demanded our best at all times. From play to play and from game to game the entire team always knew that every player and coach would continue to give his very best. That confidence was a major factor in the comeback and late game wins during the '60 and '61 seasons. Those teams just did not crack. "Do your job" at all times was not yet a well-known buzz phrase, but it was a part of every Flyer's mindset.

When I stood at the podium at the press conference presenting me as the head coach of the New York Jets, it was gratifying to see two of my most influential mentors, Joe Thomas and Charlie McGuckin, proudly sitting in the audience. During the season I also enjoyed several phone conversations with Mr. Thomas in the days following a game, when he would voice his insights on how the game had gone.

Pictured above at a press conference at Hofstra University on January 24, 2000, Al Groh was introduced as New York Jets head coach. He was joined by (from left) Chuck Mansfield, Coach Charlie McGuckin, then a Jets scout, and Coach Joe Thomas (right).

(Photograph courtesy of Al Groh and used with permission.)

THE TEAM

The Flyers' varsity football team was generally made up of juniors and seniors. How quickly and completely they meshed into a cohesive, unified unit was the most critical element in the team's success. Moreover, it is important to emphasize that the story of the perfect season is about every player on the team, not just the senior class. Without major contributions from members of the junior class, the first perfect football season in Chaminade football history would not have occurred.

It takes a great deal more to make a single-minded team in pursuit of a common goal than just pulling on the same color jersey. It is an entirely different process to build the trust, respect and dependability among players that mark a genuine team than just learning the plays. A true T-E-A-M is one that has built strong player-player and player-coach relationships. It was rigorous to be a four-year Chaminade football player. Only a total commitment to the entire process would work. Thus standards were set and not going to change for any individual. A guy had to really like rugged physical contact, daily competition, and selfless teamwork.

When the 1958 Chaminade freshman team gathered for the first time, very few of us knew each other. We had come from all over Long Island. At that first practice we were not a team, just a collection of young athletes. Over time every interaction in the locker room and on the field saw the players build the player-player relationships that would turn individuals into an unbeatable team.

These relationships continued to grow in 1959 during the JV season. At the same time the players who would be the '61 juniors were starting their process of brotherhood. In the summer of 1960, we moved up to the varsity to partner with the seniors of that team to create the 1960 CHSFL champions. We experienced what it took to earn the trust and respect of older teammates. Twelve months later, as the senior class, we would use that experience in team-building to welcome the rising juniors. A special team was in the process of being born.

The point about the preceding paragraphs is that the dynamic of creating a cohesive, unified, collaborating team of players and coaches whose commitment was totally focused on winning was a uniquely different process at Chaminade than it was at any of its rivals. It is unusual that fifty percent of a team's roster turns over every season, thus necessitating an annual reestablishing of the critical relationships that turn a gathering of players into a team. This is when consistent, continuous leadership by the coaches and team first buy-in by players come together in partnership. The leadership of Coach Thomas and Coach McGuckin and each team's senior leaders was there to reinforce the standards and expectations that all the players had been raised on. The quality of this leadership caused this amazing feat to happen. It is unlikely that the New England Patriots would be consistent Super Bowl contenders and frequent champions if they needed to replace half of their players every season, but that is just what the Flyers did.

The meshing of two classes went pretty seamlessly because all players were basically the same guy, having been shaped by the same training and development process during the freshman and JV seasons. This process created a team of guys who were ready to wear the Crimson and Gold and eliminated those who were not able to make the type of commitment necessary to play for the Flyers. The things that make a team win became ingrained habits that repeated from season to season and became the team identity. The way things were done and what was expected didn't change from year to year.

I certainly did not understand the reasons behind what we did while I was playing. I just did it. But, when I started coaching, I looked back on my time playing in order to formulate my own beliefs and style. It was then that I began to see the plan behind everything we did and how it was all tied together to produce four titles in the first eight seasons of the CHSFL. The talent at Chaminade was always good, but there was talent throughout the League, especially at our principal rivals, St. Francis Prep, Stepinac and Mt. St. Michael. Talent alone didn't do it but, when magnified by the four cornerstones of Flyer football – constant competition, fundamentals, physical, mental and competitive toughness, and superior conditioning – that talent became extremely difficult to beat. I soon realized that the process all started with competition. It was the focal point of every practice, and competition was a big reason why the freshman and JV teams played two games a week. Sure, it was to refine our skills and fundamentals, but it was very much to compete as often as possible against a new opponent. Many young players confuse playing really hard and giving great effort with actually competing. Every opponent presents a different challenge and competing is simply finding a way to win by doing whatever it takes. Competition was always a major part of our practices. The Oklahoma drill had a winner and loser, boards were competitive and physical, there was physical competition at the end of the tires, and, of course, scrimmage was competitive on every play. Some teams just know how to compete better than their opponent, and our competitive toughness gave us confidence and a competitive advantage. I sure learned to make competitive drills a core part of my teams' practices.

All offensive and defensive plays look good in the playbook, yet it is execution on the field that brings the play to life and makes it successful. The mastery of the fundamental techniques at each position gives the players the tools to defeat the opposing player. The Flyers did not have an extensive playlist. We did not trick or outsmart opponents. We ran our core plays over and over and we ran them better than the other team could defend them. It was the fundamentals built by drill after drill that gave our players the winning edge. Coach Thomas coached the linemen and Coach McGuckin coached the backs without any assistants and did a terrific job building our skills.

A lot more often than not the toughest team becomes the winning team. Toughness comes in three areas: 1) physical toughness, i.e. just playing at a more rugged contact level, 2) mental toughness, the ability to deal with any and all situations and to forge forward to become a team that will not crack, and 3) competitive toughness, which is a team's collective ability to size up an opponent and the game situation and to quickly adjust to what must be done to win. It was a core belief of Mr. Thomas that consistent and relentless toughness, as much as any factor, would make a team a winner. And toughness became an integral part of our team identity.

We were a confident team but never a complacent or comfortable team. Winning brought with it all the needed positive reinforcement, and the coaches made sure we stayed humble and hungry. Those Monday afternoon reviews of the previous day's game film (Did we actually win?) kept us humble and the daily competition kept us hungry. There was a prevailing mindset that nothing – not playing time or victory – is ever handed to you. Everything is earned by your performance.

With superior conditioning in every game, a team can overcome two opponents, the other team and fatigue. Each of these can cause a team to lose, but fatigue is the one that can be defeated beforehand and turned into an ally. We can all remember the seemingly endless wind sprints after practice. I especially recall running sprints on the game field in the dark with the only light coming from the garage. And even these end-of-practice sprints included competition and mental toughening, as we ran in tandem with somebody just about our own speed. We were not only challenging ourselves to keep pushing and defeat fatigue but we were competing against the guy next to us. As the sprints grew in number, the challenge to never give in grew as well. We were building the physical stamina to wear down opponents late in the game, learning to constantly compete in a challenging situation, and strengthening the mental toughness to never give in to fatigue. We were confident we would outlast any opponent. And the '60 and '61 teams were rewarded for these efforts as three of those teams' fourteen wins came in the final two minutes of games.

If my players ever wondered why we conditioned as diligently as we did, they could trace it back to my having played for Coach Joe Thomas. It paid off for us too, as our winning percentage in games decided in the final minutes was extremely high. Thanks, Coach!

The senior members of the 1961 Flyers had an amazingly successful football career. In four seasons of CHSFL matchups these veteran Flyers were 23-0-1, and were 30-6-3 overall, with four of the losses coming during freshman year. Over the final three seasons these seniors were in two losing games, certainly one of the greatest runs of any class in the history of Chaminade football. It all started and ended in Flushing with shutouts against the same opponent, Holy Cross. On September 29, 1958, Earl Kirmser scored in the fourth quarter for a 6-0 win, and three seasons later Frank Biasi and Tom Higgins scored as the Flyers won 16-0. Our time wearing the Crimson and Gold was bookended with two happy bus rides home.

THE PLAYERS

A great symphony plays beautifully composed music led by an accomplished conductor. But it is the individual musicians all blending their sounds together that make for spectacular sound. While there may be talented soloists in the orchestra, it is the cumulative sound that the orchestra is known for. The 1961 Chaminade Flyers had the plays and the coaches and, certainly, some all-star players but, in the end, it was the collaborative efforts of every player on the roster that produced a memorable season-long performance. It was a total T-E-A-M effort.

The '60 Flyers had some real standouts including Skip Orr, Jack Wehrum, Ed Finegan and Pat Higgins. As much as the game-changing plays they made, I remember how all the seniors welcomed us onto the team. They set a good example for the players who would have the same responsibility the next season. Many of those juniors (the seniors of the '61 team) played a great deal during the 1960 season, but there were some missing pieces in the lineup and the '61 juniors were quickly welcomed the same way that we had been.

The dynamics of the locker room are an admirable example of what would be a good way for many elements of society to operate. Guys from diverse backgrounds and locations, who might never find themselves in the same place if not for football, are brought together because of one common interest, their desire to play football. Despite their outward differences and various backgrounds, players quickly learn that what they do have in common actually makes them the "same guy;" thus a strong connection is made among the players. The code of the locker room is that if a player is "all in" with the team goals, is a good teammate, and can help the team win, he is quickly accepted. A football team is a true meritocracy where nothing is given, everything is earned. If a new player beats out a current player, even if that player is a good friend, the new player is quickly accepted because he has demonstrated that he can advance the team's objective – to win. It was this "same guy" mentality and the code of the locker room that made the task of joining junior and senior players quickly into a cohesive team a smooth process.

By Chaminade standards this was a veteran team with a lot of returning starters, or players who had played a lot of minutes in 1960. There were standouts like co-captains Earl Kirmser and Bill Sellerberg, Tom Kiley, Mike Reisert and Dave Tuohy, but there were still some spots that needed to be filled for the team to be of championship caliber. To follow Skip Orr as the Flyers' QB would have been a challenge for anyone, much less a QB moving up from the JV squad, but John Zimmermann did it beautifully, and Bobby Bowman gave us much needed athletic ability in the secondary and big-play ability on offense. The perfect season would not have happened if Zimmy and Bobby had not connected on pass completions on the last two plays of the game to beat St. Francis 6-0. Skip Rottkamp was another key addition to the secondary and Kemp Hannon played valuable minutes at center. Bruce Salerno showed that he had the talent to be an all-star lineman. We could see early that we had a chance to do something really special and quickly came together to "play some beautiful music."

And during every game the Flyers had the benefit of a 12th man in the stands, the Chaminade student body. When we had a home game, the support and energy of our schoolmates was on display at a raucous Friday afternoon pep rally, then during the game, and, finally, at a happy post-game sock hop, when the team assembled on stage. (Or was it really the female fans that our friends were happy to see?) Every away game felt like it was at the Chaminade Bowl with hundreds of students in the visiting stands. The team's entrance onto the Chaminade Bowl field was a unique and special ritual that began with a silent walk from the locker room to the Courtyard of Our Lady to say three Hail Marys, then running down through the stands before bursting onto the playing field in front of 5,000 to 6,000 fans. It was classic high school football at its best.

This was the scene in the old Chaminade gymnasium at the sock hop following the Flyers' September 1961 Hicksville victory.

THE SEASON

The accomplishment of the 1961 Chaminade Flyers football team is recognized in its entirety by a perfect 8-0-0 record. But for the coaches and players it was eight one-win seasons that at the end added up to an undefeated and untied season. There was no grand quest to win 'em all, just total focus on each opponent. Quite likely, Coaches Thomas and McGuckin were doing some long-range planning, as all coaches do, but they had the players tightly focused on two weekly objectives: 1) what to do to get better and, 2) how are we going to beat this team? Our coaches were always positive but also were always pushing us for more.

The season started with two impressive road wins at Hicksville and Stepinac, which showed how strong our team could be if we kept pushing. The next weekend brought our biggest rival, St. Francis Prep, to Mineola. With the score tied at zero and with under a minute left in the game, Zimmy hit Bobby Bowman with two passes, the last on the final play to give the Flyers a second-straight last-minute win over the Terriers. The way we won reinforced the way we were built: competitively tough, resourceful, in shape to play as long as needed, and with a defense that was extraordinarily difficult to score against. It was a win that really kick-started us into high gear. Wins over St. John's and Iona Prep set up a showdown at Mount St. Michael. Dave Tuohy had two long touchdown runs and Tom Kiley seemed to make every tackle. The 34-6 rout of the Mounties was the second signature win of the season and positioned us to finish strong. We did just that by beating Cardinal Hayes and Holy Cross. The '61 Flyers had beaten the odds to finish undefeated and untied and were CHSFL champions.

Pictured above are (left to right) Anne Groh, Al's wife, Bill Parcells and Al at a New York Giants' team reunion.

(Photograph courtesy of Al Groh and used with permission.)

There is a football axiom that "Defense wins championships" and the Flyers definitely confirmed that, as eight opponents were able to score only thirty-three total points, only twenty- five against the defense. No opponent scored more than one touchdown, and the Flyer defense allowed only one touchdown in the final four games. This is truly remarkable! Talent, fundamentals, physical ruggedness and toughness, and superior conditioning all added up to make the Flyers of 1961 unbeatable.

After the season, George Vecsey of *Newsday* asked Mr. Thomas if these Flyers were his best team. Coach responded that "I don't know if this is the best team I ever coached. I wouldn't say it is. It's all relative. They are good kids. They try hard. But, are they the best I ever had? Well, they certainly have the best record." Mr. Thomas was my first coaching mentor and many of his principles and lessons stayed with me, but here is where I must disagree with him. Often I emphasized to my teams that "The most talented players don't always make the best team, but the best T-E-A-M always wins." Every game for eight weeks we found a way to win. Teams are not judged on talent, they are judged on wins, and no team before won as many games as the '61 Flyers. There was nothing relative about it; we were the best team Mr. Thomas ever had as the head football coach of the Chaminade Flyers.*

Yeah, there may have been some skeptics when the season started but, as Bill Parcells addressed his New York Giants team in the locker room after a Super Bowl win, "FOR THE REST OF YOUR LIFE, NOBODY CAN EVER SAY THAT YOU COULDN'T DO IT."

* *In a* TARMAC *article back in the day Rev. John Worthley '62 wrote, "When asked what he thought of the team Coach Thomas replied, 'Because of the undefeated season I'd have to say this was the best team we've had.'"*

*Don't ever promise more than you can deliver,
but always deliver more than you promise.*

— Lou Holtz

TWO PLAYS THAT SHOOK OUR WORLD

*I can't imagine Coach Thomas not calling the last play of the game. ...
And I was certainly not thinking of a perfect season during this game.
I was thinking the same thoughts as in every game – how can we win
this game!*

— John Zimmermann

*Below are comments from teammates and fans, as well as the
1962* Crimson and Gold *yearbook, about the significance and effects
of the two last-minute passes completed by junior quarterback John
Zimmermann to junior halfback Bobby Bowman to break a scoreless
tie and give the Flyers an electrifying 6-0 victory over archrival St.
Francis.*

*The first remembrance, one of the longest, is from Zimmy himself
and almost certainly the most accurate. Interestingly, the reader will
find differences in the recollections of others, whose names appear
alphabetically, along with their recollections, after Zimmy's.*

Thanks to all for sharing their perspectives.

John Zimmermann: "Happy to take a trip down memory lane –
with a happy ending. What pleasant and exciting memories. I'll be
happy to share them. But understand, they are just that – my memories.

"The game as I remember was a defensive slugfest, fought
primarily between the 30s. The game was in the closing minutes.
I'm pretty sure the long pass call came from the sidelines. I believe
we were around mid-field. I'm not sure if Bobby Bowman lined up at
right halfback (going through the line and breaking deep across the
middle) or right flanker. It was not a "corkscrew" pattern. We had a
"z" pattern in our play book, but our big play wasn't that. He ran a
post pattern and broke open. I'm sure I was under pressure. The ball
came out poorly from my hand – extremely wobbly. It got there but

Bob had to slow up for it, allowing the defender to tackle him from behind. Had I thrown a good pass I think he would have scored easily, but we wouldn't have had the drama of the next play, which was my sweetest on-field memory of my Chaminade career.

"I can't imagine Coach Thomas not calling the last play of the game. Don't remember if we took a timeout to talk about it. Funny that we did not have a field goal play (or extra point kick) in our play book, but it ended up being much more memorable doing it our way. I sure wish Bob B was still here to share his memories on his two great catches.

"So I'm pretty sure the play came from the sideline – a slant to Bob B. My recollection is that he lined up on the right side and I moved him to the left side. I don't remember why, other than the play might have been called for the left side. I do recall speculation later that St. Francis thought the shift was a decoy. As there was no clock to look at like today, I didn't know how much time was left in the game or on the play clock. I took the snap, stood up, and hit Bob in the stomach – that one was a perfect pass. Bob fell to his knees in the end zone. I remember the agony on the defensive side immediately following the TD signal. At least one player – the middle backer as I recall – collapsed to the ground in despair, probably in tears.

"I had felt no tenseness or nervousness. That ends for me after the first snap. I recall this game being in the middle of the season but I am not sure of that. And I was certainly not thinking of a perfect season during this game. I was thinking the same thoughts as in every game – how can we win this game! I am very happy to be able to share my memories sixty years later."

Star juniors, quarterback John Zimmermann (left) and halfback Bobby Bowman, are pictured here in the Flyers' locker room after their two spectacular aerial hookups in the game's final seconds beat St. Francis 6-0.

Ed Christie: "From my perspective from the sidelines, the game I most remember from that championship year was the game with St. Francis. It was a home game early in the season. The Flyers won 6-0 with that game being the closest and most intense of the year. Both teams played their hearts out, with the Flyers scoring late in the game. After the game I witnessed the St. Francis team members going into their locker room. Many of the players seemed to have tears in their eyes! They gave it their all, but so did the Flyers! The Flyers' team really showed what they were made of during that game and set the winning tone for the rest of the season."

Ray Condon: "It was one of those days when you never got the sense that the clock was ticking.

"I was standing behind [back coach] Charlie [McGuckin]. I remember him calling Bowman over and giving him the fly pattern call (a rarely used play). The next thing you know Bowman was wide open (10 yards at least). It seemed like an eternity for Zimmy's pass to land. The excitement was palpable, even to this day.

"The next play – The Touchdown – seemed almost anticlimactic. Charlie, with a sense of urgency, now sent the call: The corkscrew (left side), once again to Bowman. (We practiced this play, but I had never seen it used before; nor had St Francis.) There he was, wide open again, Bowman standing alone in the end zone. Perfectly timed throw from Zimmy. Bedlam!

"It was the first time that I remember [head coach] Joe [Thomas] and Charlie smiling so broadly in unison. It was almost as if they had rehearsed the ending."

Tom Condon '65 (Ray's younger brother): "Great stories about a memorable one-of-a-kind season. I was sitting in the stands around the 20-yard line and, as I remember Bobby Bowman's touchdown catch on the right side of the end zone, he was on his back when he caught Zimmermann's pass. JZ did a slight roll out to the right to avoid the pass rush and he hit BB with a laser pass. And yes, I went crazy with the rest of CHS.

"In my day as part of the legacy to that play and your team I always thought of the corkscrew play as the Bowman Special.

"Go Flyers!"

Crimson and Gold **yearbook**: "[T]he scoreless deadlock remained. … John Zimmermann pulled out all the stoppers and tossed three long aerials. The first two were incomplete but the third wasn't. Junior Bob Bowman outhustled his man down field and hauled in the 52 yard heave on the 2 yard line. With a first down and goal to go, Zimmy fired one into the waiting arms of Bowman all alone in the end zone."

This is the individual 1961 League championship
trophy given to each member of our team.

(Photograph courtesy of Mary Ann Mansfield and used with permission.)

Rod Dwyer: "From the sidelines, I just remember seeing Bob Bowman, running full-tilt towards the end zone, turn his upper body almost 90 degrees and clasping the ball to his right hip. I thought to myself that it would be a miracle if Bob could gain full control of the ball – and the miracle happened! Bob got that ball and kept control as he was tackled, putting us inside the five-yard line. It was closer than either team had come to the goal line in the whole game.

"I confess I can't recall a pass pattern called 'the corkscrew.' (That's troubling to an old QB – is it age or is that another play I never learned?) I do remember some zig-zag routes and that seems to be what put Bobby Bowman in the absolute clear in the end zone. Zimmy's arm was like a sharpshooter's rifle – two passes dead-on target.

"We'd had that awful half-time with Coach Thomas not talking to us. Just dead silence. Some words from Coach McGuckin on coverages, running plays, patterns but mostly just silence, until Coach

Thomas finally – and oh so briefly – told us how disappointed he was in our performance, and asked us what we were going to do if we really wanted to win this game. He put it right where it belonged – on each one of us and all of us together.

"When Zimmy hit Bobby with that touchdown pass, it seemed to me that an immense weight was lifted off all our shoulders. We'd struggled that day against a very good team, but we'd finally put it together. I think that's when it became clear to me that we really could – if we kept our focus and kept working our butts off – go undefeated. After those two plays, I never ever thought of anything but winning and it made me work even harder on the scout team to push the starters as much as I could.

"Tom [Kiley] has written when he was headed to the locker room after the game, he saw the St. Francis fellows headed for their bus, and that some of them were crying. I can't blame them for that. They played their hearts out, too, and the loss had to hurt.

"At the end-of-season League Communion Breakfast and awards ceremony, we were seated immediately behind the St. Francis team. Our team was called up one-by-one by name, to receive recognition as League champions. When Bobby Bowman's name was called, and he walked up the aisle, just about every St. Francis player stared at Bobby, and I heard whispers from the St. Francis guys in front of me: 'That's him!' 'He's the one!' It wasn't really nasty, but it was very clear how much those two plays meant not only to us, but to the St. Francis team as well. (They got it wrong, though. It wasn't just Bobby; it was Bobby, Zimmy, and everybody else who did it.)

"I recently read a coach's statement about losing a championship basketball game in triple overtime. She said: 'This could only happen when two great teams played each other.' I'd like to think that could be said of the '61 game between us and St. Francis."

Bobby Bowman at halftime in the Hicksville game.

Al Groh: "Since the first request for remembrances of SFP win, I've tried to recall those final minutes and plays, and my reactions. I've been somewhat amazed that of the many recollections of specific games and plays that season, I don't really have many dramatic memories of those final two plays. Here's what I do recall: 1. I remember the final two SFP plays, especially their going for it on fourth down at midfield. I guess they thought there wasn't enough time for us to score if we got the ball (we certainly weren't known for a quick strike passing game). 2. I remember Mr. Thomas's calm on the sideline; he wasn't celebrating but gathering the players to give direction.

3. I was at my usual spot, right end. When Bowman caught the pass I remember sprinting to the ball, knowing there was little time left. I don't recall actually seeing the catch. I think the last pass was on the left, opposite my side. Bam, it happened and we won.

"When the celebrating ended and I could think for a moment, I remember 'Wow, we won,' but I wasn't all that surprised because we just always thought we'd win.

"Since then, I've been in a lot of last-minute endings like NYG Super Bowl win over Bills, and The Monday Night Miracle, but none that were more dramatic and thrilling. I wish I could have as vivid a mental picture of those two plays as I do of so many others over the next 45 seasons.

"While recognizing that win as quite a game, I never really thought of it as the signature win of the season, so I don't have a lot of definitive recollections. I celebrated at the moment, but then moved on to the next game. I actually remember other events of that season more clearly. Therefore, don't take my recall as the way it was. I'd go with what the QB remembers. I am quite sure that the play basically ended the game; if it wasn't the actual final play, then there was only time for the kickoff. I do remember NOT immediately leaving the field.

"Actually, the 28-22 win vs. SFP the previous year made a greater impression on me because of the significant deficit we had to overcome. It was a lasting lesson on 'just keep grinding' no matter what, and the game will come back to you. There is a way to beat every team, you just gotta find it. Sometimes you gotta figure that out as the game evolves (kinda like a pitcher who gives up a HR on a hitter's first AB, then Ks him three times). Coming back like that was the first time a team I was on had done that to win. Over the years, after comeback wins I sometimes thought back to that '60 game as the starting point for the mindset. As Yogi said, 'It ain't over till it's over;' so right!"

Barbara Ramsey Kiley (Our Lady of Mercy Academy '64 and Tom's bride): "While Bobby Bowman was running a quick slant into the end zone for the winning touchdown, I was making an end run out of the stadium in order to be first on line at the sock hop. OLMA girls always had to be close to the stage when Tony [Alfano] and Vinny [Testa] sang the opening bars of *Shortnin' Bread*."

While the boys were croonin', the girls were swoonin'.

(Photograph courtesy of Tom Kiley and used with permission.)

Tom Kiley: "It was one of those games when the offense just couldn't get going. I remember it as a struggle between one perfect defense and one that was almost perfect. On that day almost perfect was not good enough. In retrospect, I figure Vince O'Connor thought if he stopped Kirmser off tackle, he'd stop us. And he was almost right. But two talented juniors foiled his plan. Even the legendary Saint Francis coach could not have accounted for that.

"As the last seconds ticked away, I was standing on the sideline near the coaches who were conferring. Then Bowman ran into the huddle. He lined up as a wingback, I think. I can't remember us using a flanker very much that year. I think he ran a post pattern or at least John Z. hit him in the middle of the field, a kind of wobbly pass but good enough. A touchdown, yes? Then, no! Ball placed on the two. The last seconds ticking away. Not enough time, I feared. Remember, the only clock back then was on the line judge's wrist. Hard to know just how much time remained. All of a sudden, Bobby runs a quick slant-in pattern. Zimmermann hits him perfectly over the middle in the end zone. I am stunned. Victory snatched from the jaws of a deflating tie and the end of our perfect season. I watch the Saint Francis middle linebacker pound the ground in frustration. He figured Kirmser off tackle for sure. So would I have. Did Zimmy call that last pass or did the coaches? I don't know.

"We needed no goal line stand in the Francis game. They never got that close. Most of the game was played between the thirties, a defensive struggle of the highest caliber. We almost scored just before the half but time ran out. However, one nugget has been lost in the fog of time and the general euphoria concerning the last two plays of the game. Francis was at mid-field with a fourth and short on the third to last play of the game. They thought they still had enough time to win if they could make a first down. But our defense rose up when it mattered most, as we always did, and stopped them short of the line to gain, giving Zim and Bobby a chance to make Chaminade football history. If we had not, a different ending might have been written.

"A lasting impression: After much congratulations from fans, friends and family, I bounded up the stands and walked toward our locker room. Just then the Francis players began exiting the visitors' locker room, walking with pads in hands to their team bus. Several of them were openly crying; several others were fighting back tears. For me, only the joy of victory that day and the thought of a glorious sock hop to follow. As the song says, "You gotta be a football hero…"

Carl LoGalbo: "I was on the sideline next to Charlie, and Joe was about ten yards down from us. Bowman ran a short route into the end zone but then struggled to get into an open space. I estimate the pass to have traveled about nine or ten yards. Bowman caught it two or three yards deep in the end zone. We were on the two or three. Zimmy dropped back maybe a yard or two. As soon as Bobby caught the ball, Charlie leaped into the air and yelled to Joe, 'He caught it, he caught it!' And yes the pass was caught by Bowman between his legs after finding a clear space in the end zone. I do not remember the long pass to Bowman but do remember Al Groh making a catch or two. And I'm pretty sure about Al because it was such a big game. I remember saying to myself that Al came through with a reception, which really wasn't his strength. As we know, it was his defense.

"Finally, I remember it being a defensive struggle, and Kiley not having a typical Kiley game – no blocked punts or interceptions or turnovers. Just a head-to head-struggle in the middle of the field. They figured out how to stop Kirmser, and that made it tough."

Paul Lombardi: "I do remember the end of the St. Francis game when Bob Bowman caught the pass from Zimmy and the reaction of the Prep players at such a bitter defeat."

Chuck Mansfield: "The St. Francis game, our third of eight, proved to be a unique and pivotal moment, as well as a substantial catalyst, in our perfect season. Indeed, it was arguably the epitome of our perfection.

"Our defense was ferocious, thanks largely to Tom Kiley's power tackling, and denied Francis any points but we were ineffective offensively – until the game's final seconds.

"I was on the field at the time and watched Bobby catch Zimmy's late first pass, an unprecedented thrill, especially because at first I thought he had made it into the end zone, the game was over and we had miraculously won. Alas, I was momentarily deflated to learn otherwise but realized we, now on the two-yard line, were in easy striking distance of an actual score. And YES! Zimmy and Bobby connected again to ice the game. I believe it may well have been the most exhilarating moment of my life up to then."

Bill McGovern: "I do recall the last two plays as part of that 'story book' chapter of the season. I was aware of how good John and Bobby were, and, if given the chance, they could pull through in a clutch situation...and they did....twice. I think that win helped us for the rest of the season; that if we were in a tight situation, we had the talent, strength, and determination to get through it."

Anthony Mercogliano '64: "We had defeated St. Francis, a perennial rival, in a close game the previous year, ending their chances to be League champs, so they were 'out for blood.' The game was scoreless until the final set of downs in the fourth quarter and then finally junior quarterback John Zimmermann did it on two passes to junior receiver Bob Bowman for a 6-0 victory. The crowd went berserk!!"

Patricia Mansfield Phelan (Chuck's sister): "Chaminade immediately won the game, and the stands and players went a bit mad with joy."

Charles Raubicheck '64: "The pesky Terriers, supported by their speedy ball carriers, were deadlocked with the Flyers in a scoreless duel until only ten seconds remained in the game. On 3rd down Zimmermann lofted a 52 yard desperation pass which Bob Bowman hauled in on the 2 before being pushed out of bounds. The Flyer QB then hit Bowman with a scoring pass in the far corner of the end zone as the 4600 fans in Chaminade Bowl poured out on the field to congratulate their fellow classmen."

Mike "Tiny" Reisert: "Before I begin about the last two plays, I always remember two plays whenever I think about the '61 team. Against St. Francis it was either the first or the second play from scrimmage, St. Francis had the ball and was handing off to their big fullback, Ed Fabre. I met him in the backfield head to head, he went down, one of my best moves. The second play I always think of was against St. Michael's up in the Bronx. Sellerberg, DeMeo, Reisert, the left side of the line, we were good. What I remember it was either Tuohy or Biasi running down the field for a touchdown. That was all she wrote, we went on to beat the team who had the meanest looking football players. Coach Thomas would say, 'Don't look at them.'

"As to the last two plays against St. Francis, I knew they wouldn't score but couldn't figure out why we couldn't score. I'm sure I used some colorful language in the huddle about getting the job done. Frustrated, nervous and angry, what the hell was wrong? What I do remember is blocking for a pass play, not watching anything but my man. It wasn't till I heard the crowd that I looked up and saw we had a long completion. Running to the huddle for the next play, I was sure that we would win; we just had to do what the Coaches had us practice every day. Stay on your man until the play is over. A win is a win. We won and the rest is history. Coach Joe and Charlie made this team, and I am forever proud to have been a part of it and played with some of the best guys and friends in my life."

Bill Sellerberg: "I remember snippets from that game. I remember our many first-half frustrations. The St. Francis players couldn't move the ball on us but we just couldn't move the ball on them either. It was the kind of defensive struggle you come to expect on a muddy day, only it wasn't raining. I remember a play, a lost opportunity that happened just before the end of the first half. St. Francis was deep in their own territory (east end of the stadium field) and it was fourth down and time for them to punt. I was determined to make something happen by blocking a punt. On the snap I broke through the line and attempted to leap over a blocking halfback on my way to where I thought the ball would leave the kicker's foot. Unfortunately, the halfback's shoulder pads caught my ankles mid-stride. I wound up doing a complete flip over him and landing on my butt. Of course, the kick was a beauty. I got up and retreated to provide blocking coverage. Next thing I remember, George Ackerson had caught the ball and was weaving his way through a pack of Terriers in an effort to give us the lead. Somehow he managed to work his way through the entire bunch. I realized that he had a chance to go all the way. There was one Terrier left and I had a pretty good blocking angle on him. Down George went because I arrived about a half second late. The first half ended. The score was zero to zero.

"The second half seemed to be a carbon copy of the first half – defense vs. defense. Late in the game we managed to stop their final attempt to win the game and gave ourselves an outside chance with little time left on the clock. I was one of the offensive blockers trying to provide Zimmy with protection to find an open receiver. We had two strikes against us. I thought we had failed on the third attempt when suddenly the crowd roared. Bob Bowman made a great catch but it wasn't over yet. We hustled downfield and tried again. This time Bob was wide open. What a finish!"

Elsewhere herein Bill has written: "Our game vs. St. Francis Prep was one for the ages. St. Francis was an excellent team and a formidable opponent. It was amazing how our 'junior' players made all the difference."

George Valva: "I remember being on the sidelines with my 'game-day buddy,' Cliff Molloy, bemoaning the fact that a tie with St. Francis would ruin our 'goal' of being the first Chaminade team to go undefeated and UNTIED in its glorious football history. While we did not give up hope of winning the game, both teams were playing tough on defense and were so well matched that a win seemed highly unlikely. This seemed especially true in light of the fact that this was only Zimmy's third game as a starting varsity quarterback!

"With only two precious minutes left in the game we had the ball on our own 48-yard line, a long way to go for a new varsity quarterback. Zimmy took the snap from the center and looked downfield toward the St. Francis sideline. He heaved the ball into the air, and, at that point, I lost sight of the play. I was aware that there were players from both teams and a referee sprinting downfield and then... a roar from the crowd!

"'What happened?' I blurted twice to Cliff.

"'I think DeMeo caught a pass and the ball is down near the end zone.'

"We went wild when the referee confirmed Cliff's call! Not a touchdown but a great pass, catch and run – two yards left to pay dirt but by no means a sure thing! Time out called... I was sure we were going to try to run it in as our offensive line was tough and Mr. Thomas, our head coach, always 'preached' that anything less than three yards on a run play was a fail! So what happens next? Zimmy goes back to pass...Oh, no...not a pass! Yup, a pass! The ball goes up in the air and into the arms of my good friend and fellow senior classmate Billy DeMeo who runs it in for the score. We won, we won!!! Thank God for Billy, I thought! But wait.... it wasn't Billy after all, it was Bob Bowman, another junior who made the catch and run on both plays and went in for the TD. Holy cow, how can that be? It was then that I knew that the Men of '62 and the Men of '63 could and would combine to go down as the greatest football team in Chaminade history!"

Frank Zaino '62: "What I remember from the St. Francis game as I stood on the track with the rest of the cheerleaders was Bill Sellerberg coming off the field covered in mud with an unbelievable look of determination on his face. He reminds me of that famous picture of [Green Bay Packers middle linebacker] Ray Nitschke sitting on the bench covered with a tarp also covered with mud. Go Flyers '62!"

This was the scene at the Chaminade Bowl following the '61 Flyers' last-minute 6-0 victory over St. Francis. The team rejoices, a cheerleader exults and Coach Thomas strides to meet his opposite number, Coach Vince O'Connor.

(Photograph courtesy of Chuck Mansfield and used with permission.)

Once in a while you are lucky enough to have the thrill and satisfaction of working with a group of men who are willing to make every sacrifice to achieve a goal, and then experience the achieving of it

with them. ... In this, believe me, there is a payment that cannot be matched in any other pursuit.

— Colonel Earl "Red" Blaik in
When Pride Still Mattered:
A Life of Vince Lombardi
By David Maraniss

A SONG OF TRIUMPH BY "THE VALVE"

By Tom Kiley and Chuck Mansfield

We laughed and sang as though tomorrow wasn't there.

— Tom Kiley

"Send in The Valve!" was the passionate cry of our cheerleaders and spectators that was often heard at our football games. "The Valve" was our stalwart lineman George Valva, whose relatively low center of gravity made him impossible to move. He was also a ferocious blocker and tackler. Off the gridiron George was an accomplished singer, a legendary doo-wopper from the hard-bitten streets of Freeport. This aspect of his spirit and personality has remained fresh in our minds all these years later, especially his impromptu performance on our team bus after our eighth consecutive and championship victory over Holy Cross High School in Flushing, N.Y., in November 1961. Unforgettably, George stood in the aisle of the bus as we rode back to Mineola, and paced slowly up and down as he sang with gusto his own lyrics to the Shirelles' 1958 hit song, "I Met Him on a Sunday," while teammates provided the backing vocals, "Doo ronde ronde ronde pa pa doo ronde." If only we had a video, it would have gone viral on YouTube.

With our readers' indulgence we have taken some lyrical liberties because, alas, we don't actually have The Valve's own wonderful original lyrics, nor does he. Oh, cell phones, where were ye?

Thank you, George, for a great season and an awesome memory of a spectacular and spontaneous performance.

George's essay, "I Stood on the Sidelines Praying the Memorare*," appears later herein.*

WE BEAT THEM ON A SUNDAY
(By George C. Valva, 1961)

Sung to the tune of

I MET HIM ON A SUNDAY
(By The Shirelles, 1958)

Hicksville was first on a Saturday
(Ooo)

Edged Stepinac the next Sunday
(Ooo)

Nipped Francis on the last play
(Ooo)

Shutout the Gaels on a home day
(Ooo)

Saint John's they were easy prey
(Ooo)

Climbed the Mount on our best day
(Ooo)

Nipped Hayes much to their dismay
(Ooo)

Nailed the Cross on our last day
(Ooo)

Time to say bye bye baby

Doo ronde ronde ronde pa pa
Doo ronde ronde ronde pa pa
Doo ronde ronde ronde pa pa
Doo oo oo oo ooo

We played hard. We won. We sang all the way home. We were looking for an echo, an answer to our sound. A place to be in harmony. A place we almost found.

— Tom Kiley and Kenny Vance

COACH JOE THOMAS:
EXHORTATIONS TO EXCELLENCE

By Chuck Mansfield

Follow your bliss. If you do follow your bliss, you put yourself on a kind of track that has been there all the while waiting for you, and the life you ought to be living is the one you are living. When you can see that, you begin to meet people who are in the field of your bliss, and they open the doors to you. I say, follow your bliss and don't be afraid, and doors will open where you didn't know they were going to be. If you follow your bliss, doors will open for you that wouldn't have opened for anyone else.

— Joseph Campbell

Coach Thomas passed away on January 6, 2011, at the age of 95. The following article about him was first published in the Syosset Advance *newspaper circa 1990 under the title "Lessons from a Legend."*

In his final years Coach was very much my surrogate father, and we saw each other about twice weekly. He was an epic leader, a hero and a friend whose favorite quotation was "Follow your bliss."

May he rest in peace.

There is a strong link between my experience at Chaminade and that I would gain years later in the Marine Corps. (Conveniently, both institutions have the same colors: Crimson and Gold.)

I entered Chaminade in September 1958 as a thirteen-year-old freshman. At an even younger age I had arrived at the decision that, if accepted by the school's admissions apparatus, I would enthusiastically attend. I readily admit that part of Chaminade's attraction for me derived from the spirited support that its administration, students and their parents, as well as its neighbors, accorded its football program. For me as a boy, attending Chaminade football games was probably my top priority, at least in the autumn.

Perhaps the most prestigious athletic award given annually at Chaminade goes to the outstanding varsity football player. It is the Terzi Award, named in memory of Marine Corps Captain Joseph Terzi, a 1937 Chaminade alumnus, of whom the eighteenth Marine Corps Commandant, General Alexander Archer Vandegrift, wrote the following on the occasion of a banquet honoring Terzi's memory in 1944:

> Three years after our country was treacherously attacked by the enemies against whom he later so gallantly fought, I wish to join you in paying honor to a brave and able officer. As his commanding general during the campaign on Guadalcanal, I take particular pride in his fine record during those difficult months. There he won the Silver Star medal for remaining in an exposed and isolated outpost overrun by an enemy night attack against our lines, eventually directing four of the five men in the outpost to safety when they were surrounded and could no longer hold their isolated position. The day after Christmas last year he received the wound that cost his life while leading his company in a savage frontal assault during the attack on Cape Gloucester, New Britain. His brilliant leadership and great courage on that occasion won him the high honor of the Navy Cross.

> When Captain Terzi first entered the Marine Corps we learned from his friends, associates, and teachers that he excelled on the football field no less than in the classroom. Those qualities of grit, determination, intelligence, and leadership which he developed in sports and studies in his community are the qualities that made him a distinguished officer in

the Marine Corps. His brother officers and I salute his memory.

Another young military officer, this one a U.S. Army lieutenant who was awarded two Bronze Stars for his courage and leadership in combat in the European theater, was Joseph F. Thomas. Many Long Island readers and sports fans, as well as some in New York City, will still recognize his name. From 1948 to 1988 he distinguished himself as coach and teacher at Chaminade. Indeed, many of the school's alumni and their parents, not to mention fellow coaches, faculty members and competitors, will remember the dedication of this extraordinary Christian gentleman who has become a virtual legend in his own time.

A native of Philadelphia born in 1915, a product of Marianist education both there and at the University of Dayton, and today still a remarkably youthful presence, Coach has given of himself selflessly to many Chaminade men and their families, as well as to many others. To be sure, in the minds of many who know him, he is one of the rarest of men and could well have achieved in coaching the status of, say, a Vince Lombardi, a Don Shula or a Bill Parcells. Coach chose instead to devote his life to the young men of Chaminade, to whom he has imparted the richness of his spirit, as well as memories to last a lifetime.

Sporting his iconic sunglasses, Coach Thomas dispatches his star linebacker, Tom Kiley, to do some more defensive damage. Tom has written, "I think he said, 'Now get in there and block that damn punt.' Easy for him to say."

*Authors' note: In the photograph above, Coach appears to be holding Tom's shirtsleeve but some have noticed that there may be an object clenched in his right hand, perhaps a shortwave radio. After a canvassing of teammates, however, the consensus is that Coach is merely grabbing Tom's jersey. Of this, Tom Condon '65, Ray's younger brother, who played halfback for Chaminade in 1963 and '64 and coached high-school football for 40 years, has written: "It's a classic photo of Coach Joe Thomas in action with his trademark aviator sunglasses. He is definitely holding the jersey with his right hand to make an emphatic coaching point. He is making sure that Tom K. is listening to this **one-way conversation** that needed no verbal response, just action and results. I am positive that the coaching points were clear and brief and that TK got the message. That's why it was the perfect season."*

Now in my late fifties, I remember. These memories—and there are many—are still with me but among the most vivid certainly are those moments of inspiration and exhilaration that always came on autumn Sunday afternoons. It is these memories that were provided, actually created, by Coach Thomas, for his energy and spirit were palpable.

Sometimes, as my mind looks back, I believe I may have taken Coach for granted. In other words, I would ask myself then: Isn't everyone this good? Anyway, my first close-up experience with him came as a fifteen-year-old junior on Chaminade's 1960 varsity football team. His reputation, of course, had preceded him. He was universally said to be a great coach, demanding and hard-driving, as well as a special sort of man. Still, how were my teammates and I to have known that he was in fact any different from other high-school coaches or teachers?

And in truth, I've never known a man worth his salt who in the long run, deep down in his heart, didn't appreciate the grind, the discipline. There is something in good men that really yearns for discipline and the harsh reality of head to head combat.

— Vince Lombardi

Well, we learned; did we ever! Yet, the lessons he taught and the mark he left on us, be it in gym class, on the basketball court, on the football field or on the track, were not fully understood or appreciated by us while we were still Chaminade students. He made us winners while at the same time instilling in us humility when we savored victory. As juniors, we became League champions with a 6-1-1 record. A year later, we went 8-0-0 and became Chaminade's first undefeated and untied varsity football team, as well as League champs for the second consecutive year. This was the first time in Chaminade's history that back-to-back varsity football titles had been won, a feat that wouldn't be repeated at the school until seventeen years later.* (A large black and white photograph of that first undefeated and untied team still hangs on the second floor of the west wing of the school just off the main lobby.)

That unforgettable thrill produced a deep and abiding sense of pride, not only in us players but throughout the entire student body (Chaminade's 1962 yearbook theme was "The Year of Champions"). Furthermore, everyone knew and readily acknowledged that the achievement would simply not have been, were it not for Coach's leadership and motivational skills. In the last analysis, regardless of the rigorous conditioning and precision drills he put us through, the key to our success was that he enabled us truly to believe in ourselves.

Coach's pre-game and, particularly, half-time talks with his team were the most compelling motivators I have ever heard or seen. Significantly, it mattered not that we were winning or losing. (Make no mistake; clearly, he preferred the former.) What did matter, and mattered most in his mind, was that there was a game or another half to be played, and played as well as it could be, for the real name of the game called football, as he never failed to communicate to each of his players, is excellence. He has often said to me, "Show me a student's school notebook and I'll tell you if he'll make it on our team." Football or not, academics always came first. And before *and* after every game, win or lose, Coach made sure his team knelt to pray together.

I strongly believe there's another reason Coach's exhortations to excellence were so powerful: Although his coaching responsibilities necessitated his being on the sidelines, he was, in a very real sense, *in* the game. While each of us players was concerned with managing his position and executing his assignments as well as he could for as long as he was in the game, Coach was in there too—intellectually, viscerally and spiritually—on every play at every position—"110% for forty-eight minutes," as he used to say. Not only did he take the game seriously, I believe he took it *personally*. His players knew it, and we all felt it.

I don't say these things because I believe in the "brute" nature of man or that men must be brutalized to be combative. I believe in

God, and I believe in human decency. But I firmly believe that any man's finest hour —his greatest fulfillment to all he holds dear—is that moment when he has to work his heart out in a good cause and he's exhausted on the field of battle—victorious.

— Vince Lombardi

Incidentally, among the hundreds who also played football for Coach are two-time Tony Award winning actor Brian Dennehy (who passed away on April 15, 2020), retired Boston Patriots All Pro defensive end Larry Eisenhauer (who passed away on January 29, 2020), retired IBM CEO Louis Gerstner and former New York Jets head coach Al Groh. Former U.S. Senator Alfonse D'Amato ran track for Coach.

When I went off to play college football, I wondered and even partially dreaded what it would be like. You see, I had figured that college competition, practices, workouts and the like would be, by definition, more difficult than those in high school. It was not so; they were non-events.

In college we were expected to stay in shape on our own time, and our coach there even told us not to smoke in public! Be that as it may, Coach Thomas's approach to physical conditioning included summer double practice sessions, running through stacks of tires, three-man rolls, bull-in-the-ring and seemingly endless wind sprints, to cite a few of my personal favorites. For me it was to prove a valuable vaccine of experience three years after my Chaminade graduation when I attended my first Marine Corps summer camp, and again a few years later as a Marine lieutenant in Vietnam.

Pictured above are (left to right) Coach's son Jeff, Coach, son Mike, wife Kay and daughter Kathy Cybriwsky. The photo was taken on September 30, 1995, at Jeff's home as the family celebrated Coach's 80th birthday.

(Photograph courtesy of Tom Kiley and used with permission.)

Coach has also been a wonderfully dedicated husband and father; he is also a grandfather and great-grandfather. His wife, the late Mary Kathryn Herrold Thomas, and he met while both were students at the University of Dayton. As unusual as it may seem to some, Coach's love affair with "Kay," as she was called, has never ended, despite the fact that she passed away in 1996. He has told me that every Sunday, as a rule, he visits her final resting place and speaks to her of the week just past and the beautiful life they shared.

Kathy Thomas Cybriwsky, Joseph F. (Jeff) Thomas, Jr. and Michael Thomas are Coach and Kay's children. Already mentioned, Jeff is a Chaminade classmate of mine, and Mike attended both Chaminade and Dayton with my brother Mike. Thanks to his three kids, Coach today delights in his nine grandchildren and three great-grandchildren.

Next to my parents, Coach Joe Thomas, more than any other person, has been the single greatest influence on who I am. He is, in my own view and that of thousands during his forty years at Chaminade who have benefited from his leadership, or even simply known him, the quintessential role model. He was always there in our midst, and we had only to look to him.

"The Chaminade Man" is the moral standard that Chaminade endeavors to inculcate in every student. *(Authors' note: Please see "Criteria for the Chaminade Man Award" later herein.)* He does the right thing at the right time for the right reason no matter who may be watching. Ironically, although Coach never attended Chaminade as a student, he was and always will be for many, including me, *the* Chaminade Man. I feel privileged to know him, and it is a badge of honor and pride for me to say: I played football for Joe Thomas.

* The 1977 Flyers matched the '61 team's 8-0-0 record while the '78 squad achieved the so far unmatched perfection of 10-0-0, a CHSFL record. It should also be added here that the 1962 team also won the League title, the only "threepeat" in Chaminade football history.

When we see men of worth, we should think of equaling them.

— Confucius

THE MASTER MOTIVATOR

By Clifford F. Molloy

Talent alone didn't do it but, when magnified by the four cornerstones of Flyer football – constant competition, fundamentals, physical, mental and competitive toughness, and superior conditioning – that talent became extremely difficult to beat.

— Al Groh

Cliff is a 1962 classmate, a 1961 Flyer teammate and, along with Mike Reisert, Bill Sellerberg and Dave Tuohy, a 1966 Notre Dame alumnus. At graduation he was commissioned as an officer in the United States Navy and assigned immediately to a Carrier Strike Group in the Far East for two years. He subsequently served in the Riverine Forces for a year in Vietnam's Mekong Delta.

After leaving the Navy Cliff remained on the West Coast and began a long real estate career that included work on both coasts leading to a return to the East Coast some years ago.

Cliff, his wife, Jeanne, and their two daughters, Casey and Erin, live in Glen Ridge, N.J.

Thank you, Cliff.

We have to be humbled that someone as accomplished as Dr. Kevin R. Loughlin would reflect so warmly on our small accomplishment, which pales against his contributions to humanity.

The seeds for perfection were planted freshman year on a dirt practice field running along Jericho Turnpike. This field, in lore and in fact, was covered with rocks. You could sense the collective, "Are they serious?" We didn't know where we were going but we knew if we wanted to play Chaminade football this is how we had to get there.

The perfect block, the perfect handoff, the perfect route, the perfect pass, the perfect stance, the perfect tackle were all forged here. Over the years how many times did Coach McGuckin or Coach Thomas hit your helmet in the practice huddle to correct a small detail in your execution?

"FIRE OUT!!" Coach Thomas would exhort. For emphasis he would punch his cupped left hand with a weak right fist with the thumb pointing up. "FIRE OUT!!" We are going to go on "GO!" not hut. "GO!"

Coach Thomas surveys his players on the field.

"GO!" "FIRE OUT!!" He would always be walking among us, not missing a thing. In what appeared to be a man moving among giants in pads was in actuality a giant moving among men.

We came into the skull session Monday before the St. Francis game and Coach had listed the football champions of the Catholic High School Athletic Association (CHSAA) for the previous five years.

1961	?
1960	Chaminade
1959	St. Francis
1958	Chaminade
1957	St. Francis
1956	Chaminade

Next to that he listed the winner of the Chaminade-St. Francis game for each year. It read:

1960	Chaminade
1959	St. Francis
1958	Chaminade
1957	St. Francis
1956	Chaminade

The die was cast. In one stroke of genius Coach Thomas elevated everything we were to do to a higher level. We all knew St. Francis was a big game but only a game on the way to the championship. Irrespective of the opponent, we knew we could do this if, on each and every play, we "FIRE OUT!!"

We did.

There's an old fable that a guard is a fullback with his brains knocked out – but it's only a fable. I'm not saying guards are smarter than fullbacks or other ball carriers, but their blocking assignments lead them to see more of what makes a play succeed or fail.

— Vince Lombardi in
*When Pride Still Mattered:
A Life of Vince Lombardi*
By David Maraniss

CHAMINADE HOLDS MEMORIAL FOR FORMER FOOTBALL COACH

By Geoffrey Walter

The coach had taught them how to win, lifted their self-image, challenged them to accomplish things that they had thought might be beyond their reach.

> — David Maraniss in his book
> *When Pride Still Mattered:*
> *A Life of Vince Lombardi*

Geoff is an award-winning journalist and award-winning photographer. He is a graduate of Chaminade (2001) and Fordham University (2005). He has extensively covered the Flyers since 2010, with his work appearing in numerous publications both in print and online, including Newsday, The New York Daily News, The Garden City News, Mineola American, Manhasset Press, Mineola Patch, The Williston Times *and* The New Hyde Park Herald-Courier, *among others. He is a lifelong Long Islander and resident of Garden City, N.Y.*

Thank you, Geoff.

Not everyone is eulogized by a co-owner of an NFL team or a two-time Tony award winner of both stage and screen, even if it is just by letter.

The remarks of both Dan Rooney and Brian Dennehy were read to a crowd 160 strong last Saturday at where a memorial Mass was held in Darby Auditorium for former Flyers football coach Joseph F. Thomas, who passed away on Jan. 6 [2011] at the age of 95.

This photo of U.S. Army Lieutenant Joseph Thomas, displayed alongside the urn holding his cremains at a Memorial Mass for him at Chaminade on February 5, 2011, was taken in England in 1944.

(Photograph courtesy of Geoff Walter and used with permission.)

During his four decades at the school until his retirement in 1988, Thomas compiled a 120-46-7 record during his time as the varsity head coach from 1948-69 – 18th all-time in Nassau County history and 32nd in Long Island history – seven Catholic High School Football League Championships – including an undefeated season of 8-0-0 in 1961 – and was named CHSFL coach of the year seven times.

"Joe Thomas has been a powerful part of my life for over 60 years now and that's not going to change now because of his passing," Dennehy, one of the "pillars of strength" of the 1955 football team, wrote. "I can't think of another man whose impact was more powerful in my life. The essential purpose of the man, his rock-solid character, his profound faith, his love for and dedication to the young men he worked with, his enthusiasm for football – for all sports – and for life in general made him a great teacher and an extraordinary example of how life should be lived."

Rooney, the American ambassador to Ireland, wrote of Thomas that "he did so much for me as a young man playing football at North Catholic, as he did for all the players and students he instructed. No one other than my parents did more to motivate and push me to the right path to become a man of integrity, character, honesty; Joe was that person."

Thomas left school in his sophomore year to work on a milk wagon during the Great Depression before finally graduating from St. John the Baptist High School in Philadelphia and was given a full scholarship to the University of Dayton by Harry Baujan, who had once played for Knute Rockne.

Thomas would go on to become the star quarterback of what became known as the Quaker State Express.

Thomas also worked as the North Catholic basketball coach before leaving for WWII. Thomas's son, Joseph "Jeff" Thomas Jr., quipped that the other coaches couldn't figure out his dad's zone defense, and told his father to "use it until you lose... and they never lost," going 28-0 and winning the state championship.

"You do not coach lacrosse, you coach young men," Chaminade coach Bob Pomponio said, recalling Thomas still doing laps in the pool at 60. "It doesn't matter what sport it is, what matters is you coach the young men."

The junior Thomas also told a story of how his father went to Art Rooney, telling the Steelers' owner that he had no uniforms for the North Catholic High School football team, and ended up getting the practice uniforms of the Steelers, which the high school players used in 1946-47.

The entire memorial service was coordinated within two weeks after Thomas' death by the school.

"I'm sure my father would be surprised and delighted to see you all," the younger Thomas said. "My family greatly appreciates your hospitality." Also present were Coach Thomas' three sisters from Philadelphia as well as nine grandchildren and five great grandchildren.

"Dad did not just have a daughter and two sons," Thomas Jr. said. "He had a daughter and 10,000 sons and he knew you all and he remembered names and places and events and plays and who did what, where and when."

The Gospel reading that night was Matthew 5:3-10, better known as the Beatitudes.

"They fit so well for Mr. Thomas," Fr. James Williams, S.M., said in his homily. "God calls all of us to be a superhero and Mr. Thomas heard that call. Wasn't he a man detached from worldly honor? Wasn't he a man who avoided money or pleasure or power as his top priority? Wasn't our experience that of someone who brought out mercy; for whom God's will was most important?"

Fr. Williams also read from several letters from former students, including one that stated "it seems clear to me that you were placed, indirectly, in the perfect spot where you could be a beacon of light and provide such a powerful image for so many thousands of young men," and "football or not, academics always came first."

The younger Thomas also recalled an incident where his father was cut off on Hempstead Turnpike in Levittown by another driver which he felt summed up his persona.

"There wasn't anywhere in his body for negativity. I never saw my father angry," he said. "The perception was always in that vein of positive energy. He was one who understood on a fundamental level that what you keep in your head is what you get in your life."

Recalling his father's half-time talks to the teams, Thomas Jr. said that they were "so powerful I didn't want to interfere for fear he might hold back because I was in the room – and never with foul language, never with some of the stuff you see today. He helped people believe in who they could be and what they could be."

In what appeared to be a man moving among giants in pads was in actuality a giant moving among men.

— Cliff Molloy
on Coach Thomas

FLYER FOOTBALL: WHAT PRIORITY?

By Chuck Mansfield

*Desires dictate our priorities, priorities shape our
choices, and choices determine our actions.*

— Dallin H. Oaks

As I have written elsewhere herein, even as a small boy I dreamt of playing Flyer football, despite the fact that I was, well, *small*. Watching home games at Chaminade with my Dad and friends was always an exciting fall pastime. Still, even my vivid imagination could barely picture me wearing the Crimson and Gold and playing on that football field.

In the spring of 1961, my junior year, unforgettable events occurred that involved and affected me personally. First, I tried out for the varsity baseball team, having played for the Chaminade JV nine in 1960. Three years earlier at age twelve I pitched a perfect game in the Garden City Little League. Moreover, I was on Garden City's 1960 Babe Ruth League All-Star team, which I considered a plus but never advertised. Perhaps most importantly, the fact that Flyer head varsity baseball coach Charlie McGuckin and I already knew each other from the 1960 varsity football season was, in my view, highly positive. I tried out at third base, fielded well, batted righty, hit mostly line drives to left field and failed to survive the first cut.

Next, I was elected president of the student body and Student Council, undoubtedly the highest honor of my young life. Preceding me among holders of these offices were Chaminade legends Jack Lenz, Charlie McGuckin, Jim McLain and Skip Orr, among others.

At the same time, I was chosen by the board of Garden City's *Experiment in International Living* to represent the village and

Chaminade in a European country for the summer of '61. My wife, Mary Ann, then my secret high-school sweetheart, was also selected as Garden City High School's representative and spent three months with a family in Bielefeld, Westphalen, Germany. While there she actually witnessed the beginning of the erection of the Berlin Wall.

My selection was another great honor. Alas, I had little interest in leaving home for the entire summer because it would mean missing Chaminade varsity summer double-session football practices and possibly sacrificing a position on the '61 Flyer eleven. This was a risk I could not and would not take. Stand by.

When I told Chaminade's powers that be that I would not accept the exchange-student honor, a firestorm erupted! Next, the school's administration dispatched two Marianists to my parents' home to implore them to drive some sense into their errant son who was about to walk away from the opportunity of a lifetime for a high-school student. They were the same two good men who later visited my folks to recruit me for the Society of Mary.

As I eavesdropped on the conversation between the brothers and my parents, I was worried at first but soon soothed when I heard my father say, "Brothers, I understand your concern and Chaminade's position but the right answer is to let Chuck make his own decision, one way or the other, for he will have to live with it." I was elated, and that was the end of the meeting. Thanks, Dad.

Chaminade was not pleased with me, to say the least, but soon announced that my St. Anne's School and Chaminade classmate, as well as my freshman football teammate and a fine student, the late Jeff Zabler, would take my place. Happily, he did and the furor died down quickly.

In retrospect, my decision was the right one, at least for me. I was extremely happy *not* to have gone to Europe for the whole summer and couldn't wait for football practices to commence. Despite the often grueling drills of our summer daily double-sessions, I looked forward to the excitement and motivation of another football campaign under the brilliant tutelage and leadership of Messrs. Thomas and McGuckin. In the last analysis, I re-made the varsity, started on both offense and defense, and enjoyed immeasurably our unprecedented perfect season.

*Let Chuck make his own decision, one way or
the other, for he will have to live with it.*

— Charles F. Mansfield, Sr.

A TRIBUTE TO COACH CHARLIE MCGUCKIN

By Tom Kiley and Chuck Mansfield

He was the Flyers' co-captain and starting quarterback although he played only intramural football in his first two years and varsity football in his junior and senior years. Still, Charlie received All-Scholastic and All-Catholic honors, and was the Terzi Award recipient.

— Kiley and Mansfield

Coach passed away on January 15, 2017, at age 84. The following citation, which we wrote, was presented to Mr. McGuckin, who was honored by our team at a dinner celebrating the 50th anniversary of our perfect season on September 16, 2011. The document was encased in an attractive plaque that Coach's daughter Mary said he hung on his living room wall the next day and treasured for the rest of his life.

May he rest in peace.

The members of the Chaminade Flyers First Undefeated and Untied Varsity Football Team, 1961 Catholic High School Football League Champions, hereby recognize, congratulate and thank

CHARLES GERARD MCGUCKIN

for his outstanding leadership, talent, tutelage and coaching abilities on the occasion of our team's fiftieth anniversary of its extraordinary championship season.

Coach Charlie McGuckin is a born leader. Chaminade's 1950 Crimson and Gold yearbook says of him: "Charlie was the smoothest athlete in the school as could be seen by his exhibitions on diamond, gridiron and hardwood. His ready smile and excellent class work (that earned him four years on the Honor Roll) made him an outstanding Flyer." In April 2000, Coach Joe Thomas, Charlie's coach, mentor and friend, told a small group of some here present that Charlie was the greatest athlete he had ever seen in his forty years at Chaminade and many years before that in Pittsburgh. The same yearbook also tells us that "The 1950 Chaminade baseball team will go down as one of the best in Flyer history." An outfielder who played varsity baseball all four years, he was also team captain, batted an impressive .317 and went on to play college and semi-pro ball. He was Flyers team co-captain and starting quarterback although he played only intramural football in his first two years and varsity football in his junior and senior years. Still, Charlie received All-Scholastic and All-Catholic honors, and was the Terzi Award recipient. On the basketball court he was the Flyers varsity squad's third-highest scorer with 150 points. To top it all off, Charlie was class president and president of the Student Council. Space does not permit a recitation of his myriad other achievements and endeavors. For many of us, Charlie will always be "Mister McGuckin" and "Coach." Not only did he coach and train us, he served as the perfect exemplar of The Chaminade Man. To him go our most profound gratitude, our best wishes and a heartfelt *Fortes in unitate!**

* Fortes in unitate *is Latin for 'Strength in unity' and Chaminade's motto.*

Coach McGuckin, Chaminade's 1949 varsity quarterback, won
All-Scholastic and All-Catholic honors, plus the Terzi Award.
He also starred for the Flyers in basketball and baseball.

(Photograph courtesy of Tom Kiley and used with permission.)

*[For Vince Lombardi] Both [the Jesuits and Army Coach Earl Blaik]
emphasized discipline, order, organization, attention to detail,
repetition, the ability to adjust to different situations and remain
flexible in pursuit of a goal while sustaining an obsession with one
big idea.*

—David Maraniss in his book
*When Pride Still Mattered:
A Life of Vince Lombardi*

IN PRAISE OF CHARLIE MCGUCKIN

By Tom Kiley

Charlie was the smoothest athlete in the school as could be seen by his exhibitions on diamond, gridiron and hardwood. ... To top it all off, Charlie was class president and president of the Student Council.

— Chaminade's 1950
Crimson and Gold
yearbook

The obituary read:
McGUCKIN Charles Gerard of Syosset and Sarasota, FL on January 15, 2017, at 84 years of age.

Coach McGuckin in his later years.

(Photograph courtesy of Mary McGuckin and used with permission.)

It contained the usual language of farewell, mentioning his beautiful wife Maggie and his five children and nine grandchildren. It referred to the Alzheimer's Association and his forty-year career as coach, teacher and mentor in Long Island sports. It did not chronicle the wins and many fewer losses or the half dozen or more championships he was a part of, much less the lives he touched along the way or the respect and admiration his players had for him. It did not speak of his personal generosity, his kindness to defeated and deflated young coaches or his crankiness when losing, while remaining the sportsman always. Nor did it reveal the single expletive he would let fly when he had reached his limit. "Son of a buck!" he would mutter, which never failed to bring a smirk to the faces of his players. But run for the hills and God forgive you if he saw that smirk!

Just six years before, he had been honored at the 50th anniversary reunion of our undefeated, untied team. Back in '61 coaching had just begun to be the engine of his working life, his thoughts of law school having finally faded. Through a combination of personality, passion and an immense will to win, he came to transcend football coaching to become a master teacher, mentor and, finally, a legend. Now he was gone, the last coaching link to our glorious season. It was hard to imagine that enormous vitality finally, fully exhausted. Perhaps not only soldiers just fade away.

A couple of years before, I had heard through the ever-thinning Chaminade grapevine that Coach McGuckin had left his retirement home in Sarasota, Florida, and was back on Long Island, residing with his beloved Maggie in a nursing home in Melville. I resolved to visit whenever I could, usually on a Wednesday. At first it was startling to see Coach in a wheelchair, but his eyes were still bright and blue. Over time we reminisced about football, his coaching career at Chaminade and Holy Family and the players on our '61 squad. Then there were times when we slid into the blurred places of memory.

It seemed to me he remembered our '61 team with greater clarity than he did the great players and teams he coached at Holy Family.

He always brightened at the mention of Kirmser and LoGalbo; or Zimmermann or Bowman or Rottkamp. They were his guys, talented, yes, but tough as well. The rough exterior was gone now, abandoned in favor of pleasant memory and sentiment. Of course, they were his baseball guys too, so that may provide a partial explanation.

He loved baseball, a game he also knew inside and out. One Sunday morning in the early sixties I saw him throw out, Furillo-like, a runner trying to go from first to third on a base hit to right, the grass he patrolled for Creedmoor Hospital. A few innings later another runner tried the same trick with the same result. I was reminded of the old Dizzy Gillespie line, "The professional is the guy that can do it twice." Back then Creedmoor had a small baseball stadium and a semi-pro team that played against teams from other hospitals for the entertainment of fans and patients. It was a fast league, populated by top amateurs and some ex-minor leaguers, just like Coach was.

As we were conversing one day, my mind wandered back to my first varsity encounter with Mr. McGuckin. I say "varsity" because he had been my freshman basketball coach. It happened in 1960 just before our first pre-season scrimmage was about to begin. Typically, it was brief and to the point. Without prior notice he pulled me by the sleeve to get me away from our team, which had gathered on the sideline. Pure McGuckin, it was short and sweet.

"You ever play linebacker?" he asked.

"No, sir."

"Well, you're starting at linebacker."

And for the next six years of playing ball, I was a linebacker. That is a pleasant memory.

After a while I became familiar with his caregivers at the nursing home. One day I asked his nurse if she knew for whom she was caring.

"Why, of course," she replied, "That's my friend Charlie!"

"But do you know he is one of the most famous coaches in the history of Suffolk County?"

"Why, Charlie," she exclaimed, "I didn't know you were famous!" I left some evidence of his tremendous coaching career pinned to his door to ensure his anonymity would not continue.

"Hey," I wanted to yell, "this man is not just another old man in a wheelchair."

It was on a bleak day in December in 2016, with darkness coming on, that our late afternoon conversation was interrupted by a call to dinner, after which exercise was scheduled. Coach suggested I stay, but I couldn't or wouldn't, so I wished him a Merry Christmas and gave him a hug. Then we shook hands. The handshake was warm but not as strong as before, and I noticed his hands seemed small for an all-star quarterback. We said goodbye for the last time although I did not know it at the time.

Christmas and New Year's came and went swiftly, as the holidays often do, so I was not prepared to read the obituary of Charles Gerard McGuckin in *Newsday* on January 17. Death often comes disguised as surprise. But this one hurt more than most.

The wake was quiet and dignified and surprisingly small. I met his family for the first time. Our old coaches were not our pals. The curtain of their personal lives was rarely lifted. I did not stay long. None of his old players were there, which gave me pause. Perhaps, I thought, they would come in numbers to his funeral, as they had done for his mentor. Of one thing I was certain. Charlie McGuckin would be buried with the bright gleam of honor still attached to everything he had done in life. And, most important to all the young men he coached, he had modeled the life of a Catholic man, a family man, a communicant, a genuine part of an older America. A fine person, he practiced virtue beneath a tough and sometimes irascible exterior, when much of America was beginning to question what virtue was or had become unsure of how to define it.

He was certainly one of a kind. Like his mentor and friend, Coach Thomas, he will always be remembered in the hearts of our championship team, still undefeated after all these years. Rest in peace, Coach McGuckin. Son of a buck!

Tom Kiley
Linebacker 1961

Charlie made sure that all of the seniors saw some playing time.

— Ray Condon

"I ALWAYS WANTED TO BE LIKE MR. MCGUCKIN AND STILL DO."

By Carl T. LoGalbo

Not only did he coach and train us, [Mr. McGuckin] served as the perfect exemplar of The Chaminade Man.

— Kiley and Mansfield

I always wanted to be like Mr. McGuckin and still do. He was my high school football and baseball coach. And he was my idol back then and still is. Coach McGuckin always knew what to say and how to say it. Always balanced, never excessive. Always supportive, never critical. Always imparting a winning attitude, never negative. And he always guided me on how to do the right thing on the field. More than anything I wanted to please him and make him proud of whatever success I had.

I badly sprained my right ankle early in the Stepinac game when I tackled the returner on a kickoff. It was the second game of the football season and I sat out the next three games. When I got back to playing, mostly in the defensive backfield, I became a spot player. The defense was all set building a reputation as the best in the CHSFL. My special relationship with Coach McGuckin developed with my being the first baseman for our championship baseball team. He was a baseball man, having played in college and in the minor leagues with the Chicago Cubs. He knew the game and taught me how to play it the right way. How to grip the bat without squeezing it. How to swing the bat to get the meat of the wood on the ball. How to expect the fast ball and adjust to the curve. How to put a minimum of body movement in a balanced swing using hips in tandem with arms and shoulders. How best to field my position at first base. And he did this in a way that always built my confidence, which helped me finish my senior year with a .325 batting average and a team-leading four home runs with a league reputation of being a good glove at first.

Coach McGuckin was not only a great teacher and coach but also the kind of man you wanted to be like – a true gentleman, a leader, an advisor and a good family man. He led us to the league championship game against Stepinac in our senior year after beating Holy Cross for the conference title, a game I think we could have won if there was a fence in right field. In about the seventh inning, I hit a high shot deep into right field, maybe 400 feet, that the right fielder turned on and caught just before the bleacher seats. With a man on base it would have been a two-run home run. We lost the championship by one run. Coach was also assertive but not in an irascible way although he could be a bit peppery at times, especially when we lost, which was seldom. He knew what he wanted from his players and we would run through a brick wall to meet his expectations. And he also knew how to handle disappointment, sometimes with just a look. For example, in my junior year against Monsignor McClancy, Coach had me leading off for the first time. I usually hit from three to five in the lineup. There were two Yankee scouts at the game, so naturally I wanted to do well, and I did. My first time up, I hit a home run over the short right field fence. Second time up, I hit the fence in deep right center field and barely made it into an inside the park home run by tripping on rounding third base. Next two at bats, I doubled down the right field line and singled between first and second base. And I played an errorless first base. Well, after the game the scouts went up to Skippy Orr who hit two long fly outs to deep right center field. Was I disappointed? Of course. I think it had something to do with my tripping around third and with Skippy being 6'2" and a superior athlete. After the game I drove back to school with Coach and the first thing he did in the car was give me a look that said, "I know how you feel, you had a great game, let's move on from here."

I loved and admired Coach McGuckin and still do. One of the many regrets I have in life is not staying close with the Coach as the years went by. My two dear friends, Tom and Chuck, the co-authors and great Chaminade men and athletes, did continue their relationship and in some small way I stayed connected with the Coach through them.

I always wanted to be like Mr. McGuckin and still do.

Charlie McGuckin would be buried with the bright gleam of honor still attached to everything he had done in life. And, most important to all the young men he coached, he had modeled the life of a Catholic man, a family man, a communicant, a genuine part of an older America.

— Tom Kiley

TEACHER, COACH, FRIEND:
CHARLIE MCGUCKIN

By Cyril J. Rottkamp

Mr. McGuckin was the epitome of The Chaminade Man.

— Skip Rottkamp

Skip was a muscular, strong and powerful running back and defensive player, who was also a brilliant catcher on Chaminade's varsity baseball team all four years. His reflection, "Chaminade High School: 1959-1963," appears later herein.

Thank you, Skip.

I was fortunate to have known Mr. McGuckin from 1959-1963 at Chaminade High School. For all my years addressing him, it was always Mr. McGuckin for total respect during varsity football (two years) and varsity baseball (four years). Growing up we all have "father figures," be it a father, uncle, neighbor or friend. Well, Mr. McGuckin fit that role for me. I remember him being friendly, approachable, level-headed, knowledgeable and dependable. After practices/games, he would drive me halfway home where my father would pick me up.

To this day in the hallways of Chaminade you hear the phrase "The Chaminade Man."* Mr. McGuckin was the epitome of The Chaminade Man. In the late '40s he played two years of varsity football, was the team captain, starting quarterback and 1949 Terzi Award winner. He played varsity basketball, was the starting guard and third-leading scorer. For four years he played varsity baseball and was the team captain and outfielder. With his extra time Mr. McGuckin was class president and president of the Student Council. He attended Villanova where he played varsity basketball, was the starting guard and the squad's third-leading scorer. He also played varsity baseball for four years and was team captain and an outfielder. He went on to sign a professional baseball contract for three years with the Chicago Cubs, batting .334 in 1954.

Pictured above are Coach Charlie McGuckin (left) and Skip Rottkamp at our 1961 title team's 50-year reunion in 2011.

(Photograph courtesy of Cyril Rottkamp and used with permission.)

Over the years I stayed in contact with Mr. McGuckin. For many years we corresponded with holiday cards, catching up on our family happenings. It was a real treat to speak with him at the 50th anniversary of the 1961 football team's undefeated and untied reunion. At the end of the evening we walked him back to his car, gave him a hug and said goodbye. Little did I realize that was the last time I would see him and share a wonderful evening. He passed away on January 15, 2017. Mr. McGuckin, 84, of Syosset and Sarasota, Florida, beloved husband of Maggie for 62 years, had five children and nine grandkids.

To this day, my four years at Chaminade High School reflect on my years of being a father, a teacher, an administrator, a coach and a recreation director. Thank you, Mr. McGuckin, for playing an important role in my life!

* At graduation each year Chaminade presents The Chaminade Man Award to the graduating senior who is "outstanding in leadership, scholarship and character." Near the end of this work is a short piece entitled "Criteria for The Chaminade Man Award."

Without a good system and great coaches who knew how to put the right talent in the right positions in that system, winning was not assured. Chaminade always had those elements.

— Frank Biasi

A LETTER OF CONDOLENCES
TO THE MCGUCKIN FAMILY

By Chuck Mansfield

CHARLES F. MANSFIELD, JR.
P.O. Box 1487
Westhampton Beach, N.Y. 11978-7487
631-288-2803
Fax: 631-898-0071
Wireless: 516-818-7030
Winter telephone: 772-232-6173
E-mail: chuckmans@aol.com

February 2, 2017

Ms. Mary McGuckin
(Address omitted in
respect of privacy)

Dear Mary,

My wife, Mary Ann, and I send our belated condolences to you and all of Clan McGuckin on the loss of their beloved father and grandfather. All who knew him will miss him terribly.

I am a 1962 Chaminade graduate who played football for your father in 1960 and '61. I managed to keep in touch with him and your mother over the years and visited with them when they lived in Sarasota. I last visited with your Dad about a year ago at his assisted-living home.

Coach was a prince! I have never known a finer gentleman or gentle man. We have all been greatly blessed to have had him in our lives. One of the things I am happy I did was to play a part in honoring him in 2011 when Chaminade's first undefeated and untied varsity football team held its 50-year reunion. Coach was the guest of honor and was presented with a handsome plaque that my classmate and teammate Tom Kiley and I prepared for him. I believe your father was very pleased by the gesture, and his acceptance "speech" greatly moved all of his players present that evening.

My wife and I are in Florida until April; otherwise, we would have paid our respects in person. Please excuse our absence but know that you and all of Coach's family are in our thoughts and prayers.

Yours sincerely,

Chuck

"TALENT WAS JUST THE BEGINNING."

By Francis X. Biasi, Jr.

I once asked '61 fullback, Carl LoGalbo, who was the most talented back he ever played with at Chaminade, and without hesitation he answered, "Frank Biasi. He really would have been something if he could have stayed healthy in '61."

— Tom Kiley

Born during the waning days of World War II in Queens, N.Y., of Italian, German and Irish heritage, Frank grew up on Long Island attending Catholic grammar school and Chaminade. He excelled in football, baseball and track. He married a "city girl," Angela, in 1966. The couple has four children and six grandchildren. Frank graduated from the University of Maryland and later attended Harvard Business School. From 1966 to 1971 he served in the United States Air Force.

Following military service, Frank's business career included positions as a financial and operations executive in packaging, pharmaceuticals and electronic industries. Frank retired in 1999 but remained active as an independent consultant and a volunteer at The Senior Core of Retired Executives (S.C.O.R.E.).

During their more than four-decade marriage the Biasis lived in Amarillo, Tex., Washington, D.C., Baltimore, Md., Scranton, Pa., Milwaukee, Wi., Lexington, Ky., Danbury, Ct., Springfield, Ma. and Charlotte, N.C.

Frank and Angela moved to the Sacramento area in 2008 where he was inspired to write his first novel, The Brother-in-law. *He wrote two additional books,* The Tanner Extraction *and* Slaughter House Chronicles. *His pen name is F.X. Biasi, Jr.*

Frank passed away on April 8, 2019. May he rest in peace.

He submitted the following reflection on August 1, 2011, in anticipation of our team's 50-year reunion.

Thank you, Frank.

To me it was not surprising that we were undefeated and untied during the '61 football season. From my first day as a freshman on the hot and dusty practice field, I was in awe with the talent of my teammates. However, in time I came to realize that winning resulted from more than talent. Talent was just the beginning. Without a good system and great coaches who knew how to put the right talent in the right positions in that system, winning was not assured. Chaminade always had those elements. But, beyond talented players, great coaches and a sound system, one element that is essential to winning is desire. My teammates in the fall of 1961 exuded desire and, because of that element, we couldn't lose.

Frank Biasi
Halfback

Ability is what you're capable of doing. Motivation determines what you do. Attitude determines how well you do it.

— Lou Holtz

FRANK BIASI: A TEAMMATE REMEMBERS

By Tom Kiley

Once again I saw Frank flying around left end on the old 27 Fly, me at left tackle leading him down the field. Frank was not only a talented runner, but a clever one, who would slow down to allow me to get out in front and then set up my block on cornerback or safety by faking to the inside before going outside or vice versa. He gobbled up hundreds of yards on the play that season.

— Tom Kiley

I wrote the following shortly after Frank's passing in the spring of 2019.

It being Good Friday, I woke up thinking about our friend, Frank Biasi, and what a shame it was that such a wonderful, creative Chaminade '61 teammate had left us way too soon.

And so my mind wandered back to those old, sentimental Flyer football days and settled down in the autumn of 1959, our junior varsity season. There, for old time's sake, once again I saw Frank flying around left end on the old 27 Fly, me at left tackle leading him down the field. Frank was not only a talented runner, but a clever one, who would slow down to allow me to get out in front and then set up my block on cornerback or safety by faking to the inside before going outside or vice versa. He gobbled up hundreds of yards on the play that season and was a big part of a rather prodigious offense and our 10-1-1 season.

I once asked '61 fullback, Carl LoGalbo, who was the most talented back he ever played with at Chaminade, and without hesitation he answered, "Frank Biasi. He really would have been something if he could have stayed healthy in '61." So today, Good Friday, my mind lingers on a healthy Frank Biasi, and those days when Frank's football success seemed assured, as he scored touchdown after touchdown for the JV Flyer eleven. In particular, it gives me great pleasure to remember Frank's 50-yard fourth-quarter run against Holy Cross, which clinched the game and locked up our undefeated, untied season. Frank deserved that.

Fifty years later, as we embraced at the reunion of our 1961 undefeated, untied football squad, Frank whispered in my ear, "27 Fly!"

Rest in peace, Frank. We love you.

Of all losses, time is the most irrecuperable
for it can never be redeemed.

— King Henry VIII

A LETTER OF CONDOLENCES
TO ANGELA BIASI

By Chuck Mansfield

CHARLES F. MANSFIELD, JR.
P.O. Box 1487
Westhampton Beach, NY 11978-7487
631-288-2803
Fax: 631-898-0071
Wireless: 516-818-7030
Email: chuckmans@aol.com
Florida tel.: 772-232-6173 (until 4-22-19)

April 11, 2019

Mrs. Francis X. Biasi, Jr.
(Address omitted in
respect of privacy)

Dear Ange,

Mame and I are deeply saddened by the news of Frank's passing. As my classmate, teammate and loyal friend of more than sixty years, he was a man of enormous talent, and the loss of him already brings grief and sorrow of major proportions to all who knew him. You and your family have our heartfelt condolences. May Frank rest in peace.

The years have passed far too quickly for all of us, I'm confident. Still, for myself, Frank has enriched my life with his goodness and love, and I will always remember him with love and admiration. His books are treasures for humanity and especially for his family for they will be with you always. May God bless you, your children and your grandchildren.

I miss Frank already and believe that God has welcomed him home with open arms.

Respectfully and affectionately,

Chuck

"WE COULD PLAY BALL."

By J. Michael Reisert

By God, I have ability and I know it too well to blush behind it.

— Tom Kiley

A friend of almost sixty-three years, Mike is a 1962 fellow graduate of Chaminade and a member of our first undefeated and untied varsity football team, who was named a High School All American. He is also a 1966 alumnus of the University of Notre Dame.

Mike writes that from the time he entered Chaminade through his senior year, he had Mr. Valva, the father of our teammate George, and our coaches to thank for making him what he became, "a decent football player" who was offered scholarships to a number of schools. When his mother mentioned to him that his Dad would love for him to attend Notre Dame, that's what he decided to do. Teammates Cliff Molloy, Bill Sellerberg and Dave Tuohy joined Tiny in South Bend. Unfortunately, Mike suffered several serious injuries that ended his playing days. Happily, his scholarship was honored through graduation by Notre Dame, unlike many of the other schools that offered him scholarships that would not have been as generous. Many of us have continued to stay in touch thanks to an annual get-together in Florida. As Mike has written, "Thank you, Chaminade Family."

A financial executive, he and his wife Vicci live in Melbourne, Fla. Thank you, Mike.

In September 1958, we were all gathered around each other, in shorts and t-shirts. I didn't know anybody. This was my introduction to the guys who would become my teammates on the Chaminade Flyers football team.

I considered myself to be a decent size until the JV and the varsity teams came through. At that point I was scared, as these were big guys. It was around this time that I got the nickname of Tiny. If my memory serves me, John Stampfel was the boy who initiated that name.

Freshman, sophomore and junior years were somewhat of a blur but our senior year will forever be etched in my mind. Three-man rolls, bull-in-the-ring, boards, calisthenics and wind sprints at the end of practice. Lining up at the goal line and off we go, from five yards to the entire 100 yards. I can vividly recall us cursing, waiting for the end.

Coach Thomas preached to us that the team who is in better shape will in the end win. He was right. There was no question in my mind that we were better prepared and in better shape than any team we played against. We would still be hitting in the fourth quarter when our opponents were getting tired and sloppy.

Bill DeMeo (right foreground) shows his All League pass rush.

My good friend George Valva's Dad would pick him up after practice; he always spoke with me. Sometime early in the year before the games, he pulled me aside and told me in no uncertain words to get tough, that I needed to be a player. It was at that point that I felt that I could be a good tackle. My favorite move was the forearm shiver. Sellerberg, left guard; Reisert, left tackle; DeMeo, left end. We could play ball.

Co-captain, guard and MVP Bill Sellerberg (left) and High School All American tackle Mike Reisert are bloodied but unbowed.

One of my weekly thoughts as we were in the locker room getting ready to play was how nervous I was. Each time I put on a piece of equipment I had to pee. Put on jockstrap, pee; put on hip pads, pee; shoulder pads, pee. Until I had everything on, then I would have to pee again. It was my nerves. How are we going to play? Are we tough enough to be on the field? Every game was the same until the first play. Thanks to our coaching, after the first hit, we knew we could play with the best. Better conditioning and better technique. We went 8-0-0.

Coach Thomas would tell us when we went out for pregame warm-ups not to look at the other team. Of course we did; half of them had beards while most of us had fuzz at best. However, once the game started we knew we could win and we did. Put your head on their numbers and drive. We could and did drive them off.

I love my teammates, classmates and coaches. I have been blessed and honored to know you all.

If you train hard, you'll not only be hard, you'll be hard to beat.

— Herschel Walker

"THANKS, TINY!"

By Kevin M. Walters

There it was: a cut on the bridge of my nose, just like the ones most of our linemen and linebackers had. I finally had my badge of honor.

— Kevin Walters

Another 1962 Chaminade alumnus and a member of our '61 undefeated and untied team, Kevin has rewritten the "Reflections" he prepared for our 50-year reunion. A great defensive cornerback, he was also one of our backup quarterbacks.

Kevin received a B.A. in Mathematics from St. John's and served as an officer in the U.S. Army Reserve.

Today Kevin writes, "As for me, I am indulging myself in the culinary arts. My New Orleans Gumbo was surprisingly tasty. Now on to baking sourdough bread and apple pie."

Many thanks, Kevin, and bon appétit*!*

I would like to share two anecdotal incidents, which involve the same teammate, Mike "Tiny" Reisert. I'm doubtful that Tiny has any recollection of either of these events.

The first occurred mid-season during an afternoon practice on our dusty practice field behind the visitor bleachers, where the only remnants of grass surviving double-sessions and daily afternoon practices were at the field's fence perimeter. The team was in the midst of one of Coach Joe Thomas' most beloved drills, the Chaminade Special. Most times, during this drill I had the enviable task, as one of the back-up quarterbacks, to hand off the ball to one of our running backs.

On this particular day I had the opportunity to be a running back. Tiny was the defensive lineman. After the snap and handoff, I veered off to the head side of his block, a key coaching point, one of many continually emphasized by Coach McGuckin. Thought I: "Not a bad block. I'm gonna make it through that small opening between my lineman and the tackling dummy defining my running lane." It was a good block, but Tiny, feeling the head pressure of the block, executed, in an instant, a 180-degree reverse pivot, arms outstretched their full length horizontally like a figure skater preparing to spin. Just as I was about to clear the hole, the back of Tiny's hand caught me on the bridge of my nose. Yep, knocked me flat on my back, bloodied my nose and dazed me, but that was one heck of a move. Had to sit out of practice for a little while. After practice, I checked myself out in the mirror. There it was: a cut on the bridge of my nose, just like the ones most of our linemen and linebackers had. I finally had my badge of honor.

Thanks, Tiny!

The second incident occurred during the waning minutes of the Holy Cross game. We were on the cusp of a defining moment in Chaminade football history. Win this game and we distinguish ourselves with an accomplishment no other Chaminade varsity football team had ever achieved. There were three to five minutes left in the game and we had a two-touchdown lead, but the Holy Cross offense was starting to have some success moving the ball. During our season the extent of any comments I made in the defensive huddle were limited to "Let's go!" as we broke the huddle, but at this momentous point in the season, I was more outspoken.

Now, instead of exhortations of encouragement or cautionary suggestions of the types of plays we might expect from the Holy Cross offense, I started haranguing my teammates with inane comments like "This game is not over. Don't be thinking about tonight's party..." blah, blah, blah. I did this continuously for two or three consecutive defensive huddles. Finally, Tiny could not endure my outbursts any longer and spoke what I suspect all in the huddle were thinking: "Shut the *bleep* up!" he shouted. And I did. Immediately. Kept my mouth shut the remainder of the game. In retrospect, I always liked to think that my subsequent silence had a positive effect on our defense's performance for the rest of that game.

Thanks, Tiny!

Thanks for the memory.

— Bob Hope

MY JOURNEY TO AN UNDEFEATED AND UNTIED CHAMPIONSHIP SEASON

By William E. Sellerberg

I still feel the sting of the first forearm shiver from Billy Sellerberg that introduced me to Chaminade varsity football.

— Larry Grassini

Like Cliff Molloy, Mike Reisert and Dave Tuohy, Bill is a 1961 Flyer teammate and a 1966 Notre Dame alumnus. He worked for a CPA firm in the city of Chicago until Uncle Sam called him to duty. After his discharge in 1971 the now former U.S. Army officer and a Vietnam War veteran returned to the New York area where he enjoyed a long and successful career with the Long Island Rail Road.

As a teammate Bill distinguished himself as our team's co-captain, Most Valuable Player and recipient of the Lou Gehrig Award.

Avid golfers and skiers, he and his wife Carole have two grown children and are retired in Northport, N.Y.

He has written. "Here is my Chaminade High School football story. It starts with a failure. It continues with priceless comradeships and I hope they will never end."

Thanks, Bill.

As a freshman in the fall of 1958 I remember trying out for the Chaminade football team with what seemed like a hundred other prospects. I was wearing high-top sneakers and hadn't quite figured out how to keep them from untying themselves. I remember being disoriented by all the action taking place on the field and I remember looking at the freshly posted list of players who made the team. My name was not on the list and I was very disappointed.

I wanted so much to be a part of the football program at Chaminade. I needed to find something else to do. I was assigned to homeroom 1G with Mr. Joseph Fox as our moderator. Sitting next to me was this big guy by the name of Mike Reisert. I remember congratulating Mike for making the team and telling him about my disappointment. Mike thought maybe I would get bigger and be able to play football next year. He suggested I turn my attention to the track team where I could work on building my strength and endurance. He gave me hope by telling me that I might even grow a few inches. So, I signed up for cross country track.

The cross country team attracted a much smaller following. Any student who was willing to run made the team automatically. This was meant for me or so I thought. We started with at least 30 freshman hopefuls. After just one week of practice the number of runners had dwindled considerably. I persisted. I wasn't going to quit. I trained most of the season as a scrub just doing the best I could. We ran through the streets of Mineola and we ran sometimes at Van Cortland Park and other places. I was resigned to be a member of the scrub group yet happy to be a part of the team.

I do remember running my last cross country race for Chaminade. It was a relay race at Van Cortland Park. To my surprise our coach, Bro. Jim Abel, designated me to the anchor position on the Team B. For me this was an opportunity to watch most of the race progress and assess our team's chances before I got started. My outlook was not very optimistic. After the first runners completed their laps we were somewhere in the middle of the pack. After the second group of runners our position improved only slightly. After the third leg our position had improved further but we were still a long shot. Gene Mangiardi took over for the fourth leg. Gene was by far the strongest of the Team B runners. He somehow managed to bring us much closer to the leading runners. When I successfully grabbed the baton from Gene the race suddenly became very exciting. I was really psyched as I headed for the woods as we had a chance to finish in a decent position if only I could do my part. I did not want to let the team down. I managed to pass a number of runners before reaching a winding and somewhat rocky, hilly and narrow portion of the trail all of us runners had to negotiate. Here in the wooded area hidden from public view I encountered two runners from another team blocking the trail and literally pushing opponents who tried to pass them off the trail. I made an attempt to pass between them and was knocked down, scraping my knee badly from the fall although I didn't notice it at the time. I immediately righted myself and tried again. This time I broke through. I also found that there were only a few runners in front of me. As we came out of the wooded area and back into public view I could see plainly there were only four or five runners in front of me. I decided to begin my move to the front.

About 100 yards from the finish line I passed the runner in second position. I then approached and passed the leader. As I passed him he noticed me to his left. He put on a burst of speed and again took the lead. With less than 25 yards to the finish line I had gained the lost distance and was about to pass him a second time when he purposely stepped to his left and forced me to break stride. Frustrated, I wacked the back of his head with my baton and down he went. I crossed the finish line followed by the former third-place runner.

Everyone was screaming at me, even my own coach. Of course, there were all sorts of protests. Had this incident happened back in the wooded area where I was pushed to the ground nobody would have heard about it, but a few yards from the finish line? Bad timing. My meager complaint about being pushed to the ground even as evidenced by my very bloody leg just didn't cut it. In the end, the guy I wacked – his team was declared the winner. My team – the Chaminade B Team – was moved all the way to last place.

After the race, Bro. Gohring retrieved his first-aid kit from the Chaminade school bus and patched me up. Once we had all returned to the bus Bro. Abel explained the final outcome in more detail. He thought I was a bit overzealous coming down the stretch. According to Bro. Abel we deserved an "A" for our effort and he was looking forward to our continuing progress in the fall. As for Sellerberg, instead of running track in the fall maybe he should try out for the football team. It might be a more prudent vocation. I guessed that maybe he was correct. Still, he was a great coach.

Cross country led to spring track and interaction with some wonderful people. I especially remember Bill Boyle and his accomplishments. Of course, my grammar-school friend, Ed Dean, and his gang of talented runners were people I also greatly admired. Little did I know that he, Doug Casey, Art DeLeo and later Jim Meehan et al. would mature to become a Team of Champions in their own right.

In the fall of 1959, I tried out for the football team once again. The first thing I noticed was that most of the kids were wearing real football cleats. Some wore high-top cleats and others wore low-cut cleats. I was wearing my high-cut sneakers similar to the ones I wore at tryouts the previous year. The only difference was that this year I could tie my shoes.

I tried as best I could with all the calisthenics – the jumping jacks, the stretches, pull-ups, push-ups, etc. Routinely included in these exercises were such things as wind sprints, three-man rolls, tires, sleds, tackling dummies and the ever unpopular neck bridges. One day after a grueling practice, Mr. Ed Flynn, Athletic Director and our J.V. football coach, called me into his office for a private meeting, where there was a variety of brand new football cleats in boxes on the floor, and he had me try some on for size. When I found a pair of the high-top variety that fit my feet nicely he gave them to me and informed me that football players wore cleats, not sneakers, and that since I was now a member of the team he didn't want to see those darn sneakers ever again.

I was pretty happy when I got home that night. I told my dad I had made the team and showed him the new cleats Mr. Flynn had given me. Dad congratulated me on making the team and asked me how much the shoes had cost. He was upset when I repeated that they were given to me by the coach. Before I went to school the next morning, dad put a twenty dollar bill in my hand and insisted that Mr. Flynn be reimbursed. That was my dad. I love him and miss him every day.

Sophomore year was the big year for learning the basics about how to play football. Mr. Flynn turned out to be a great line coach instructor as he found ways to get into your head, make you a better player and make you a better person. He believed that teamwork and hard work led to opportunity, and opportunity led to a chance for victory. He advocated for the 110% principle regarding effort – always try your best and, when that doesn't work, try harder.

The entire J.V. season was a crazy time. We had six or eight League games scheduled but they were minor compared to the scrimmages Mr. Flynn arranged with other schools in the area. I'll bet we played ten or fifteen scrimmages and they often were more grueling than a regular game. Sometimes we performed well and other times we were beaten pretty badly. The scrimmages afforded us an opportunity to rerun plays and review our propensity for making both offensive and defensive blunders. Our level of play improved dramatically. By the end of the season we were functioning much better as a team. We were beginning to understand that we really could win if we worked together. Most of us were ready to move to the varsity level where our point man, Earl Kirmser, was already playing.

As a junior-year player, I was in awe of the senior players and worked hard for an opportunity to play. We started the season with a devastating 14-7 loss to Hempstead High School. I can remember our center, Jack Wehrum. He took the loss very badly and told me then we weren't going to lose another game. For the next four games we rolled to victory on the passing arm of Ed "Skippy" Orr and the running prowess of seniors like Greg Shorten, Art Marvin, Steve Colucci and Jay DeMeo [elder brother of our '61 squad's Bill DeMeo]. On the line we had Jim Clinton, Pat Higgins, Bob Woods, Ross Roper, Ed Finegan and Pete McDougal. These guys were top players. Where possible the coaches provided each of us junior-year players with as much playing time as possible. We then played Mount St. Michael to a 12-12 tie. We didn't lose the game but Jack Wehrum reminded me that a tie was not a win. Both Jack and Pat Higgins were great mentors. They took time to encourage me and show me how to operate on the interior line. We finished the year with a 26-16 victory over Holy Cross and the 1960 CHSFL championship.

Our senior year began with a great deal of uncertainty. We desperately needed a quarterback to replace Skippy Orr. Most of us were trying to figure out what Coach Joe Thomas had up his sleeve. John Zimmermann, a young unproven player, was in his junior year and he was our best candidate. Well, Mr. Zimmermann proved himself in the very first game of the season as we defeated Hicksville by a score of 28-7. As my teammate and friend Al Groh has written, "A football team is a true meritocracy where nothing is given, everything is earned."

Our first CHSFL competition was against the Crusaders of Archbishop Stepinac. The game proved to be highly competitive and much closer than the final 14-6 score. Chaminade got off to a quick start thanks to a blocked punt by either Tom Kiley or Bill DeMeo – both were great players. We were on our way to a second score as the first half ended. On that last play of the first half it appeared to me that Dave Tuohy had scored another touchdown. The referee, however, thought otherwise so the half ended with Chaminade leading by 6-0. Stepinac woke up later in the game and closed the gap to 14-6. On the ensuing kick-off they tried an on-side kick and recovered the ball. We seemed to have lost our momentum. They marched all the way down the field to a first down inside the ten-yard line. We somehow held on with the big play coming from Kevin Walters when he swatted what appeared to be a touchdown pass from the fingertips of the receiving player.

We got the ball back and still had the lead but were in total disarray and there seemed to be an eternity of time left on the clock. As the offense huddled, a timeout was called. During the timeout Chuck Mansfield opened up on all of the players in that huddle and somehow let us know that it was up to us to win this game and that we could win the game only if we gave it everything we had. His words were very inspiring but I think he sent the oranges back just when we could have used them. Anyway, it worked. With Earl Kirmser acting as our main battering ram we began a methodical Ohio State-type attack that boosted our confidence as it built our momentum. We didn't score but kept the ball and marched steadily ahead to our first CHSFL victory.

Flyer 1961 co-captain, guard and MVP Bill Sellerberg receives the Lou Gehrig Award from Eleanor Gehrig, "The Iron Horse" MLB Hall of Famer's widow.

Our game vs. St. Francis Prep was one for the ages. St. Francis was an excellent team and a formidable opponent. It was amazing how our "junior" players made all the difference. Congratulations to Mr. Zimmermann and to Mr. Bowman for their stellar clutch performances. Congratulations also to the rest of those "junior" players who made up a significant percentage of our squad. They helped us throughout the season which we rolled through to clinch the CHSFL championship with a victory over Cardinal Hayes at Chaminade.

With our victory over Cardinal Hayes only one more week of practice and one more game vs. Holy Cross High School remained between us and an undefeated season. I can remember that week of practice before the game and how difficult it was to practice. As a team we seemed to be more tuned in to enjoying our championship status than to looking ahead to the last game of the season. To me a recipe for disaster was brewing. I kept thinking about what my mentors, Jack Wehrum and Pat Higgins, had told me last season. I knew that just as a tie was not a win, a championship was not an undefeated season.

The game turned out to be much more difficult than anyone could imagine. Our offense just didn't seem to click. We couldn't maintain the consistency needed to score. Fortunately, we were playing fairly well defensively. The score at halftime was 0-0. Sometime in the third quarter our junior fullback, Tommy Higgins, broke loose and scored on a 30-yard burst, another impressive contribution from one of those "junior" players. I was very happy for him. For the first time in the game we had the lead. Still, there was much work to do. The game went back and forth and was full of frustration on both sides. Near the end of the game Frank Biasi finally closed out the season with a 51-yard dash through a minefield of Holy Cross players. We were true champions and we were undefeated! I wondered what Coach Thomas was going to say about this.

Bill Sellerberg
Class of 1962

If you don't invest very much, then defeat doesn't hurt very much and winning is not very exciting.

— Dick Vermeil

THE ENIGMATIC IRISHMAN: ED FLYNN

By Tom Kiley

Ed Flynn was a joy to play for. Everyone got a chance to play and, believe me, we played a lot.

— Ray Condon

It has been interesting to read in these pages just how many Flyer football players have tried through literary exertion to belatedly repay Ed Flynn for their early football training at Chaminade. He was an old school guy for sure, often inscrutable in his ways, and he certainly made an interesting contrast with Coach Thomas whom he hired in 1948 and with whom he worked for 13 years. For many of those Coach Flynn worked as Coach Thomas's JV football coach. These many years later, I have concluded that Ed Flynn and Coach Thomas were, to a degree, a mismatched pair, temperamentally very different types. In a way I instinctively understood Ed better than Joe, maybe because we were both Irishmen. He could have been one of my uncles. I had no uncles like Joe Thomas.

For many years, after the football season was over, they reversed positions, Joe coaching JV basketball for Ed who coached the varsity. True to his instincts and credo, Coach Thomas would one day have us playing with a medicine ball and the next with a rubber ball, running around, passing and shooting a Spaldeen Hi-bouncer. Only he could explain what was behind that. Coach Flynn had success doing it his way, regularly going to the CHSSA playoffs and getting to the finals during the '60-'61 season, while collecting a Brooklyn *Tablet* coach of the year award ('57-'58) along the way.

For me to write about Coach Flynn is pure pleasure because he gave me one of the most enjoyable years of my Chaminade football experience. Of course he was first and foremost a basketball coach. Football was secondary.

I learned many things from Coach Flynn during my sophomore year. One of them was how to relax before a big game. Another was that it is important for a coach to realize that what he doesn't say is often more important than what he does say. And Ed generally didn't say too much. "Less said, less mended" was his motto. And yet I never spent one practice under his tutelage that was dull or purely a grind. He brought an enormous amount of energy and fun to those who were lucky enough to play for him and he was an important influence on many Chaminade football lives. "Remember you are as good as the best thing you have ever done," he once told me before one of the biggest games of the '61 season, which inspired me to have one of my best games. Ed was an unsung hero of our '61 team's football success and he has only rarely been given proper credit.

He not only introduced a little humor into our generally grim football proceedings, but he was much more relaxed than his varsity counterpart, and was more fun to be around. Indeed, one of the contributors to *The Perfect Season* has declared that playing for Ed Flynn was the most fun he ever had playing sports. In addition, Mr. Flynn gave Coach Thomas a steady, experienced hand at the JV level for most of the years Joe coached at Chaminade. The importance of this relationship can easily be underestimated but it shouldn't be. Moreover, Ed scouted all the big games for Joe and was a shrewd evaluator of who and what would work well against our upcoming opponents.

Although he may have seemed unapproachable, at least as far as I could discern, Coach Flynn was capable of sudden and great kindness as several writers have revealed herein. He was also capable of giving you the old "Flynn Flam" for good reason or for no reason at all. All in good fun of course. I was its victim several times during my career at Chaminade. To wit:

One day after a certain home JV football game in 1959 – which we won handily as we did most games during a terrific 10-1-1 season, taking on all comers, public and Catholic – we gathered in the small locker room just like the varsity did, as our game had been filmed for the first and only time that season. This was very exciting. Finally, we would be complimented on just how well we had played. Well, not quite, as it turned out.

From the start the whole team got a Flynn Flam special, a humorous critique as only Coach Flynn could deliver it, which elicited peals of laughter from the whole squad. The good I had done that day was buried, like Caesar's, with my bones. On one play the film showed me missing a block badly. Coach Flynn re-ran the play over and over again. With each repetition, he seemed more and more to enjoy himself. Finally, he said, "Kiley, you and Tuohy look like the two of you just can't wait to go over to the park to have a smoke." My teammates roared. I laughed myself. You just couldn't help it. My dreams of football glory had gone up in smoke. Why poor old Dave Tuohy was brought into it, I shall never know. What Ed meant by this remark will never be known either. I did know one thing for certain. It meant I was not as good as I thought I was.

Once in a while I felt that Coach Flynn didn't think JV ball was all that important. He seemed not to possess the love of precision and technique that Mr. Thomas did. Therefore, he scheduled two games a week and we scrimmaged Mineola High School every Wednesday, sharply limiting our practice time. We learned the game by playing the game, not by breaking it down into its component parts, as our varsity coach loved to do. Not a bad way to learn how to play football I later came to believe. Sometimes Mr. Flynn did things with an Irish twinkle in his eye, for his own amusement. One day in the middle of the week, the Mineola squad appeared on our game field. We were scheduled to scrimmage them across its width rather than lengthwise. As we were about to begin, Coach Flynn said to me matter-of-factly, "Kiley, you'll be starting at quarterback today." At first I thought he had to be kidding. It had to be the first time a down and dirty offensive and defensive tackle like I was ever played quarterback, but there I was, taking a few practice snaps, getting ready to go.

My quarterback career lasted exactly two plays. On the first, I made five yards on a sneak. Felt pretty good about that. Next I called for a quick slant-in pass to my flanker, the late Jimmy Gerstner. I dropped back and saw him running diagonally across the field. All hell broke loose. Everything was mass confusion. Defensive backs converged from the rear. Linebackers dropped back into the passing lanes. I started to throw, hesitated, started to throw again, hesitated again. Finally, I let it go, five yards behind Jimmy, no chance that the ball could be caught. In fact I was very lucky it was not intercepted. Sufficiently amused, I guess, Coach Flynn said, "That's enough. Danny, get back in there." And so ended the shortest quarterback career in Chaminade football history. But that was Ed Flynn. What the hell! It was only a couple of plays in a scrimmage. What did it matter? I am sure Coach Thomas would not have approved, but Coach Flynn seemed amused, as were all of my teammates.

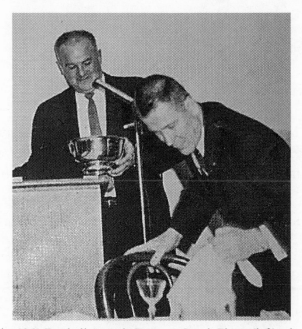

At the 1961 Football Awards Banquet Coach Flynn (left) admires the bowl presented to him by Coach Thomas in recognition of his lengthy service to the Flyer football program. Mr. Flynn would leave Chaminade in June of the following year.

(Photograph courtesy of Tom Kiley and used with permission.)

Ed did not leave Chaminade until the end of the 1962 school year, which enabled him to share in our glorious undefeated season, and rightly so, as it represented the apogee of the football program he had built starting in 1948 when he hired Joe Thomas. Sadly, after he left Chaminade I never saw or spoke to Coach Flynn again. First I heard he had assumed a position at Massapequa High School. Then, that he had re-joined his brother Frank and his other brothers running his family's iconic and eponymous Flynn's Fire Island, a well-known local restaurant and summer hot spot. This was the Irishman in his element. A man about town restaurateur and raconteur meeting and greeting the general public with a glad hand and a big smile.

Pictured outside their iconic restaurant in the 1960s are the founding brothers of Flynn's Fire Island. Coach Ed Flynn is on the left.

(Photograph courtesy of Tom Kiley and used with permission.)

Unfortunately, the young often do not pursue their affections, only to regret it later. Ed Flynn is one such regret. In retrospect, I am sorry I never told him how much I had liked and respected him nor did I ever thank him for all he had done for me on the gridiron. Eventually, I came to understand that it was an indication of the esteem he held you in that he gave you the old Flynn Flam from time to time. Just to cut you down to size when he thought you needed it.

Our '61 football team owes a substantial debt of gratitude to the inimitable Coach Edward J. Flynn, one that has only rarely been acknowledged. If confidence is born of demonstrated prior performance, then his relaxed, somewhat idiosyncratic approach to coaching football, leading us to a 10-1-1 record while taking on all comers, laid the groundwork for the next two seasons when, reunited with arguably the best fullback in Chaminade football history, we would win back-to-back CHSFL titles. Due to the training Flyer elevens received while in Ed's capable hands during their sophomore years, the Golden Age of Chaminade football reached its height. Perhaps it is not coincidental that the sun set on that Golden Age shortly after Coach Flynn left Chaminade in 1962. Flynn Flam indeed!

Tom Kiley
Tackle and Quarterback
1959

Sometimes Mr. Flynn did things with an Irish twinkle in his eye, for his own amusement.

— Tom Kiley

MY CLOSE ENCOUNTER OF
THE COACH FLYNN KIND

By Chuck Mansfield

It was very humbling for us for the rest of the [varsity basketball] team was in the locker room and we felt we were not part of the team that day. The Coach said, "You Rinky Dinks go and get some shooting practice in." After the last game of the season [Fred Capshaw, Bob Peterson and I] had a surprise, however. We were in the locker room cleaning out our lockers when Coach Flynn came to us and gave all three of us a varsity letter!

— Ed Christie

Since I was a young boy I had wanted to go to Chaminade. Yes, its rigorous academic reputation was important and I was a good student but all I really wanted to do was play football for the Flyers. Of course, the big question in my mind was: Am I good enough? As a 12-year-old eighth-grader in 1957 I played for the near-championship Garden City Rams and was named "Best Lineman," which was a great and gratifying surprise, as well as the first trophy I was ever awarded; I still have it.

In 1958 I was admitted to Chaminade and that September tried out for the freshman football squad. As Chaminade teammates have written elsewhere in these pages, there were scores of frosh who tried out and many of them were bigger, stronger and faster than I. Moreover, there were only five whom I knew: Tom Greene, Brian Maxwell, John Schmitt and Jeff Zabler, each a St. Anne's School classmate, and Jim Meehan from St. Joseph's School, also in Garden City. Most of those trying out had already turned 14 and I was a full year younger. At a mere 110 pounds and just over five feet tall, I was hardly an imposing physical specimen. As my dear friend and late teammate Frank Biasi has observed earlier herein, "From my first day as a freshman on the hot and dusty practice field, I was in awe with the talent of my teammates." Indeed, I recall thinking I would probably get cut but resolved to give it my best shot.

Well, to my happy surprise, I made the team! However, as the season progressed I became increasingly concerned that I wouldn't get to play in 14 different quarters, which was required if a freshman football player was to receive his '62 numerals for his Crimson and Gold "letter" sweater. Again, happily, I got to play in exactly 14 quarters and was very pleased.

During freshman year and the following summer I grew naturally and also undertook a weight-lifting program and a running regimen. When it came time for JV football I recall that I was about 140 pounds and considerably stronger. I remember my pal and teammate, George Valva, referring to my increased size and strength, exclaiming "Good Lord, what happened to you?!" I thought he was being funny but he had actually noticed and seemed impressed by the muscular improvement in my physique.

Edward J. Flynn, a longtime fixture at Chaminade, was the school's Athletic Director, our JV coach and the man who recruited Coach Thomas and brought him from North Catholic High School in Pittsburgh to Chaminade in 1948. To me Mr. Flynn seemed to run our practices quite differently from the way Coaches Jerry Rossi and Bob Antolini did in our freshman season. Still, I was content with my position and enjoyed far more playing time, both offensively and defensively, than in the preceding season.

On a sunny and pleasant fall Saturday morning in '59 our JV team faced an opponent in a home game. (I don't recall which team it was but would hazard a guess it was St. Francis.) I started both ways but was challenged by the defensive player who was my responsibility. I didn't think my play was poor, merely somewhat tempered by my able opponent. Alas, Coach Flynn saw things differently.

At halftime, before addressing the whole team, Mr. Flynn walked me to the west end zone for a private chat. Indeed, it was a 'behind-the-woodshed' tongue-lashing and an unforgettable watershed moment.

"Mansfield," he seethed, eyes glaring, visibly angry and grasping the front of my jersey, "have you got crap in your blood?" My coach was now the first person in my life to insult me, and I was frustrated and mad.

"No, sir," I replied sheepishly and terrified.

"Now, do your job in the second half!"

"Yes, sir."

I followed Coach briskly back to the bench where the rest of the team awaited us. No one asked me what had transpired but I'm confident Mr. Flynn's grabbing my shirt and gesticulating as he did gave my teammates all they may have wanted to know.

Suffice it to say that in our game's second half I took care of business, and never heard a discouraging word from Coach Flynn for the rest of the season. And we won too.

Amazingly, shortly after writing those words I read the following passage in David Maraniss's book, *When Pride Still Mattered: A Life of Vince Lombardi*: "Lombardi confessed in *Look* that he considered football 'a game for madmen' and that he once pounded on a huge lineman with his fists to get him to 'hate me enough to take it out on the opposition.' He struck the player, the coach said, because he believed that to play football well you had to have 'that fire in you,' and there was 'nothing that stokes that fire' like hate. Hit or be hit, that was the reality of football, Lombardi believed."

Mr. Flynn's strong words echo still, have provided me a valuable life lesson and factored substantially in my positive motivation for the next two Flyer varsity football championship seasons.

THE PERFECT SEASON

The perfect block, the perfect handoff, the perfect route, the perfect pass, the perfect stance, the perfect tackle were all forged here.

— Cliff Molloy

THOUGHTS AND MEMORIES: OUR '61 TEAM

By Raymond F. Condon

From the first whistle – ours was a dominant performance; the line was firing out in unison on both sides of the ball (that would be the '61 team's calling card, dominant line play) in typical Chaminade fashion; once game control was apparent there were liberal substitutions, everyone got to play on TV and grandparents were happy.

— Ray Condon

A friend of almost sixty-three years, Ray is a 1962 Chaminade alumnus who is also our classmate and football teammate.

He lives in Southport, Ct., with his wife Claire and daughter Caitlin and is a Senior Advisor to Shenkman Capital Management in Stamford, Ct., where has worked for the past 18 years as a Principal, Senior Vice-President and Portfolio Manager. Prior to joining Shenkman, he spent 26 years in various firms where he obtained unique experience in all aspects of the securities business including capital markets, management, sales, trading and research.

Like many of us, Ray thought his active contact team sport participation had ended post-high school and certainly post-college. However, after joining the New York Athletic Club in 1971 while going to night school at nearby Fordham for his M.B.A., he joined the newly founded rugby club in 1973 and played for over 30 years. He served as Captain, Chairman and Coach and has been elected to the NYAC Rugby Hall of Fame. Ray has served on the boards of the Bridgeport Hospital Foundation and Caroline House, a center for disadvantaged women and their children in Bridgeport.

Thank you, Ray.

My biggest thought and memory of it all was that we were a team not just in descriptive words but in how we acted on and off the field then and in all the years since. A bonding that will never go away. No egos, all for one, humbleness and pride in accomplishment, discipline, confidence, respect for each other and our opponents, an abiding faith, and a willingness to adapt to the here and now. It all adds up to a winning combination that many more talented than we have tried but have never accomplished.

In many ways what makes the '61 team even more remarkable was that we were (by Chaminade standards) just average as freshmen (6-4-1) (except Earl who would be promoted straight away to varsity the next year). A definite ragtag bunch with little experience. I recall that about 90+ incoming freshman tried out for the team (the only other fall sport was cross country). The initial selection process had to be difficult/chaotic in some ways for the coaches. The improvement would come gradually, especially as we became more accustomed (both on and off the field) to what I would call the 'Chaminade Experience.' Happy ending: We took a small travel squad up to the Mount for our last game and not only won our final game (20-0) but looked and played like a Chaminade team.

JV year '59 was the most fun that I ever had in sports. Ed Flynn was a joy to play for. Everyone got a chance to play and, believe me, we played a lot. Tuesday was usually live 'scrimmage day' with uniformed referees against worthy public-school foes: Jefferson, Freeport, Lawrence, Brooklyn Tech etc.) Thursday was once again live against our 'friendly' rival Mineola. I think we wore on each other over the next three years with each side going undefeated as seniors. Saturdays were set aside for a regular League match. Our team was noticeably improved (10-1-1) not only by growing with more everyday experience but also by being bolstered by the welcome addition to the team of several classmates who did not play as freshmen, among them Billy Sellerberg and Rick Darby, the first of a long line of 'Darby Brothers.' We were now ready (with some uncertainty) for the challenges and pressure that would await us on the varsity.

Junior year, 1960. A bit of a blur. Recollections: We were reunited with Earl; 'Tiny' started to come into his own; teammate Ed "Skippy" Orr, the best player in the League; the loss to Hempstead in our first varsity game (14-7). Hempstead's Joe Blocker (*Newsday*'s top five athlete of the 20th Century in Nassau County) scored on a long run late; the dreaded practice week that followed; the TV win against Stepinac; the extremely hard-fought win over St. Francis (28-22); Jack Wehrum climbing over the top of a three-man wall at Iona to block a punt; 6-1-1 League champions and the accolades that followed.

Despite the successes, even though it was never spoken, there was a cloud – you could see it in the coaches' faces and the seniors' eyes – a deep sense that the team did not quite play up to their ability and lofty expectations. A bright light in the tunnel: Charlie announced in the locker room, concluding the season that he was going to keep the juniors (except Earl and Tiny) and selected members of the JV for an additional week of practice. It was here that the '61 team was born. Football was fun again; Charlie and the JV coaches seemed to be enjoying themselves, intros and bonding with new and, it turns out, invaluable future teammates (Zimmy, Bowman, Grassini, Ken Darby et al.); a self-confidence was built that was never to be diminished.

Pictured above (left to right) are our '61 teammate and halfback Ray Condon, Coach Charlie McGuckin and Tom Condon, Ray's younger brother, who played halfback for Messrs. Thomas and McGuckin in 1963 and '64. The photo was taken at the Cherry Valley Club in Garden City, N.Y., in 2005 at the celebration of Coach Thomas's 90th birthday.

(Photograph courtesy of Tom Condon and used with permission.)

Senior year 1961. Double-session days were maxed out in nearly two weeks, with Labor Day and school starting late. The heat – mid-90s every day – was so oppressive that the coaches even decided to take 'mercy' and split the practice schedule (early morning and early evening).

No doubt, a bit of a sluggish start. Coaches on edge. The first Friday pep rally, with the entire school amped up, Coach Thomas put a damper on things and I believe shocked most of us by stating that he was disappointed in the way the team was shaping up. Our first game was on TV against Hicksville, the top-rated public-school team in Nassau County, featuring Chris Coletta (that year's version of Joe Blocker), with game announcers Elston Howard and Marty Glickman scouting us at practice the day before. On game day we changed into game uniforms at Chaminade, rode the bus to Hicksville, heat still oppressive and no breeze. The stands were packed on both sides, it was quiet, lots of stares; nobody had ever seen a Chaminade team east of Mineola.

From the first whistle – ours was a dominant performance; the line was firing out in unison on both sides of the ball (that would be the '61 team's calling card, dominant line play) in typical Chaminade fashion; once game control was apparent there were liberal substitutions, everyone got to play on TV and grandparents were happy. Joe's pep rally speech was never mentioned again. No looking ahead – Stepinac, a win; now the tension facing St. Francis Prep – our fierce rival from Brooklyn (Red Hook), tough city kids, ably coached, unparalleled fan base (no home field, up to 40 bus loads to surround our entire block); standing room only, up to 10k estimates, people standing on neighborhood roofs and in trees to get a view, black-and-blue game fought in mid-field, neither side had the advantage, scoreless, time stood still. With a minute left, Coach McGuckin calls the fly pass ('Zimmy' to Bowman), unexpected since we never threw downfield; Bowman well clear, ball hung in air forever, bedlam. Seconds left to score, McGuckin calls the 'corkscrew' (pattern where receiver runs an in slant, reverses in corkscrew fashion and does an out slant), 'Zimmy' to Bowman again, perfect execution. Ecstasy!

We roll through most of the balance of the schedule, uneventfully, until the highly anticipated away-match in the Bronx against the Mount. It was another tough city-kid team that was well coached but this team was different from others in that they had an unpredictable offense built around a 'scramble' QB with a very strong arm who seldom ran the ball. This game was not going to be black-and-blue; it was a wild card and did not play to our strengths.

In four years at school I do not recall more pre-game enthusiasm. "Beat the Mount" signs were plastered all around the hallways, students were wearing "Beat the Mount" buttons and the Friday pep rally, far more than routine, was tumultuous. We went off to the Mount that Sunday quietly confident both in spirit and knowing that we were well prepared.

AD Ed Flynn had spent the last several weeks scouting our opponent and, armed with recent game film, the coaches dissected a game plan: Maximum outside rush, both strong and weak sides, to minimize the scramble; defensive backs were well rehearsed to stay glued to their coverage well past the normal allotted time and to go wherever that took them; the offense was pressed to reemphasize the potential of the option attack to be more open than our usual ball control game; several trap plays were added to take advantage of Mount over enthusiasm and the speed/flexibility of the offensive line. Game day was a joy. Everything designed on defense worked to perfection; the option attack flourished. Mount had obviously over-scouted us, employing what seemed like their entire team to tackle our 'Go to guy,' Earl, and leave a gap for Dave Touhy to run for daylight to score on the Flyers' opening play from scrimmage in each half. I can still picture Howie Smith, the famous/infamous Mount coach, hysterically running up and down the sidelines berating his players each time Dave scored. It was a pleasant ride home.

Our last match – Holy Cross, another tough city-kid team, this time from Queens, an away-match for us at a public park, no locker room, little in the way of grass, minimal stands, lots of graffiti. Little did we know at the time the venue was probably the perfect setting for the *Look* article featuring our game that was to be published almost a year later (8/28/62): 'The Danger in High School Football.' Silence was deadly the week before at practice, nothing was said by either coaches or players about what was at stake: Undefeated/ Repeat League Championship. There even were no complaints about extra wind sprints in the post-daylight-saving dark. We knew we were going back for this one to our basic game plan. Four yards and a cloud of dust (Earl) and impregnable line play. Opening kickoff: I got the wind knocked out of me. (That was me in the *Look* article being hoisted up by Joe and the team doctor.) I came back to play in the second half. Despite the pressure, it was a typical game for us: played within ourselves, scoreless first half, impregnable D. I do not think the Cross played outside their 50, (we) built a modest lead (16-0), coaches substituting freely to try different combos. I think that Charlie made sure that all of the seniors saw some playing time.

After the game: there was no gloating, only pride in accomplishment that was only to grow over the years.

The only qualifications for a lineman are to be big and dumb. To be a back, you only have to be dumb.

— Knute Rockne
Notre Dame

Flyer-Holy Cross Photos Highlight LOOK Feature

Some of the photographs of the 1961 Flyer-Holy Cross game that appeared in LOOK magazine.

Chaminade, Mineola has made the big time! Four pages of pictures of the Flyers in action against Holy Cross appeared in the August 28 issue of LOOK magazine, along with an article on the merits and dangers of high school football, which detailed the qualifications for playing and conducting the game properly and safely.

The article pointed out that "football's values are priceless to any youngster who wants to play; its danger and pain are part of its value.

Football teaches a boy to cope with the risks of physical danger and pain, risks often inseperable from the act of living itself. The game also demonstrates the value of work, sacrifice, courage, and perseverence. Football, nevertheless, is only for the boy who is physically qualified to play it and for the high school that conducts it properly."

The article in its entirety will be up on display outside the TARMAC office for the next few days.

(Article courtesy of Chaminade High School and used with permission.)

Coach Thomas preached to us that the team who is in better shape will in the end win. He was right. There was no question in my mind that we were better prepared and in better shape than any team we played against. We would still be hitting in the fourth quarter when our opponents were getting tired and sloppy.

— Mike Reisert

"I STOOD ON THE SIDELINES PRAYING THE MEMORARE"

By George C. Valva

In truth, I believe [our coaches] thought my small stature would serve me well in that [onside kick] situation since I would not have far to fall to secure the football.

— George Valva

A 1966 Villanova University alumnus, George is the retired CEO and a founding partner of DVC Worldwide, Inc., a marketing, communications and technology company once headquartered in Morristown, N.J.

His brilliant impromptu parody of a Shirelles hit song appears earlier herein under the title, "A Song of Triumph by 'The Valve.'"

George submitted the following reflection on June 17, 2011, in anticipation of our team's 50-year reunion that September.

Thank you, George.

My most memorable moment of that season was being asked by Coach Thomas and Mr. McGuckin to play the "center front" line position on the kickoff return team. For some reason they thought I had "good hands" and that I would be able to handle an onside kick. In truth, I believe they thought my small stature would serve me well in that situation since I would not have far to fall to secure the football. Needless to say, at the beginning of the fourth quarter of the Stepinac game we had a 12-point lead when Stepinac scored.

They decided to try an onside kick. My knees were knocking uncontrollably as I ran on the field. I prayed the ball would fly over my head or sail to the end of the field. BUT NO, it was kicked right to me! Sure enough I grabbed the ball and fell on my belly with the ball under me UNTIL a big Stepinac lineman fell on top of me and the ball slipped out of my grasp. Stepinac recovered on our 40-yard line and their fans were in a frenzy as they took over the ball on their home field!

Our defense had to go back on the field and they were pissed, especially Sellerberg and Reisert. It was a sunny and very hot day and the field was dusty and throats were parched. I stood on the sidelines praying the *Memorare** that they would not score, but the "Mo" was on their side. Stepinac easily marched down the field to my horror, all the way to our ten-yard line. And then…Our Lady kicked in, our defense miraculously caught a second wind and courageously stiffened, yielding no more yards or points! Our offense ran out the clock and we won by eight! Other than the Saint Francis game the following week, it was the closest call we had that season of losing the distinction of being the first undefeated, untied team in Chaminade's football history!

P.S. I never played that position again, nor did I want to!

* *The* Memorare, *Latin for "Remember," is a Catholic prayer of petition for help from Mary, the mother of Jesus. As George has so faithfully put it, "Our Lady kicked in."*

I'm excited about the opportunity to get out there and show not only what I can do but, more importantly, what this team can do with me in there.

— Philip Rivers

"DREAMS OF PLAYING AT CHAMINADE"

By Paul A. Lombardi

We'd struggled that day against a very good team, but we'd finally put it together. I think that's when it became clear to me that we really could – if we kept our focus and kept working our butts off – go undefeated.

— Rod Dwyer

A friend of nearly 63 years and a '61 title teammate, Paul played football for four years at Chaminade and was a tough competitor, who wrote this reflection in the summer of 2011 in anticipation of our team's 50-year reunion. He received the nickname (expletive deleted) Masher from a very literary-minded classmate after applying a competitive football technique to that classmate's unprotected cranium during a game of backyard basketball.

Thank you, Paul.

My recollections go to the locker room and the hangers we had to air out our sweaty equipment. Also I recall the managers – Bob Pacifico, Ray Hess, Bob Lewand and George Meng – recording our quarters played so that we would get our letter for our sweaters. I do remember the end of the St. Francis game when Bob Bowman caught the pass from Zimmy and the reaction of the Prep players at such a bitter defeat. Also Coach Thomas using the two wide-outs or split ends against St. Michael's and then running bandy-legged Dave Tuohy up the middle on a dive for a 44-yard TD on Chaminade's first play from scrimmage after the opening kickoff. Dave did the same thing for 54 yards on the Flyers' first play from scrimmage in the second half! Also the Holy Cross game half-time when we were sitting on the bus with the windows all fogged up and receiving a stern warning about what was at stake. Of course, winning that game led to the *Look* color pictorial that came out in August of 1962. Two-a-days [summer practice double sessions] are always a fond memory, and coaches telling us to drink carbonated soda to overcome nausea or whatever ailed you. Water breaks were not in existence to my memory but drinking quarts of water would have been more beneficial to the sweating bodies.

I will admit that dreams of playing at Chaminade or in games of that '61 season still occur and I was a spectator more often than not. I know Al Groh went on to play football at UVA and also lacrosse. I did not play football at Cortland but did play lacrosse and felt that the tough training of CHS football helped me in a sport in which I did not have a lot of skill. Thank you to all the teammates that will be in attendance and will contribute to this momentous event. God bless you and thanks for the memories.

Gratefully yours,
Paul Lombardi

The St. Francis game, our third of eight, proved to be a unique and pivotal moment, as well as a substantial catalyst, in our perfect season. Indeed, it was arguably the epitome of our perfection.

— Chuck Mansfield

HAPPY BIRTHDAY, MR. THOMAS

By Chuck Mansfield

He helped people believe in who they could be and what they could be.

— Joseph F. "Jeff" Thomas, Jr.

MASTER OF CEREMONIES SCRIPT
A Celebration of Coach Joe Thomas's 90th Birthday
Cherry Valley Club, Garden City, New York
September 10, 2005

Reverend fathers and brothers of the Society of Mary, Senator and Mrs. D'Amato, Senator Hannon, Judge Hurley, Judge Flanders, Thomas family members, fellow Chaminade alumni, members of the greater Chaminade family, admirers of Coach Joe Thomas, former athletes, ladies and gentlemen: Good evening and thank you for coming here to honor a very special and truly outstanding human being.

My name is Chuck Mansfield and I graduated from Chaminade in 1962.

COACH, HAPPY BIRTHDAY!

Fifty-seven years ago this month, Mr. Joseph F. Thomas began his extraordinary forty-year career of service to the men of Chaminade. Indeed, he has been honored innumerable times throughout that career, most recently on September 11, 1988, at the Joe Thomas Testimonial at the time of his retirement, and many of you were present that day.

I played football for Coach in 1960 and '61. In 1960 our team won the Catholic High School Football League title with a record of six wins, one loss and one tie under the leadership of Jack Wehrum, Skip Orr, Pat Higgins, Greg Shorten, Lou England, Steve Colucci,

Ed Finegan, Pete McDougal and Ray Pezzoli, all of whom are present this evening.

The following year we were League champions again and became Chaminade's first undefeated and untied team with an 8-0-0 record. We did it with the likes of Earl Kirmser, Tom Kiley, Al Groh, Ray Condon, Rod Dwyer, Carl LoGalbo and Kemp Hannon, who are also here tonight. Still, both of these championship seasons would not have been were it not for Coach Thomas's leadership and motivational skills.

For the record, Chaminade football teams coached by him from 1948 through 1969 won 120 games, lost 46 and tied seven. They captured six League championships, five of which came during the eight-year period from 1956 to 1963, with a record during that period of 52 victories, nine losses and two ties.

Among many other honors during his eminent career, Coach Thomas was named Football Coach of the Year seven times in the years 1951, 1956, 1958, 1960, 1961, 1962 and 1965.

But what I really learned from you was how to live. For thousands of young men you have always been a living example of honesty and dignity, of dedication and discipline, and a simple Christian goodness.

— Brian Dennehy in a 2005
letter to Coach Thomas

As I have written elsewhere, "Although his coaching responsibilities necessitated his being on the sidelines, he was, in a very real sense, *in* the game. While each of us players was concerned with managing his position and executing his assignments as well as he could for as long as he was in the game, Coach was in there too – intellectually, viscerally and spiritually – on every play at every position – '110% for forty-eight minutes,' as he used to say. Not only did he take the game seriously, I believe he took it *personally*. His players knew it, and we all felt it."

"I feel privileged to know him, and it is a badge of honor and pride for me to say: I played football for Joe Thomas."

Pictured above (left to right) are Skip Orr, Bill Basel, Tom Kiley, Chuck Mansfield, Carl LoGalbo, Ed Finegan, Jack Wehrum and Jeff Thomas. The photo was taken on September 10, 2005, at the Cherry Valley Club in Garden City, N.Y., at a celebration of Coach Thomas's 90th birthday.

(Photograph courtesy of Tom Kiley and used with permission.)

I am delighted to serve as your emcee for the evening, and it's time to get on with our program. Before I introduce our first guest speaker, however, I would like to acknowledge two Chaminade alumni who have done and continue to do a great deal for our *alma mater*: Craig Tigh of the class of 1972, chairman of Chaminade's Torch Fund, former alumni president and a Terzi Award recipient, and Larry Mahon of the class of 1978, president of the Chaminade Alumni Association, as well as president of the Friendly Sons of Saint Patrick of Long Island.

Ladies and gentlemen, the president of Chaminade High School today is unmistakably a strong leader for the twenty-first century. He is a visionary and a man of decisive action who is not only spiritually uplifting, as one might expect of a Catholic priest, but also an individual who would be a positive moral force in the world of American business. It is my honor and privilege to introduce to you Chaminade president Father James Williams of the class of 1987. Fr. James...

Coach Thomas had another, earlier and very remarkable chapter in his wonderful life and brilliant career, one about which some Chaminade alumni know very little. In fact, he coached not only football but also basketball at the Marianists' North Catholic High School in Pittsburgh, Pennsylvania, in the early nineteen forties. If you look on the back page of your dinner program, you will find near the top of the page a quotation from Barney Joseph Thomas Otten – how's that for a name?! – who is one of Coach's players and admirers from that time.

Another North Catholic stalwart of that era, I am pleased to tell you, is actually with us this evening. He and his wife Patricia have made a special trip to Long Island today to honor Coach Thomas. They will return to Pittsburgh tonight in order to attend the Steelers' season opener against the Tennessee Titans tomorrow. Ladies and gentlemen, please extend a warm Chaminade welcome to Dan Rooney,* the owner of the Pittsburgh Steelers. Mr. Rooney...

To many of us the Thomas family may be renowned for sports but this clan's talent in the arts and music is equally prodigious. Jonah Thomas, the son of Michael Thomas and Jo Valens and Coach's grandson, is an all-star basketball player and a world-class concert cellist. He will be accompanied musically by his friend and pianist Stephanie Wu in a rendition of *Hungarian Rhapsody, Opus 68* by David Popper. Please join me in welcoming Jonah Thomas and Stephanie Wu.

The next person I am privileged to introduce I am also privileged to know. He provides a unique perspective on Coach Thomas for he both played for and coached with him at Chaminade. I first came to know him in 1960 when he was Coach Thomas's varsity football assistant and back coach. For those of us who played under him, he possesses the same great attributes we have all witnessed in the man we honor this evening. Indeed, theirs is an epic friendship. Coach Thomas himself has called him the finest athlete ever to play at Chaminade during Mr. Thomas's forty years at the school. A Terzi Award recipient and president of the Chaminade class of 1950, our next speaker also excelled at basketball and baseball. Indeed, some have called him "The Natural." Please join me in welcoming Charlie McGuckin of the class of 1950, who will introduce Coach Thomas. Coach...

Pictured above (left to right) are Tom Kiley, Chuck Mansfield, Coach Thomas, Earl Kirmser and Carl LoGalbo. The photograph was taken on September 30, 1995, at the home of Coach's son Jeff, who that day hosted a celebration of his father's 80th birthday.

(Photograph courtesy of Chuck Mansfield and used with permission.)

Two-time Tony Award winner and star of stage and screen Brian Dennehy of the Chaminade class of 1956, who played Flyer football for Coach Thomas in 1954 and 1955 and passed away in 2020, could not attend Coach's 90th birthday party but sent him the following letter, which was read aloud at the celebration.

Saturday, September 10, 2005

To Coach Thomas,

Happy Birthday, and greetings from London. We had two performances of "Death of a Salesman" today, so it was impossible for me to make it to Mineola this evening. Only my long-standing commitment to Arthur Miller for this London engagement could have kept me from your birthday celebration.

It is interesting that you and Arthur are almost exact contemporaries. He would have been 90 this year, and I consider myself very fortunate to have known and worked with him in the bruising arena that is professional theatre.

And I was fortunate to have known and learned from you, Coach, all those years ago. How do you measure the impact of a great teacher on your life? You taught me how to play football, of course, how to push my body a little further, a little harder. How to win, and also how to lose. A valuable lesson in my business.

But what I really learned from you was how to live. For thousands of young men you have always been a living example of honesty and dignity, of dedication and discipline, and a simple Christian goodness.

So for me, and so many Chaminade men like me, I want to say… Happy Birthday, Coach, and thanks, thanks for everything.

Love,
Brian

* In the early 1990s Coach Thomas told me he had been invited by Pittsburgh's North Catholic High School to an alumni dinner honoring Dan Rooney. This event would take place some 45 years after Coach left North to move to Long Island to begin his stellar career at Chaminade. Coach, then in his late seventies, said he would

love to attend the event, and that his son Jeff would accompany him, but the round-trip airfare was prohibitive. Since I had a ton of frequent-flyer miles accumulated over many years, I offered to procure the airline tickets, a no-brainer. Coach and Jeff were grateful, and I was thrilled that Coach could now make the trip, which greatly energized and excited him.

Upon his return after the weekend in Pittsburgh, I visited Coach and asked him about the dinner. He actually became emotional as he described seeing his old North Catholic players, including Dan, who Coach had assumed was the keynote speaker. Instead of speaking at length, however, Danny, as Coach called him, used his remarks to extol Coach Thomas and introduce him as the guest speaker. At that moment, the dinner hall erupted in a thunderous standing ovation for Coach Thomas. Now, in his telling, Coach was clearly embarrassed and profoundly moved, overtly reliving the uplifting moment and the highlight of the preceding weekend. Epic humility was always his hallmark but this honor and recognition clearly touched his soul and gave him great joy.

This was one of the best things I had ever done for anyone, and I couldn't have been happier that it was for Coach Thomas at that time in his life. After all, what he had done for me in mine is incalculable.

We are such stuff as dreams are made [of], and
our little life is rounded with a sleep.

— Prospero
in *The Tempest*

THOUGHTS OF A QUARTERBACK

By John T. Zimmermann

To follow Skip Orr as the Flyers' QB would have been a challenge for anyone, much less a QB moving up from the JV squad, but John Zimmermann did it beautifully.

— Al Groh

A 1967 graduate of the University of Notre Dame, John or "Zimmy," as many of his teammates came to call him, was a major catalyst in our perfect season. Thanks to his brilliant quarterbacking talents and leadership, the '61 Flyers rushed for 1,925 yards and passed for 500. His contributions to our championship are the stuff of legend, and he was greatly admired even among the seniors on our team, many of whom were two years older than he. In his senior year he was the recipient of the Terzi Award and received other well deserved honors.

Zimmy was awarded a B.B.A. from Notre Dame and an M.B.A. in marketing from Columbia University. He served as an Army officer in Turkey in 1968 and '69 and later married his wife, Robyn. Married for 38 years, they have four grown children and eight grandchildren. Having spent his career in auto sales, primarily in Denver, John and Robyn are now retired in Boise.

Thank you, Zimmy.

By the time I became a 15-year-old junior at Chaminade I had progressed from a freshman who cried his first day of school – I had to leave my neighborhood friends in public school in East Meadow. I was a tackle in junior high, playing quarterback (QB) only in street ball, a lot of street ball.

One of the best things about playing football under Joe Thomas at Chaminade was the continuity. From the first day of tryouts as a freshman to the last snap as a senior, the system was unchanged. I could run our offense from the early '60s right now, 60 years later. Repetition, repetition. In my opinion, having a consistent system with intelligent, disciplined players was one of the secrets of our success.

My high-school football life changed radically in spring workouts in '61 when Coach Thomas took me aside and told me I was going to be his starting QB. The presumed starter was kicked out of school – leaving an incredibly strong returning class without its senior QB. From that moment I constantly prayed that I wouldn't screw up this potentially terrific team.

Zimmy speaks at a 1961 Flyer pep rally as teammates (left to right) George Ackerson (42), Rod Dwyer, Earl Kirmser (39), Chuck Mansfield (63) and Dave Tuohy (41) look on.

My memory highlights of the season are many. Our domination of the public school powerhouse Hicksville, our struggle with mediocre St. John's, our fantastic offensive line, our dominating defense, our bruising fullback. I was blessed to have one center in my four years playing for the Flyers – Bruce Salerno. I'm probably wrong but I don't remember ever having a fumbled snap. A strong memory stands out – against Stepinac. We had one play close to the goal line before halftime – Hand it to Earl Kirmser, right? – Not me. I overthought it and tried to catch them off balance with a sneak. (Didn't make it of course.) Looking back, I'm shocked Coach Thomas didn't yell at me coming off the field – he calmly said it would've probably been better to run his play to our stud fullback behind our stud line. Ya think! Fortunately, it didn't cost us the game.

Many pleasant and exciting memories. Two last-minute passes to fellow junior Bobby Bowman to win the St. Francis game – and seeing the agony of their defense after the touchdown. Then there was the game-changing run by fellow junior Tom Higgins off tackle after Earl was helped off the field in the last game against Holy Cross. (To the delight of the other team's players.) That followed the most passionate and inspiring half-time talk ever – on the school bus during halftime by Coach Thomas. He obviously sensed that we were at the doorstep of making history.

Looking back, I think the coach Mr. Thomas most resembled was Bear Bryant. He wanted players that were tough, quick and well disciplined. Size back then was not an issue. Both men (as well as my favorite college coach ever, Ara Parseghian, observed during my years at Notre Dame) had integrity, class and were true Christian gentlemen on and off the field. Next to my dad, Joe Thomas had the most positive influence on my life. I had the pleasure of meeting with Coach in his later years during my visits to my hometown on Long Island.

I am blessed, thankful, honored and humbled to be part of the 1961 Chaminade undefeated and untied football team* – the first one in school history. Thank you, Chuck, for keeping the memory special and alive all these years later.

* *Chaminade's first undefeated varsity football team enjoyed that then-unique status for ten years. That 1951 team, also coached by Mr. Thomas, was indeed undefeated but, alas, logged a scoreless tie against Cardinal Hayes, a minor blemish on its otherwise stellar and unprecedented record.*

On August 21, 2011, in anticipation of our team's 50-year reunion the following month, Zimmy penned the following:

I tell all of my friends that I had the privilege of playing for the high school version of Bear Bryant – assuming all the legendary stories are true. A personal example: At the end of the first half of the Stepinac game I outsmarted myself and tried to sneak in instead of giving the ball to our horse (Earl Kirmser). Most coaches would have chewed my butt – Coach Thomas told me in a very encouraging way that Earl would have been a better option (not to mention the play coach had called). Fortunately, that play did not cost us the game. A great person, a great Christian man, a great example for us all and, yes, a great football coach. I thoroughly enjoyed talking with him a few times for hours over the past ten years.

At the end of the St. Francis game I had Bob Bowman open and threw a crappy pass causing him to have to wait, thus necessitating the dramatic ending.

The Holy Cross game [our eighth and last]: Coach Thomas's incredible half-time tirade on the bus. Then Earl passes out on the field in the second half and the other team is cheering his demise. Tom Higgins comes in at fullback for Earl, totally pumped up, runs the first play for us – a 36 power – and races to the end zone, seemingly untouched. Game, set, match – sealing our legendary season.

On another occasion Zimmy reminded us:

The 1962 Chaminade varsity football team also won the League title with a 7-1 record.

(Francis was the spoiler, beating us 14-0.) Still, the greatest significance of the '62 season championship is that it marked the first and only "threepeat" in Chaminade varsity football history, that is, three consecutive League titles in 1960, 1961 and 1962. Four of the '62 Flyers' seven victories were shutouts, eclipsing the '61 squad's three. To add to this lore, Coach McGuckin recalled that there would have been a fourth consecutive championship in 1963 but the Flyers couldn't put together any substantial offense and lost a must-win game to the Cross late in that season by a field goal.

We did a very good thing for the team—having Zimmy as the starting QB was a wonderful change!

— Rod Dwyer

1961: CHAMINADE'S FIRST PERFECT FOOTBALL SEASON

By William J. McGovern

There was something about that team, and, frankly, everything about Chaminade football that I believe has contributed greatly to whatever family or professional successes I've achieved.

— Larry Grassini

Like Zimmy, Bill graduated from Chaminade in 1963 and Notre Dame in 1967 with a B.S.B.A. in marketing. He was commissioned an officer in the Navy in 1968 and flew as a radar intercept operator in the F-4 Phantom *fighter jet. While in Pensacola in 1973 he earned an M.B.A. in marketing from the University of West Florida and later sold hospital supplies for 27 years, retiring from Cardinal Health in 2007. In 1968 he married Denise Sullivan, an alumna of St. Joseph's Academy in Brentwood, N.Y., with whom he has two children and five grandchildren.*

He wrote the following essay in anticipation of our team's 50-year reunion in 2011.

Thank you, Bill.

As a junior I was assigned mostly to all of the special teams – kickoff, kickoff receive, punt and punt receive. I was an offensive end and not a starter. However, I relished playing on the football field with a group of guys that I had played with the two years prior on the freshman and JV teams.

I had played in the band and it was exciting to be part of the entertainment at halftime my first two years at Chaminade. As much as I enjoyed that, it was much better for me to be in the locker room at halftime with the whole varsity strategizing for what we would do in the second half.

Our first game was against Hicksville, which was one of the better public schools on Long Island. I started on the special teams and, early on, Coach Ed Flynn suggested to Coach Joe Thomas that he put me in at offensive end. John Zimmermann ended up throwing a few passes to me, one for a touchdown. It was a televised game-of-the-week in the New York area, and friends of my Dad called him at work on Monday to see if I was related to him (his name was also Bill McGovern). He said. "Yes, he is my son," and it was a very proud moment for him and my Mom. We won 28-7.

When we played Iona, we were 4 wins, 0 losses. We were halfway through the season, and a win would kick off the second half of the season on a great note. I was fortunate to be playing in the first quarter on offense. I had just turned in the end zone on a hook pass, and a bullet from John Zimmermann came right at me, perfectly thrown and just missing the hands of many defenders. I caught it for our first touchdown of the game. It was a spectacular pass from John. We won 28-0.

Our sixth game was at Mount St. Michael on McGovern Field. This was a big game for us. I started on special teams and played them the whole game. I had played a little defensive end during the season and, very close to the end of the game, Coach Thomas put me in at left defensive end, replacing Al Groh. Mount St. Michael was on our six-yard line, and they called an option-right running play toward me. As the quarterback came down the line, he pitched the football to his halfback. In the air I picked off the lateral and ran 94 yards for a touchdown. No one was near me, except for Al Groh running down the sideline yelling at me to keep running and don't look back. When I came off the field, Al was waiting for me and said that he had played a lot of football up until that time, and that opportunity at defensive end had never happened to him. I go in for one play, intercept a lateral, and run for a touchdown. Still, Al was very happy for me, and I was excited to help the team at McGovern Field. We won 34-6.

It was a tremendous season and a wonderful accomplishment. When you think of the two-a-days [double practice sessions] we had during the summer before the season started and all of the late practices we endured, it was a phenomenal accomplishment to win week after week. The teamwork and camaraderie between juniors and seniors were inspiring. I held them in my Navy years and work career. Thank you to all, coaches, seniors, juniors, managers, for contributing to my formation.

The Holy Cross College Club of New York awarded the Crusader Cup shown here to Chaminade in 1961 for the second consecutive year. The award is emblematic of metropolitan New York Catholic School football supremacy.

Rev. Joseph A. Glavin, S.J., of the College of the Holy Cross presents the Crusader Cup to Chaminade as Coach Thomas (left), Earl Kirmser and Tom Kiley (right) look on.

On August 21, 2011, in anticipation of our team's 50-year reunion, Bill wrote the following:

The 1961 football championship season was one of the most exciting years from different aspects: team achievement, team camaraderie, and team personality. It was unknown at the time what kind of impact the championship would have on our lives, but now, 50 years later, it most likely shaped our lives in many positive ways. Thank you for this opportunity to reflect on what we accomplished as teenagers and how it molded our future years as adults.

I am looking forward to seeing you and all of those alumni that can make this reunion. Thank you, again, for putting it together.

Best regards,
Bill McGovern

A coach "must be a pedagogue," [Lombardi] once explained. "He has to pound the lessons into the players by rote, the same way you teach pupils in the classroom."

— David Maraniss in his book
*When Pride Still Mattered:
A Life of Vince Lombardi*

CHAMINADE UNDEFEATED VARSITY FOOTBALL 1961

By Philip J. Pignataro

Looking back on my time at Chaminade, I see how it formed my life and that goes double for my football experience there.

— Phil Pignataro

Shortly after graduating from Chaminade in 1963, where he was elected president of the student body and the Student Council, Phil entered the Air Force Academy Prep School. This led to the Air Force Academy itself and a commission as a second lieutenant in 1968. Thus began a 21-year USAF career flying tankers and various transport aircraft, including a 1971 tour in Viet Nam flying the C-7A Caribou and a 1985 assignment in Washington, D.C., carrying military and government VIPs on worldwide diplomatic missions.

In 1990, he retired from the service and joined United Airlines. While a Captain on the Airbus A-320, he reached the mandatory FAA retirement age in 2005 and left UAL for his final piloting job, NetJets, Inc. After a two-year stint in the Cessna Citation X, he retired from flying. With time to spare, he worked as a barista for Starbucks, then Borders Books and finally Barnes & Noble. He left the work force in 2015 to spend more time with Martha, his spouse of 38 years. They have two adult sons, Greg and Taylor, who live in Phoenix and Chicago, respectively.

Thank you, Phil.

My memories of that season drift toward the practice sessions. Practices were tough. Coach Thomas definitely embraced the theory to practice hard made the actual games "easy." Even the practice field was memorable. Located behind the visitor's bleachers and extending to the school's boundary at Jericho Turnpike, it was mostly smooth and completely covered in grass. That was in August. However, within a month or so, the grass was gone and it was dusty, hard-packed, and full of pebbles. Lots of scrapes and cuts ensued – no gloves back in the day!

Warm-up calisthenics, blocking and tackling drills, and scrimmaging were the usual order of the day. I was a long way from the starting squad, so during those scrimmages my role was to play with the unit that mimicked the next opponent's formations for the starters. During one of these sessions early in the season, I played as a center linebacker (all 150 pounds of me). After the snap, a hole opened to my left and I headed for it. I soon saw our star fullback, Earl Kirmser, charging fast for the same opening. I was pretty sure this was going to hurt – and it did. He was low, so I got lower and I think my helmet collided with his knee. Stars appeared everywhere and I remember looking up into Coach McGuckin's face. When he quizzed me to assess my condition, I knew my name but not much else. I was out for a week after a doctor's visit, lots of ice packs and rest.

My most vivid memories of that season were my blowing a hike on a fourth down punting situation during the Hicksville HS game (my home town) and coming up on the short end of a tackle on Earl Kirmser during a practice scrimmage.

— Phil Pignataro

Practices ended with the dreaded series of wind sprints. Our coaches were fond of wind sprints. To stay fit for the games, I was determined to "win" as many of these as I could. I often managed to do so since I mostly raced with linemen. As a result, I did participate in the season's games on the kick-off and kick-receiving squads.

In this capacity, my job was to use my speed (relative term) to get downfield for a tackle or to help our receivers by blocking for them. I used a *Kamikaze* approach and just threw my body in the path of opposing players.

I personally don't recall the fact the team was headed for an undefeated season as a big motivational factor until the last couple of games. From the beginning, Coach Thomas had ingrained in us the spirit of winning through hard work, so I didn't feel the added pressure of being the first undefeated team until very late in the season.

The lesson of success through hard work and dedication to a job well done stuck with me all through my schooling and subsequent careers. Coach Joe Thomas and Coach Charlie McGuckin were true gentlemen and great role models for us. I look back with pride on playing a small part on Chaminade's first undefeated and untied varsity football team.

The game itself was the superficial part of coaching for Lombardi. He had already done his work getting his team prepared.

— David Maraniss in his book
When Pride Still Mattered:
A Life of Vince Lombardi

CHAMINADE HIGH SCHOOL: 1959-1963

By Cyril J. Rottkamp

Chaminade football on Long Island was very prestigious. We set the standards for other teams – character and winning tradition.

— Skip Rottkamp

Skip penned the following reflection on August 22, 2011, with a view to our team's 50-year reunion. His essay, "Teacher, Coach, Friend: Charlie McGuckin," appears earlier herein.

Thank you, Skip.

I grew up on Long Island, the son of a proud farmer and a farming family. My parents wanted me to attend the best parochial school on Long Island. Having had some success with baseball and football at an early age, I chose Chaminade High School. Little did I realize how important a decision was made at that time.

Academics at Chaminade were a real challenge. The Brothers were patient and dedicated to get me through the rigors of four years of high school. Summer school became an added tool to get me graduated on time.

Athletics at Chaminade were my outlet for friendship and coaches who taught me about dedication, hard work, sportsmanship, team work and winning. Four years of baseball (Mr. McGuckin) and two years of football (Mr. Thomas) laid the groundwork for me for the rest of my life.

Flyer football marked great character at Chaminade. Freshman and junior varsity prepared me for the varsity. In 1961 I was fortunate enough to make the varsity. Chaminade football on Long Island was very prestigious. We set the standards for other teams – character and winning tradition. Looking up to the upper classmen and getting a chance to play was a "big deal." Chaminade football got the "cream of the crop" of athletes on Long Island and 1961 was no exception. Mr. Thomas got the most out of us resulting in a championship season – an undefeated season – an untied season! What a thrill! All the sprints, three-man rolls and running plays paid off.

After receiving a four-year scholarship to Long Island University for baseball, I settled in Wappingers Falls, New York. I had the opportunity to play baseball in the Kentucky-Indiana College League in 1967 and the Cape Cod College Baseball League the following year when I replaced at catcher the great New York Yankees Hall of Famer, Thurman Munson.

I retired from the Wappingers Central School District in 2000 after 33 years (17 years Physical Education teacher, 15 years of coaching baseball, 25 years officiating soccer and 13 years in Administration). After all the years of 'receiving' it was time to 'give back.' I joined Fishkill Rotary 27 years ago, drove for the Meals-On-Wheels, raised money at the Cancer "Relay for Life," and ran a yearly golf tournament to raise money for the Meals-On-Wheels. Lost my wife to cancer in 2006 but my six grandkids keep me very busy. I was honored to be inducted into the Wappingers Central School District Hall of Fame, the Sports Museum of Dutchess County and the Dutchess County Baseball Hall of Fame, of which I have been president for the last nine years. As the shirt I wear says, "Life is Good."

Look, I like hitting fourth, and I like the good batting average, but what I do every day behind the plate is a lot more important because it touches so many more people, and so many more aspects of the game.

— Thurman Munson

VIEWS FROM THE BENCH: A JUNIOR SCOUT PLAYER'S PERSPECTIVE

By Lawrence P. Grassini

Hit or be hit, that was the reality of football, Lombardi believed.

> — David Maraniss in his book
> *When Pride Still Mattered:*
> *A Life of Vince Lombardi*

Larry became one of the most respected trial lawyers in the U.S., being twice recognized as "Trial Lawyer of the Year" by the Los Angeles Trial Lawyers Association. He was also elected to the Inner Circle of Advocates as one of the top 100 plaintiff's lawyers in the United States.

In the late '90s, Larry and his wife Sharon realized that the wine industry was starting to bloom in Santa Barbara County, and found that their land was the perfect spot for a vineyard. Thus, Grassini Family Vineyards and Winery was born, and their daughters Katie, Corey, Mandy and Molly have worked with their parents in support of this exciting and enriching undertaking.

Indeed, Grassini Family wines were provided by Larry and enjoyed and complimented by everyone at our team's 50-year reunion dinner in September 2011.

Larry submitted the following piece on August 18, 2011, in anticipation of that reunion.

Thank you, Larry.

As a junior on a senior-dominated team, my memories of that historic season are not of heroics on the field, but of the views from the bench. Of course, next year as seniors, we did again win the championship and remain the only Chaminade team to "threepeat."

My first memory of Chaminade football actually occurred when Pete Eisenhauer (Ike), Tommy Liesegang and I all played on our parish's tackle football team in grade school. There we learned football fundamentals, and how to lose graciously to teams twice as big and three times faster than ours. (I, an offensive guard at Chaminade, was a running back at St. Pat's – that's how understaffed we were.) There, we also learned of Chaminade football, where Ike's brother, Larry (Chaminade '57), was a star player.

We all came out for frosh football and were absolutely thrilled to be selected from among the 250 guys who tried out. Our fundamental football knowledge paid off and now we would hopefully learn to win. Frosh, JV or varsity, the football team was expected to exemplify the virtues and values that the brothers, priests, and coaches instilled in us. I recall that at some time as a sophomore, maybe the spring, we got to play against the varsity team. I still feel the sting of the first forearm shiver from Billy Sellerberg that introduced me to Chaminade varsity football. Tom Kiley, Earl Kirmser, Charlie Mansfield, "Tiny" Reisert, and Rick Darby (who I carpooled with from Huntington and who spent most of the carpool telling his brother Ken to shut up) further contributed to my football education by beating the stuffing out of me. But in true Chaminade fashion there was nothing dirty, no trash-talking – just practice like you play, Chaminade football. Double sessions before the season, late night practices in the twilight (dark) on that old rock-strewn field behind the bleachers, running the tires, back bends (aka neck bridges) on your head without a helmet, three-man rolls – we learned a lot of football, but we learned more about being a team player and a "Chaminade man." *(Authors' note: Please see "Criteria for the Chaminade Man Award" later herein.)*

I remember all the pre-game rituals that were followed religiously: Steak and eggs at six a.m. on Sunday, game day, before we dressed, the mandatory prayer before Our Lady's statue where I admit I was praying that we would kick ass as opposed to Joe Thomas's exhortations to pray for a good game and no injuries. The prayers worked, as I remember few injuries and many great games. However, all my prayers didn't stop me from feeling that steak sitting in my stomach as I sat on the bench, cheering. I do remember the water bucket with sponges in it that guys would use to wipe their sweat, clean their bloody wounds, suck on for a sip of water, and then throw back in the bucket. I still recall the excitement of the games and the respect I had for all my teammates who put in so much hard work to make that season a success.

There was something about that team, and, frankly, everything about Chaminade football that I believe has contributed greatly to whatever family or professional successes I've achieved. Moving to California has kept me from Chaminade reunions, so I can't wait to reconnect with my teammates and relive those very special years.

Larry Grassini (Gratz)
Class of '63
Offensive Guard

Know this, Chuck: You and your teammates helped inspire us runners to be a cross-country team that the football team could be proud of.

— Doug Casey

MEMORIES OF A CHAMINADE LINEMAN

By Tom Kiley

I visit the old back field for the first time in many years. But where have the rocks and dirt and dust gone? The grass is like carpet, green and soft. It seems to ask, "What are you doing here?"

— Tom Kiley

Let's see. Chuck asked me for my memories of the 1961 season. I think they're supposed to come from the corners of my mind.

I remember us beating Holy Cross to finish unbeaten, and being rather subdued afterward, very aware that this was the last time I would put on the pads for Chaminade. I envied the juniors. I wanted there to be more games, but I knew that could not be. The season was over. I was not happy about that, although I was proud of what we had accomplished. The game itself seemed anticlimactic. Hard to get up for. The league title had been clinched one or two weeks before. It took a halftime verbal lashing by Coach Thomas to get us going, but it was really no contest after that. No doubt. No chance for Holy Cross. In today's jargon, we took care of business. Then, the last bus ride home, singing all the way, our last prayer as a team before the Statue of Our Lady, and the fading sound of cleats on cement and in the locker room. Taking off the Crimson and Gold for the last time.

I still remember the rhythm of a lineman's practice very well. Without too much difficulty I could run (well, maybe walk) through the usual regimen like it was yesterday. Calisthenics and maybe three-man rolls. Afterwards, we run over to the boards. Always running – everywhere. Legs apart, wide apart. Get the air dummies out for Oklahoma. Bull the neck, drive, keep those feet moving. On defense, resist, always resist. Never back up easily. Now over to the seven-man sled. Explode, stay on your feet, head up, drive until your legs hurt. Work hard until the whistle sounds. Repeat again and again. We know this will pay off on game days. This will be our meat and potatoes. Now hit and spin out. Hit every other sled dummy. After the last, recover a fumble the right way. Always the right way and there is a right way to do everything. Now on to one on one; then two on one. Always contact first, then work for position. Never the opposite. Split the double team. Spin out if necessary. Never take the line of least resistance.

Next, run over to the tires. The ultimate test of toughness. Take on all comers, several at the same time if necessary. Let them yell and scream all they want. Do the backs ever have to do this? Run over that miserable pile of rubber or stand up like a real man at the end of it, but always hit out, deliver a blow. Never just accept one passively. We are separating the men from the boys right here.

Next, the Chaminade Special. Set up the big dummies. Hit, react to the block and make the tackle. Some would like to be a quarterback, standing there, handing off. Not me. This is what I do. Hey, don't set those dummies up too far apart. No extra room for the backs to slip through. That's just what they long for. You have two arms and two legs. Nobody can block you. Ever. Never!

Now to the tackling drills. One line of tacklers and three lines of backs. Forward roll, then get up fast. If you don't, the back may scoot by you and make you look silly, tackling air. Nothing would please them more. Get your head in front. Hit hard and bring the back down. Great to be able to get your hands on somebody. Now this is Chaminade football.

Afterwards, we run our plays on the big field, perhaps if we are lucky. 'Round and around we go – first team, second team, third team. Run in and out of the huddle fast. Get down in your stance right away. Just like we will do in a game. At Hicksville, their defensive line wilts in the 92-degree heat. We are in our element.

If we are lucky, maybe we get to live scrimmage on the big field. That's always fun. I hear an unmistakable sound. No need to turn around. It's DeMeo hitting a receiver as only he can. That can't be good for anybody. Finally, work on our pursuit angles, block downfield on every play, gang tackle.

One thing left – wind sprints. Keep your helmet on. Perhaps, once in a while on the big field in the quiet and looming darkness. In tandem, with somebody just about your own speed, so nobody loafs. Goal line to twenty and back. Forty and back. Sixty, then eighty yards and back. We are in the best shape of any team in the League. We are ready to do battle. We are truly a band of brothers. Leaving the field on a Thursday, we are like a thoroughbred being given his special oats the day before a race. We can feel it. We know instinctively the big day is not far off. The hard part of the week is over.

Pictured above is the notorious "Old Back Field" as it looks today.

(Photograph courtesy of Barbara Ramsey Kiley and used with permission.)

I visit the old back field for the first time in many years. But where have all the rocks and dirt and dust gone? The grass is like carpet now, green and soft. It seems to ask me, "What are you doing here?" Beautiful evergreens now line the old fence as stately maple trees overlook a quiet, peaceful scene. No sign of tires or sleds or the old garage we stored them in. Instead, a state-of-the-art workout facility rises majestically above a beautiful football stadium. Only young men in short pants play here now, our struggles on this field of friendly strife long forgotten, except by a few. I think I can hear faintly the grunts and battle cries of old, and can still see our excellent captains leading us to victory. A thought comes into my head now that I never would have dreamed of then. How soon the years stretch far away.

Tom Kiley
Linebacker 1961

Bitter or sweet, memories become precious as time passes. This book is a memory and I am grateful for it.

— Tom Kiley

RANDOM THOUGHTS FROM AN OFFENSIVE RIGHT TACKLE (#75)

By Richard W. Darby

I don't believe you can discuss the 1961 team without underlining the major factor in the team's success – An Abundance of Leaders.

— Rick Darby

In 1969 Rick married Bonnie R. Benedict of Santa Monica, Ca. They are blessed with three children, their spouses and seven grandchildren.

He graduated from Chaminade in 1962 where he played JV and varsity football, and was a member of the varsity rifle team. He accepted a senatorial appointment to attend the United States Military Academy at West Point, graduating in 1966 with a Bachelor of Science in Civil Engineering. While at West Point, he played on the Army Rugby Team for four years, and competed on the Army Rifle Team for one. Rick served in the U.S. Army on active duty during the period 1966-1970, attaining the rank of captain, attending Airborne and Ranger Schools and serving with the 9th Infantry Division in Vietnam (1968-1969). While stationed in California, he played rugby with the L.A. Rugby Club for two seasons.

Rick graduated from the University of Minnesota Law School with a Juris Doctor degree in 1973. He was admitted to the Vermont Bar Association in 1973, and became a partner in the Vermont law firm of Adams Meaker & Darby in 1975. He is currently practicing law with the firm of Darby Kolter & Nordle LLP, with offices in Waterbury and Stowe, Vt.

Thanks, Rick.

1. # The Team – Greater Than the Sum of Its Parts

Although there were two high school All Americans and many good student-athletes on the team, I don't think we realized there was something special about the 1961 team until the last-minute victory over a good St. Francis team. In addition to that game, of course, the "something special" realization may have had its genesis in the way we were winning (i.e. the St. Francis game), or the way we practiced, or the camaraderie in the locker room and on bus rides, or by the players' game-day intensity, or more likely – *all of the above.*

2. Practice – More Important Than We Thought

We started practicing in early July 1961, when the dreaded postcard from Coach Thomas arrived interrupting our plans for the summer. The postcard message was brief and to the point: *"Now is the time to start getting in shape."* Further, the postcard triggered weekly workouts at central locations, supervised by seniors. If you were a junior or sophomore trying to make the varsity, you attended the workouts. It was also a good opportunity to get to know the seniors who were entrusted with your fitness. Although somewhat intimidating to underclassmen, the summer practices generally worked in terms of fitness, team-building and as a rude awakening to the differences between you and the seniors – the hallmark of Chaminade football.

Team practices at school began in mid-August heat and humidity in what was less than affectionately referred to as *double sessions.* Working out in full pads twice a day in the heat, then returning home to eat and sleep before returning to school to do it all over again. The first day of the school year didn't arrive fast enough, and so did single practice sessions.

The practice sessions were designed to make us mentally and physically stronger, and to prepare for the next game. Additionally, the practices were enhanced by what can be referred to as *Chaminade*

Football Jargon. Jargon, which although a significant part of the winning culture, occasionally became a source of humor for coaches and players alike. Some of the more memorable and semi-humorous terms were the following: (1) *Three-Man Rolls*: An exhausting drill which aside from general fitness, seemed designed to foster quick and agile reactions in the chaos that exists within three or four feet from the ground. (2) *The Chaminade Special*: A meat grinder of a drill involving one-on-one contact between an offensive lineman and a defensive lineman in the narrow space between two tackling dummies. The defensive lineman tries to avoid the block of the offensive lineman and tackle a ball carrier running close to full speed into the space where the linemen are battling. Looking back on The Special, it is the closest thing I can think of which replicates the one-on-one struggles, which are a constant on the line of scrimmage. (3) *Avoiding the LLR*, or *Avoiding the Line of Least Resistance*. A pithy comment from coaches, mostly for defensive players, designed to make you react quickly when physics and opposing players are moving you *away* from the ball. To simplify, we were taught not to go where opposing players want you to go. There is one caveat – *Avoiding the LLR* may not necessarily be helpful for life in general.

Yes, the practices and related jargon were intense, physical, and sometimes humorous, but they contributed substantially to the camaraderie of the 1961 team. Camaraderie that built as the season progressed, until all the players connected as a team. When that connection was made, we were playing for each other first and foremost, then for the coaches, our families and Chaminade.

3. Leadership – An Abundance of Leaders

I hesitate to say too much about leadership. Yet, I don't believe you can discuss the 1961 team without underlining the major factor in the team's success – An Abundance of Leaders. There were numerous players on the team who could be described as natural leaders since they unselfishly led by example, by working hard, by accepting responsibility for their actions and even by admitting their mistakes. Many of them were also vocal leaders, including by leading the team in song or by participating in good-natured ribbing between teammates – such as the *right side* of the O-line being more successful in games than the *left side,* and vice versa. My fairly unbiased opinion relative to such friendly banter between right- vs. left-side offensive linemen remains the same to this date!

Although the coaches made it clear from the beginning that responsibility for leadership belonged to seniors, such leadership characteristics were evident at every level of ability and experience, in both seniors and juniors. Indeed, the Perfect Season was a consequence of seniors accepting primary leadership responsibility, and juniors providing leadership as needed, knowing they would soon have primary responsibility when the postcard arrives with the admonition: *"Now is the time to start getting in shape."*

This handsome plaque was designed by our coaches
and presented to each member of our team.

(Photograph courtesy of Mary Ann Mansfield and used with permission.)

Rick and I executed our blocks superbly, if I do say so myself, opening a huge hole through which Dave [Tuohy] galloped 44 yards all the way for a touchdown, his first of two on the day. I recall Dave running on a perfectly straight line from the line of scrimmage into the end zone. No one impeded or touched him. It was simply beautiful.

— Chuck Mansfield

"SINGING CHAMINADE SONGS"

By David J. Tuohy, Sr.

We were playing for each other first and foremost, then for the coaches, our families and Chaminade.

— Rick Darby

Dave's exploits during our perfect season were the stuff of legend. An outstanding halfback, he created some of the major highlights of that unprecedented championship year and was named All League.

A 1966 Notre Dame alumnus, along with Cliff Molloy, Mike Reisert and Bill Sellerberg, Dave enjoyed a long and successful career in the insurance business. He and his wife Marilyn reside in Coram, N.Y.

Dave submitted the following piece on August 1, 2011, in anticipation of our team's 50-year reunion.

Thank you, Dave.

My reflections:

Singing Chaminade songs on the bus led by Tiny Reisert on our returns from away scrimmages.

Hicksville: Coach giving a pregame talk that went on and on. I noticed that we still had a bus ride, and kickoff was in 35 minutes. I brought this to Mr. Thomas's attention only to be asked why I hadn't said something sooner. We arrived on time and on a hot, hot day got a feel that we were good. *(Editor's note: Flyers 28, Hicksville 7. This* High School Football Game of the Week *was televised and the announcer was the late, great Marty Glickman, who was assisted by former Yankee catcher Elston Howard and earlier in the week had interviewed players in the Chaminade locker room.)*

All League halfback Dave Tuohy romps past Stepinac Crusader
defenders. In this challenging game, the Flyers prevailed 14-6.

Stepinac: Ref on the 15-yard line when I caught a perfect pass
from Zimmy. He ruled I was on the one, and time expired. Biggest
play of the season...Kevin Walters stretching his fingers to deflect a
pass that would have meant a loss. Biggest play of the season.

St. Francis: The clock that kept going in the last quarter. Bob
Bowman making the catch that led to our only score and a win in
the final seconds.

St. John's: It was actually close for the first half. Coach was
pissed.

Iona: George Ackerson's behind-the-hip catch (of) a long TD
pass.

The Mount: Leaving on the team bus for the trip there and
passing 35 (Chaminade) student buses. Game was won before we left
Mineola. *(Editor's note: Dave scored on the Flyers' first play from
scrimmage, a dazzling 44-yard gallop. He also ran for another 54-
yard touchdown that day on Chaminade's first play from scrimmage
in the second half and was named the game's Most Valuable Player.)*

A caravan of 35 buses gets ready to head to the Bronx to cheer
the Flyers on to victory over Mount Saint Michael.

(Photograph courtesy of Tom Kiley and used with permission.)

Hayes: Scored easily right away, then almost slept through it.

Holy Cross: Back to where we started. A fun day watching Frank
Biasi run for a long TD the second time after a holding call brought
the first one back.

The egg attack by the "North Shore" boys on the "South Shore."
*(Editor's note: The first group was known as the "North Shore Party
Boys;" the latter, "The Unholy Seven.")*

In a recent email Dave elaborated on this encounter. "My memory
of that season was the infamous egg fight the Friday night before the
Mount game. I was picked up after practice that night by Captain
Sellerberg in his red chief's car. Accompanying him was the late and
beloved Frank #31 Biasi. Bill drove and Frank rode shotgun.

"As I got into the back seat, they warned me to be careful not to
sit on a brown paper bag. As Bill drove back to Chaminade, Frank
asked me to pass it up to him. To my surprise it contained four dozen

eggs. He explained that the North Shore was about to attack the South Shore. As we drove past our fellow teammates exiting practice we began hurling eggs at them with several direct hits before Bill sped down to Jericho Turnpike, escaping a lot of pissed off teammates.

"We were laughing like hell. I remember it took the edge off many of the Flyers as we were all up tight as the Mount game was that Sunday. In the end the South Shore got even the next day after our team meeting. It helped us to laugh together and relax before our biggest game of the year as, like us, the Mount was 5-0 at the time. I think it helped us to go there and kick their butts."

There's nothing that cleanses your soul like
getting the hell kicked out of you.

— Woody Hayes
Ohio State

FLYER GRIDMEN WIN 21 POSITIONS ON NEW YORK ALL STAR TEAMS

By Charles Raubicheck

Kirmser received the Terzi Award, Kiley received Most Outstanding Player honors, and Sellerberg was voted MVP. In a concluding word of praise that night, Coach Thomas summed up the entire year by fittingly commenting, "This is the best team I have ever coached."

— Charles Raubicheck

A 1964 Chaminade alumnus and one of the country's foremost Food and Drug attorneys, Charles wrote the following article for TARMAC *in the 1961 post-season. His "Undefeated Flyer Eleven Look to Mount St. Michael" appears earlier herein.*

Thank you, Charles.

Many outstanding players on our 1961 Chaminade grid squad have earned positions on various all-star teams sponsored by the New York newspapers in post-season ratings. A total of 21 places on these squads were given to Chaminade, a tribute to the success of this fall's Flyer gridders.

Besides these first team awards [Earl Kirmser, Mike Reisert and Bill Sellerberg per an accompanying photograph], a number of our players were honored on other teams. End Bill DeMeo made all-league second string; Carl LoGalbo, Al Groh, Chuck Mansfield and Dick Darby received honorable mention. In addition, Mr. Joe Thomas was voted "coach of the year," and his assistant, Mr. Charles McGuckin, was similarly recognized.

"Awards Night" capped the finale to this tremendous season. Kirmser received the Terzi Award, Kiley received Most Outstanding Player honors, and Sellerberg was voted MVP. In a concluding word of praise that night, Coach Thomas summed up the entire year by fittingly commenting, "This is the best team I have ever coached."

It isn't necessary to see a good tackle. You can hear it.

— Knute Rockne
Notre Dame

THE BOYS OF SUMMER

By Tom Kiley

As we laughed uproariously at our jokes and stories and the years began to melt away, I could not help but wonder at the strength and continuity of a friendship that has remained constant through all the years.

— Tom Kiley

In the spring of 1997, nearly thirty-six years after Al Groh, Tom Kiley, Earl Kirmser, Carl LoGalbo and Chuck Mansfield were part of our undefeated and untied '61 team, Al returned to Long Island for a new coaching assignment with the New York Jets, of whom he would become head coach less than three years later. His return occasioned a dinner in Garden City, N.Y., an evening that would mark a special reunion. It was a time instructive of just how strong the bond among us had remained. The authors believe these sentiments apply to all our 1961 teammates.

On August 6ᵗʰ of that year, Tom wrote the following letter:

Dear Al, Earl, Chuck and Carl,

It was a great pleasure seeing each of you at the Newport Grill a few weeks ago. That night brought together for the first time in a long time a group of guys that I have always considered quite extraordinary in so many ways.

As we laughed uproariously at our jokes and stories and the years began to melt away, I could not help but wonder at the strength and continuity of a friendship that has remained constant through all the years, sometimes despite long periods of enforced separation and even silence. Clearly the bonds that we began to forge nearly forty years ago bind us tightly still. Certainly they have proved far more enduring than we could have imagined back in 1958.

Therefore I am pleased to send along to each of you a copy of a picture that was taken on the evening of our reunion. I think it captures a little bit of the spirit and camaraderie of the group as well as some of the affection we still have for each other. It is rare to find such feeling among any group much less one thrown together purely by fate as we were so many years ago.

Although the circumstances that brought us together recently may change sooner or later, it is my hope that our love for each other never will. It is in that spirit of hope and love that I enclose this picture of the Boys of Summer, still young in the autumn of their years.

Your friend,

Tom

Pictured above are (left to right) Carl LoGalbo, Tom Kiley, Al Groh, Earl Kirmser and Chuck Mansfield at their mini-reunion dinner in 1997.

(Photograph courtesy of Tom Kiley and used with permission.)

THE PERFECT SEASON

Coldly, sadly descends
The autumn evening. The field
Strewn with its dank yellow drifts
Of withered leaves, and the elms,
Fade into dimness apace,
Silent, hardly a shout
From a few boys late at their play!

— Matthew Arnold
in his poem *Rugby Chapel*

SHEER TALENT OR TRUE GRIT?

By Chuck Mansfield

Which is more important, the talent of the troops or the skill of the leader? That is one of the central questions of all group enterprises and can be debated forever, but remains essentially unresolvable.

> — David Maraniss in his book
> *When Pride Still Mattered:*
> *A Life of Vince Lombardi*

As Skip Orr, Flyer 1960 championship quarterback, president of the Chaminade class of 1961 and star Navy wide receiver, has noted, "With his players at such an impressionable age, Coach Thomas each year would take a group of undersized over-achievers and mold them, through rigorous pre-season drills, discipline and execution-oriented practices, and powerful and emotional pep talks during games, into teams with rich, winning traditions."
Thank you, Skip.

On the much-discussed question of our team's talent, renowned *Newsday* and later *New York Times* sports columnist George Vecsey interviewed Coach Thomas in November 1961, as published earlier in this work, and wrote: "Maybe this wasn't his best team. Maybe he has had better material. But as he points out, 'they certainly have the best record.'" Of this exchange I have written, "Coach may have sounded a bit reluctant or diplomatically non-committal at that time but he was almost certainly thinking about his most talented team and believed – and rightly so – that we were not the most talented." Similarly, Bill Sellerberg has observed "that we weren't the greatest bunch of players." According to Al Groh, "Teams are not judged on talent, they are judged on wins, and no team before won as many games as the '61 Flyers." Joe Namath has stated, "When you win, nothing hurts." Gen. Douglas MacArthur once said, "There is no substitute for victory." Even Napoleon, when asked which troops he considered the best, replied, "Those which are victorious." *Amen.*

Our '61 Flyers were unquestionably "victorious" but let us evaluate the team's talent through the lens of accolades accorded at season's end. To wit:

> - Earl Kirmser: All American, All Met, All City-First Team, All League, All Scholastic, All Nassau-Suffolk Honorable Mention, Terzi Award
> - Mike Reisert: All American, All Met, All City-First Team, All League, All Scholastic, All Nassau-Suffolk Honorable Mention
> - Tom Kiley: All Met, All City-Second Team, All League, All-Nassau-Suffolk, Most Outstanding Player
> - Bill Sellerberg: All League, Lou Gehrig Award, All Nassau-Suffolk Honorable Mention, Most Valuable Player
> - Bill DeMeo: All League
> - Dave Tuohy: All League
> - Al Groh: All League Honorable Mention
> - Chuck Mansfield: All League Honorable Mention
> - John Zimmermann: All Nassau-Suffolk Honorable Mention
> - Rick Darby: All Nassau Honorable Mention

With ten of eleven starters and nearly twenty-two percent of our team receiving "All" recognition at some level, it may rightly be argued that we had talent in abundance. Still, there remains the question of whether it was raw talent or great grit that enabled us to achieve a perfect season. Despite my earlier assertion that we were not Mr. Thomas's "most talented team," I would agree that we had substantial talent that, when subjected to and augmented by the crucible of hard work, set us apart from our competition. In short, a winning combination of talent and grit defined us.

After the 1961 season, *Long Island Press* sports columnist Al Spitzer offered additional perspective on the relative level of talent among Chaminade varsity football teams. "Thomas doesn't think it is fair to go out on the limb to compare teams of different years. Too many factors enter into the picture such as the strength of the opposition. Some fans may argue that the current team had too many close calls, but Thomas will reply that playing in a league as tough as the CHSFL puts extraordinary pressure on a team. ... 'It's a tough league, top to bottom,' asserted Thomas." *(Authors' note: Comparative comments on several other Flyer teams coached by Mr. Thomas appear earlier herein in the chapter entitled "Which Team Was Mr. Thomas's Best?")*

My teammates have commented admirably and in considerable detail elsewhere in this work on the often grueling physical conditioning drills that Coach Thomas put us through every day at practice. Their emphasis on the competitive nature of these drills and their stamina-building objectives were, in our time, both lamented and recognized as essential and worthy.

Indeed, David Maraniss, author of *When Pride Still Mattered: A Life of Vince Lombardi*, called these aspects part of "the mystical discipline of football."

As Al Groh has written earlier herein, "The talent at Chaminade was always good, but there was talent throughout the league, especially at our principal rivals... Talent alone didn't do it but, when magnified by the four cornerstones of Flyer football – constant competition, fundamentals, physical, mental and competitive toughness, and superior conditioning – that talent became extremely difficult to beat."

In this connection, I have a keen memory of the Hicksville Comets' game, our first of the new season. It was played at Hicksville on Saturday, September 2, 1961, when the temperature at game time was 92 degrees Fahrenheit with 50% relative humidity. Moreover, it was the *High School Football Game of the Week*, which was televised and announced by the late, great Marty Glickman, a Brooklyn high-school friend of my mother, Mary. *(Please see "My Mother Mary, Non-football Fan" later herein.)*

Coach Thomas (right) prepares to send Chuck Mansfield into the Hicksville game on that sweltering day. Taking a knee (in its original and apolitical sense) in the background are Bill McGovern (left) and Tom Kiley.

(Photograph courtesy of Chuck Mansfield and used with permission.)

As Mike Reisert has recounted, "Coach Thomas would tell us when we went out for pregame warm-ups not to look at the other team. Of course we did; half of them had beards while most of us had fuzz at best." When Hicksville's players entered the field for their pregame warm-ups, more than a few Flyer teammates were struck by their opponents' size. Indeed, I recall thinking, *This is going to be tough.* After all, with the exceptions of Joe Mauro, Barry O'Connor and Mike, Chaminade's varsity players were relatively small and light. Still, at the end of the first half we Flyers were ahead, 14-7. In the second half, Hicksville's players, despite their superior size and strength, proved not to be as physically well-conditioned as we and couldn't handle the oppressive heat. Chaminade scored another 14 points in the second half and won the game 28-7. Mike has concluded that "Once the game started we knew we could win and we did. Put your head on their numbers and drive. We could and did drive them off."

Thanks to *Newsday*'s Andy Slawson, who keeps Long Island high-school sports records dating back to 1914, I was able to confirm that the Comets' bow to Chaminade was their first of just two losses in a 6-2 season in which they went on to become their league's 1961 champions!

Flyer football marked great character at Chaminade.

— Skip Rottkamp

A CHSFL SUPER BOWL:
1961 VERSUS 1962 FLYERS

By Chuck Mansfield

The meshing of two classes went pretty seamlessly because all players were basically the same guy, having been shaped by the same training and development process during the freshman and JV seasons.

— Al Groh

In my leisure moments I wonder occasionally about both our extraordinary Chaminade 1961 varsity football team and its outstanding successor. At this point in the narrative I believe there is no need to emphasize the nature and character of the teams or their coaches.

Still, in a hypothetical sense, I have recently thought about a potential "bowl" between Chaminade's 1961 and '62 championship varsity football teams. Some may regard such a thought as frivolous, inappropriate, odious or silly but it may still delight the imagination of others.

Here, with help from my co-author Tom Kiley, is my analysis, which is followed by comments from 1962 Flyer co-captains Pete Eisenhauer and John Zimmermann.

Thank you, Tom, Ike and Zimmy.

My first thought was about our great 15-year-old junior quarterback, John Zimmermann, who led the '61 Flyer varsity squad to its unprecedented perfect season and got the '62 team off to an undefeated two-game start before sustaining injury. Zimmy was the direct successor of the great Skippy Orr and Skippy's presumed successor, Danny Connors, who left Chaminade after his junior year. Undaunted, Tommy Liesegang stepped in as quarterback and led the Flyers to a 4-1 record and the League title, which was clinched before the final game, in which Zimmy returned, victorious. Net-net, the quarterback slot is a neutral between the two teams in my view, as well as a major strength of both squads, which were led by two QBs from the Chaminade class of 1963. Zimmy logged a 3-0 record on the season (11-0 for both seasons) and received the Terzi Award.

Bruce Salerno was the team's outstanding junior center in '61 and the following year when he was designated High School All American and received additional significant recognition. *(Authors' note: Please see "Congratulations to Bruce Salerno!" later herein.)*

Now, I believe the '61 team's offensive line, Bruce aside, may arguably have the edge over our junior teammates. The '62 backfield, despite the tremendous rushing performance of Earl Kirmser the preceding year, may actually have been more talented than '61's. The running back position on the '62 squad was deep and excellent in the persons of Bobby Bowman, Tom Higgins, Bill Keahon and Skip Rottkamp. They were joined by talented juniors, notably Bob Gately, Pete Groh (Al's brother), Billy Marvin (Art's brother) and Tom McKeon. The '62 team had a plethora of big, fast and skilled running and defensive backs and receivers, none of whom the '61 unit had. Indeed, some of them had breakaway speed. In Ken Darby and Bruce they had two offensive linemen who were top shelf, and Pete Eisenhauer was an outstanding end. They carried the '62 squad after Zimmy's injury. The team probably only needed Tommy L. to be competent, which, of course, he exceeded. In a way, he played the role in '62 that Zimmy played in '61. Indeed, these players proved major factors in winning the title again, especially in light of the injured Zimmy.

There's no denying that our running game in '61 sometimes had problems. As we all recall only too well, we could not move the ball all day against St. Francis because they shut Earl down. We had difficulty against Stepinac, as George Valva and Zimmy have duly noted herein. Thanks to Tom Kiley blocking a punt and giving us a short field to score the winning touchdown, we broke open that game, winning it 14-6. We managed to put up only twelve points against Hayes, who scored eight, our smallest margin of victory. And, alas, we were shut out in the first half by Holy Cross but came back to shut them out 16-0.

On a brighter note, we certainly overwhelmed some teams, with Hicksville perhaps being the best example, whom we defeated 28-7. We also beat St. John by 21 points and both Iona and the Mount by 28. Thus, what I'll call our 'overwhelming margin' (OM) was 98 points for the four games. The '62 squad did some substantial overwhelming as well, shutting out Hicksville 26-0, St. John 48-0 and Holy Cross 32-0 for a whopping OM of 106 points for just three games, all shutouts. Accordingly, the '61 team's OM was 24.5 points per game while '62's tallied 35.3, a full 44% higher. Do these numbers mean that the '62 offensive team was more explosive? Very likely.

With respect to defense my initial inclination would be to give the nod to the '61 unit primarily because of the fierce performances of our star linebacker Tom Kiley. Had our defense faltered even a little, we would have been sunk. Still, the fact that the '62 defense produced four shutouts compared to three for the '61 team may arguably give that squad an edge. Moreover, the '62 defense allowed only one more point than '61's (34 vs. 33), a highly impressive showing.

Pictured above are Coach Thomas (left), his wife Kay and co-author Tom Kiley at the celebration of Coach's eighth and last CHSFL championship in 1968.

(Photograph courtesy of Tom Kiley and used with permission.)

Both Flyer teams played the same opponents in the same order both seasons. Here are their comparative records:

Opponent	1961			1962	
Hicksville	Won	28-7	W	26-0
Stepinac	W	14-6	W	12-6
St. Francis	W	6-0	Lost	0-14
St. John	W	27-6	W	48-0
Iona	W	28-0	W	8-6
Mount	W	34-6	W	12-8
Hayes	W	12-8	W	6-0
Holy Cross	W	16-0	W	32-0

Both squads clinched the CHSFL championship with their Hayes victories.

Below are additional comparisons that focus mainly on offensive categories:

	1961	1962
Total points scored	165	136
Average points per game	20.6	17
Opponents' points scored	33	34
Average points allowed per game	4.1	4.3
Ratio of Flyer points scored to opponents'	5:1	4:1
Total rushing yardage	1,925	1,563
Rushing yardage per game	>240	>195
Total passing yardage	500	598
Total yardage	2,425	2,161

Touchdowns scored	21	19
PATs	21	12
First downs	102	85
First downs per game	12.8	10.6
Minutes per first down (assuming 30-min. time of possession)	2.35	2.82
Largest margins of victory	28, 28, 21, 21, 16	48, 32, 26, 6
Smallest margins of victory	4, 6	2, 4

Our top scorers in '61 were Earl Kirmser (66 points), Bill McGovern (18), George Ackerson (12) and Dave Tuohy (12). Their '62 counterparts were Tom Higgins (41), Skip Rottkamp (22), Tommy Liesegang (14) and Zimmy (9). Earl's 66 gave the edge to '61, 108 points to 86.

Thanks to Larry Grassini I have the eighth and ninth annual banquet programs of "The Catholic High Schools' Football League of Metropolitan New York" in which are found listings for "The All-League Team" and "The Players of the Week." I have listed only those players from Chaminade's 1961 and 1962 varsity squads.

1961 All-League Team	*1961 Players of the Week*	
	Linemen	*Backs*
Bill DeMeo, End	None	Earl Kirmser
Tom Kiley, Linebacker		Dave Tuohy
Mike Reisert, Tackle		
Bill Sellerberg, Guard		
Earl Kirmser, Fullback		

1962 All-League First Team Offensive

Ken Darby, Tackle
Bruce Salerno, Center

1962 All-League First Team Defensive

Phil Pignataro, Guard*
Cyril Rottkamp, Quarterback*

1962 All-League Second Team Offensive

Bob Swanson, End

1962 All-League Second Team Defensive

Pete Eisenhauer, Tackle*

1962 Players of the Week

Linemen

None

Backs

John Zimmermann
Tom Liesegang
Tom Higgins

By way of analysis, it is hardly surprising that Earl Kirmser was both All-League and a Player of the Week. What is perhaps surprising is that not once were Messrs. DeMeo, Reisert and Sellerberg, the entire left side of the '61 Flyer offensive line, as well as Tom Kiley, who had several explosive defensive performances, designated Player of the Week. The '62 Flyer team was well represented with four players making All-League First Team: Messrs. Darby and Salerno on offense, and Messrs. Pignataro and Rottkamp on defense. Bob Swanson and Pete Eisenhauer made All-League Second Team on offense and defense, respectively. Like its '61 predecessor, the '62 squad surprisingly had no linemen named Player of the Week.

In the last analysis, the 1961 Flyer varsity team had six players named to these designations, whereas the '62 unit surpassed their former teammates with nine players being so acclaimed, five linemen and four backs. Thus, the nod goes to '62.

* These positions are from the 1962 League dinner program listing. Our records show that Phil Pignataro was a linebacker, Skip Rottkamp a halfback and a defensive back, and Pete Eisenhauer an end.

In conclusion, a playoff between these two teams would surely be a CHSFL super bowl. As to the outcome, Tom Kiley has written, "In sum, I think '61 would win. Our offensive line was bigger and more seasoned, several of our seniors having had considerable experience on the '60 squad. And our seven-man front-run defense was nearly impregnable. Would Tommy L. have been able to exploit us through the air? Who knows? Perhaps a healthy Zim under center might have made a big difference."

As for me, I too would take the '61 squad because I believe it had the advantage on both sides of the ball. Still, such a clash may well and ever be too close to call.

Perhaps George Valva's closing sentence earlier herein about our last-minute St. Francis victory provides the most accurate and integral assessment: "It was then that I knew that the Men of '62 and the Men of '63 could and would combine to go down as the greatest football team in Chaminade history!"

*The teamwork and camaraderie between
juniors and seniors were inspiring.*

— Bill McGovern

I had sent Ike and Zimmy advance copies of this analysis because I considered it prudent to have it reviewed by men who played on both teams. For my part, I thought, who better than these '62 co-captains? Their replies follow.

From Ike: "Here are my thoughts on the '61 and '62 teams. You, Tom and Zimmy did a thorough job of dissecting the stats and personnel to come to a reasonable conclusion. I tried to look at it beyond the numbers and individuals and focus on what made each team champions. We have a sign in the weight room here at the Loon Mountain Health Club (which I now ONLY use during the six weeks before each ski season; it's like Double Sessions for geezers!): 'Hard Work and Perseverance Beats Talent!' That was the life-lesson that I took away from our playing days under Joe Thomas and, as a player with limited ability and size, it has helped me survive and succeed in sports and life.

"The analysis that you and Tom did is very detailed and even-handed and I agree with your conclusion that '61 would have the edge over '62 in a head-to-head matchup. So, what did make each team a champion? In that era, '61 was the most talented team that Chaminade ever fielded. This fact, coupled with our incredible training and coaching, enabled us to go into each game knowing that we were the best team on the field. Don't forget, the '61 team was even featured in that *Look* magazine photo of our halftime at Holy Cross!

"In '62, although we had two outstanding players in Bruce and Zimmy, the balance of our team had good overall talent and depth but not exceptional. In addition, the loss of Zimmy as our star QB and my fellow co-captain created a significant challenge for us to repeat as champs. It's noteworthy that our only loss (to St. Francis) came immediately after Zimmy's injury. Lacking the super-star factor we enjoyed in '61, the '62 team had to rely on a group of hard-working guys that 'drank the Kool-Aid' that Coach Thomas fed us about conditioning and perseverance. One of his classic lines to us during the brutal conditioning drills the week following the St. Francis loss was, "You guys are so out of shape, you should report to the sock hop!" As a result, we went into each game through the remainder of that season knowing that we were in better shape than anyone else on the field and that we could win with the talent we had, whether it was starters or subs. Two different teams with two different personalities but both champions!'"

From Zimmy: "Can't disagree with any of it. I will say, in my opinion, the '62 team would have a harder time running the ball against the '61 defensive front. Because the '61 team had a bigger, more experienced line, including All American Tiny Reisert, and a bruiser at FB in Earl, another All American, the running game would appear to favor the '61 team. The comparison of Zimm (sorry about the third person) in '61 vs. Tom L. in '62 is probably about right. If Zimm was healthy, as he was for three games (including the season finale), the '62 team would have had a more diversified attack – with more offensive weapons. Zimm was a much better QB in '62 than '61 due to experience and maturity. That said, both teams faced excellent passing attacks and gave up very few points. I think we'd agree it would be a low-scoring game. Great comparison – lots of 'what if' fun, Chuck. Thanks for your efforts."

Authors' note: Of the 46 players on the 1961 Flyer squad, 23 were members of the class of '62, 21 were from '63 and two, the Swanson brothers, were from '64.

And they shall fight every one against his brother.

— Ecclesiastes 19:2

SHOES MAKE THE MAN

By Tom Kiley

Some say shoes make the man. If so then I owe
a lot to my no-name black high tops.

— Tom Kiley

This is the story of a pair of football shoes that were part of my football life for so long that it now seems a little absurd for me to realize that to this day I never have known what brand they were or where they were purchased, though they were with me every day of my high-school football career.

They were worn every day we practiced and every day we played from 1958 to 1961, rain or shine, summer and fall, during pre-season and in-season, in the dust and mud of the back field and on the green fields of game-day stadiums. And they never let me down, not once in all that time. They were no-name high cuts and were black as the ace of spades, as befitted the down and dirty interior lineman I started out as and, to some extent, always remained. In retrospect, when their usefulness finally came to an end, I should have had them bronzed like my mother did my baby shoes. As it turned out, I was a much better football player than ever I was a baby.

When, after much consideration of other schools, I finally decided to attend Chaminade, I had not the slightest intention of playing football for the Crimson and Gold. Sixty years and more later, I still cannot remember how or why I decided to try out for the freshman football team. There was certainly no parental involvement, of that I am sure. My only prior experience was playing touch football in the streets of Elmont where the greatest danger was that a player might run over a fire hydrant or into a telephone pole. Now that wasn't good for any growing boy.

I do remember running around in gym shorts and tee shirts and sneakers the first few days of tryouts, a scenario not calculated to show me off to best advantage. But it was my sneakers that were about to become a big issue.

After a few days of no-contact tryouts, a couple of players who seemed to know each other, burst into the locker room and declared. "We made first team." In my naïveté that seemed entirely plausible. Then a rumor circulated that Chaminade kept seventy or eighty players on the freshman squad and I convinced myself that I would be quite happy to be Chaminade's seventh string guard, if only I could make the team. What did I know? When school started in earnest, practices were held afterwards and, for the first time, in newly issued helmets and shoulder pads. I had no idea how to put my pads on properly and put them on backwards at first. It also took me quite a while to learn how to operate the cinch buckle on my pants. Finally, I went out onto the back field for the first of hundreds of times in full pads and SNEAKERS!

On a day that I thought was crucial to my chances to make the team, it rained hard and the ground was muddy as hell. We blocked and tackled for the first time, but I could get no traction. I had to be shown several times how to assume a proper three-point stance and how to "pull." I thought this might be my last chance but, like the old Little Richard song, I was "slippin' and a slidin'" all over the place. But, at least I was able to crash into people, albeit without much finesse. Gradually, I began to feel better about myself. After several days of contact drills, the coach came up to me and said, "Kiley, you can't play any more without cleats. You have until Saturday to get a pair."

Now I was faced with a new crisis. It was Wednesday and I was convinced that the coach meant I would be cut unless I wore proper cleats by the following Saturday. That night I mentioned my predicament to my parents who said little. I said less. I knew that money was often an issue in my house and I rarely asked for anything therefore. Practice went well enough the next couple of days but as the week came to an end, my anxiety began to increase. I was sure I was about to be cut on Saturday morning.

On Saturday I got dressed, ran out to the back field and hid in the middle of the calisthenics formation, praying that the coach would not notice my sneakers. As cals were ending, I looked for somewhere to hide, certain the end was near. Then I heard a familiar voice call out, "Tom." I looked over my shoulder and saw my father hurling a pair of football shoes, tied together by their laces, grenade-like, like the old infantryman he once was, over the fence on the west side of the field. "Go good out there," he yelled. Then he and my brother Jimmy drove off. Dad had come through once again when I needed him most, as he always did. As the linemen were dispatched to the boards, I hung back a little and quickly put on my brand new football shoes, my splendid black beauties.

And there you have it. I felt like a real football player for the first time. Shortly thereafter the coach, reading from a list, shouted, "First team right guard, Kiley." I could hardly believe it. At that moment who could have foreseen that those football shoes would be with me for such a long time. Ultimately, their record at Chaminade was 30-6-3, not bad for a fifteen dollar pair of cleats. Well, what can I say further. Life is beautiful when it wants to be.

Tom Kiley
Freshman guard 1958

Tom Kiley receives the Most Outstanding Player award from
his father at Chaminade's 1961 Football Awards Night, as
teammates (left to right) Bob Swanson, Skip Sullivan, Bill
Sellerberg, Bruce Salerno and George Ackerson look on.

*You can learn more character on the two-
yard line than anywhere else in life.*

— Paul Dietzel
LSU

THE NIGHT I MET "THE BOILER"

By Chuck Mansfield

Although I didn't know it at the time, I was enjoying what is now called multigenerational bonding.

— Marlo Thomas

In 1962 the late Jack Lenz of the Chaminade class of 1943, class president and a Marine Corps Iwo Jima veteran, and his buddy, the late Lou Caracci '45, met with then-Chaminade principal Bro. Al Kozar, S.M. to discuss the revitalization of the Chaminade Alumni Association, which had begun briefly in *alma mater*'s early years but had since become non-existent. There was no data base, not even alumni addresses. Today, Chaminade has detailed contact information on virtually all of its approximately 22,000 graduates, which has enabled the school to build a substantial endowment via the Torch Fund, a program of annual giving designed to defray tuition for all of Chaminade's 1,700 students.

Today's Alumni Association has grown substantially in its reach and responsibilities. Indeed, it boasts a slate of officers elected every two years and a board of directors consisting of more than 40 alumni, each of whom serves on one or more committees that sponsor and organize the many alumni activities and events that take place each year.

In the early 1970s Chaminade held what is believed to have been its first Alumni Smoker. Hosted in the Chaminade cafeteria, the event was well attended by scores of graduates, many of whom were former Flyer football players. For me this was likely my first alumni event since my class's ten-year reunion in 1972. Also in attendance were former Chaminade head varsity football coaches, Frank "Boiler" Burns and Ed Flynn, as well as my teammate Bill

Sellerberg. As I remember, Bill and I were the only members of our '61 team present that evening and had played Flyer JV football for Coach Flynn.

Boiler Burns. Of course it does!

— Tom Kiley

"The Boiler," as Mr. Burns was affectionately called, was a legend in his own time. My late friend Jerry McDougal of the Chaminade class of 1945, who played for Boiler Burns, once regaled a group of mostly younger alumni with tales of The Boiler. It was that moniker that his players unfailingly used when referring to him, never "Coach Burns" or "Mr. Burns," as was the unswervingly respectful protocol in the Thomas-McGuckin era. When I recall Jerry's Boiler stories, irascibility and a certain craziness invariably come to mind.

At the smoker that evening The Boiler and Coach Flynn invited Bill and me, two '61 guards, to join them for drinks. Both coaches tippled bourbon unreservedly while we younger drinkers stuck to beer. The Boiler was remarkably entertaining, as was Coach Flynn, and our foursome enjoyed two hours of storytelling and laughter. Two generations came together totally harmoniously with Flyer football the bonding agent. Moreover, this chance meeting made clear that the culture and camaraderie that characterized the teams of Chaminade's golden era of football had their roots much earlier than the 1950s and '60s.

After Coach Flynn retired from Chaminade in 1962 I never saw him again until after his passing in the early nineties. Coach Joe Thomas had telephoned and asked me if I would drive him to Mr. Flynn's wake, and of course I agreed. In the funeral home, surrounded by family and friends, former colleagues and players, the great man who was an architect of Flyer football's golden era, Edward J. Flynn, appeared diminished yet serene in his eternal repose, his distinguished and victorious flame alas and at last extinguished. Happily, he will always be warmly remembered with respect and admiration by all those young men who benefited from his coaching, teaching and basic human goodness. Godspeed, Ed Flynn.

I didn't think much about it then but, now, nearly half a century later, I marvel at the opportunity that Bill and I had. Indeed, it was a privilege and a pleasure to share time and good cheer with these two men. The Boiler coached Flyer varsity football in the 1930s and '40s, and Coach Flynn served as Flyer varsity head coach in 1946 and '47, the year before he recruited and hired Coach Thomas to succeed him. In the Burns-Flynn era the Flyer eleven compiled a won-lost-tied record of 68-71-13. From 1948 through the 1969 football season Coach Thomas's record was 120-46-7. The Boiler coached Chaminade football from its beginning and Ed Flynn subsequently helped build it into the powerhouse it would become with the advent of Joe Thomas and Charlie McGuckin.

On that long-ago evening at Chaminade my teammate and I were in our late twenties at the time of our meeting with these two legendary and aging coaches. Indeed, they may have been wizened enough to be our grandfathers. While at the time we may not have sufficiently appreciated it, we two erstwhile Chaminade football guards had spent a memorable and mirthful evening in the presence of Flyer football's founders without whom Chaminade's golden age on the gridiron would never have come to pass.

Teams that exhibit good chemistry spend a lot of time together, getting to know each other's personalities, and becoming more in-tune with each other's perspectives and ways of thinking.

— Shea Walker

MANAGERS

By George E. Meng

I decided it might be nice to be a manager but I couldn't seem to get any coach to give me a chance.

— George Meng

As a Chaminade junior, George was one of our team's four managers. His story about the strong linkage between his athletic managerial experience and his career success as a litigator is impressive. He submitted the following essay on August 1, 2011, prior to our team's 50-year reunion.

Thank you, George.

When I was ten, my hip came out of joint – kind of similar to little leaguer's elbow. I underwent a rare surgery with what was known as a Smith Petersen nail put in. There was about four weeks in the hospital, then a wheelchair, followed by crutches, a brace and finally a cane and then normalcy after a year. Except, nobody was going to let me do anything strenuous. Interestingly, my orthopedist friends are amazed it's been in there 65 years with no trouble.

Anyway, there was no playing team sports for me. I decided it might be nice to be a manager but I couldn't seem to get any coach to give me a chance. So, in my sophomore year, I started hanging around the basketball team at the end of the season just volunteering help. Somebody got the message and offered me the manager job for varsity baseball that spring. That led to football manager for this team. And again the next year and two more years of baseball. Ended up with five letters for manager.

Here's what being a manager leads to. I graduated with an engineering degree and started working for Westinghouse where I found out about a program where they put engineers as engineering support on aircraft carriers. I signed up. But then they found out about the hip and didn't want to let me anywhere near a ship. Finally, I convinced them and they let me do a cruise on the USS *Independence*. I was an expert on the missile control system for the F4-J *Phantom* [fighter jet]. (This equipment designated as AWG-10 has since been declassified and is on display at the Steven F. Udvar-Hazy Center in Virginia.) That's when I became clear about my desire to get to be on the front lines and not in a supportive role. Unfortunately, there wasn't any way I'd ever be a pilot. That first cruise led to a promotion and my being in charge of the Westinghouse engineer contingent for a cruise on the USS *Enterprise* to Viet Nam. (It was on that cruise while we were on readiness exercise off Hawaii in January 1969 that a devastating fire occurred. This picture, the loss of life and injuries are forever etched on my brain.) My work getting the ship ready for that cruise led to another promotion and, after the cruise, another support role at headquarters. But that job gave me the chance to explore other options and a decision to attend law school.

Upon graduation, I ended up in another support role as a clerk to a judge. But, finally in 1973, I got to the front lines doing a wide range of litigation. That continues to this day and unlike a lot of lawyers, I love it and hope to be able to continue until I die.

I'm convinced that my experiences as a manager supporting the various Chaminade teams led directly to my success in life. And for that, I pass along to each of you my thanks.

A winning combination of talent and grit defined us.

— Chuck Mansfield

THE PERFECT SEASON

By Anthony Mercogliano

The secret of the success of the school athletically is mainly attributable to the excelling spirit of the school on the whole this year.

— George P. McCabe, Jr.

Born in Rockville Centre, N.Y., Tony graduated from Chaminade in 1964. He went on to Manhattan College, Riverdale, N.Y., where he earned a Bachelor of Arts in Psychology in 1968. He attended OCS earning a commission as a U.S. Navy Supply Corps officer serving until his retirement in 1989 and went on to Widener University, Chester, Pa., where he earned an MBA in Finance in 1994. After a successful career in finance and management consulting, he and his wife Kay retired in Dumfries, Va. He continued his involvement with the Marianists and the Family of Mary through his associated membership in the Christian Life Community of Long Island (formally known as the Sodality of Our Lady of the Pillar), and volunteer work at Marianist Center, Folsom, Pa., and the Marianist Christian Family Retreat Center in Cape May Point, N.J.

Thank you, Tony.

SOME BACKGROUND

For most of the contributors to this book Chaminade High School's 1961 varsity football season was the culmination of a journey; it was a beginning for me. I was entering my sophomore year just beginning to understand what it meant to be a "Chaminade Man" – the term used by the Marianists to show the importance of intellectual, spiritual, and social development during the formative years of high school. *(Authors' note: Please see "Criteria for the Chaminade Man Award" later herein.)* I was a true social "wallflower" during my first year at Chaminade, somewhat overwhelmed by the size and pace of a 1300+ student high school coming as I did from a Catholic grammar school with about 300 students (about 40 to a class). Multiple subjects and teachers, having seven minutes to change classrooms every 40 minutes at the sound of a bell was a challenge I never faced before, but gradually I mastered the routine. I was able to keep my grades up and made second honors, not quite as good as my grammar school days but acceptable to my conservative Italian-American working-class parents who would forego several summer vacations to afford the pricey $375 annual tuition. For my parents extracurricular activities were not an option – with the exception of Sodality, because it dealt with religion and only involved a one-hour commitment from 3:15 p.m. to 4:15 p.m. on Mondays – until I proved I could handle the academic workload. The one thing I could do was attend the football games. We lived about a mile from the school and when the wind was blowing toward the east, you could hear the crowd cheering the Flyers on at every Sunday home game. The football season was the high point of my freshman year.

SOPHOMORE YEAR

Sophomore year started off with more challenges. Due to a higher than normal attrition rate of the freshman class, the homerooms were "rebalanced" and I was now a 2E Continental rather that a 2F Untouchable. Unfortunately, 2E was on the second floor while 2F was on the first floor, so most of my friends were out of daily sight. But there was good news. My new homeroom teacher was Brother Carmine Annunziata, S.M., newly assigned to Chaminade from a Marianist School in Cleveland, Oh. He was also the Sophomore Guidance Counselor and the Assistant Athletic Moderator (more to come on these points later). *(Authors' note: Tony has written that "With the help of Bro. Carmine as my fact checker and content editor I put together my remembrances of Chaminade's 1961 season. While it comes from a slightly different perspective than most of the others involved in that great event, I believe it will help in your telling of the story about the Perfect Season.")*

Bro. Carmine had (and I'm sure still has) a unique ability of identifying and relating to people searching for a goal in life. That was me. At our Guidance Counseling session during the second week of the school year, he asked me about my family and how I was enjoying Chaminade. He also asked about what activities I was involved with. After I finished giving him a summary of my freshman year, he asked me if I could help him out in the Athletic Department. One of the JV football managers had chosen the marching band over his duties as a manager. He said it would be just for a few days and after checking with my parents I said "Yes." I was to meet him at "the cage" right after my classes the following Monday.

BEING A TEAM MANAGER

My first day consisted of helping with many of the routine tasks necessary to field a high school football team – handing out uniforms and towels, washing uniforms and towels, etc. But I loved it. I was part of something which was important to the school. Being able to interact with the stars of the team, both JV and varsity (even if it was indirectly), like Tiny Reisert and Earl Kirmser, was fantastic. Connecting with JV team members from my new homeroom was also great. At the end of the week Bro. Carmine asked what I thought of the experience and would I like to continue on a full-time basis as one of the JV football team managers. I was "over the moon." After some negotiations with my parents and a promise that my grades would not be affected, I began the journey.

Truth be told, the vast majority of my daily responsibilities dealt with the JV team (who by the way had a 9-0 perfect season that year). However, it was "all hands on deck" to prepare for varsity Sunday home games at the Chaminade Bowl. The work began on Saturday after the JV game when the field had to be lined. Then there was the task of wrapping crimson and gold crepe paper around the goal posts. Sunday morning began the final process before the game's 1:00 p.m. start time. During the game the JV managers were on the field doing various important jobs like scraping the dirt from the cleats of the offensive starting team while they knelt along the sidelines cheering on their defensive counterparts as the crowd roared "Push 'em back, push 'em back harder, harder" and carrying out the water dispenser during time outs. Some might consider these menial tasks, but I loved it; I was part of the team. Although we didn't travel with the team for road games, if we rode the student buses, Bro. Carmine was able to get us field passes so we could be on the sidelines to help during the game.

THE COACH

About half way into the season, Bro. Carmine asked me to deliver a group of folders to varsity coach Joe Thomas's office. Up until then my only one-on-one interaction with Mr. Thomas was in gym class as he "encouraged" me to try harder to meet the minimums of the recently introduced Presidential Fitness program better known as the JFK's (gym was not a favorite class for me). I knocked on his door and politely stated why I was there and laid the folders on his desk. As I was leaving, he stopped me and asked me to sit down. He asked me how I liked working as a manager and spent at least ten minutes explaining how important each job on the football team was to the team's overall success. I was really impressed that Coach Thomas would take his valuable time to get to know a JV team manager, but that was Joe Thomas, always a teacher and an educator first. As I got to know him better, I was impressed with the respect and dignity with which he treated all people. I could see how he was able to motivate all involved with the football team to give that 110% effort in their work.

THE GAMES

I don't believe anyone had the expectation of a perfect football season – our goal was to repeat as CHSFL champions. As the season progressed, the victories mounted. The three games I remember most were the 6-0 victory over St. Francis Prep, the 12-8 victory over Cardinal Hayes and, of course, the 16-0 victory over Holy Cross.

THE ST. FRANCIS TERRIERS. We had defeated St. Francis, a perennial rival, in a close game the previous year, ending their chances to be League champs, so they were "out for blood." The game was scoreless until the final set of downs in the fourth quarter and then finally junior quarterback John Zimmermann did it on two passes to junior receiver Bob Bowman for a 6-0 victory. The crowd went berserk!!

THE CARDINAL HAYES CARDINALS. The game with Cardinal Hayes was also a nail-biter. This was the game we needed to clinch the championship. We took an early lead into the first quarter as fullback Earl Kirmser ran the ball into the Hayes end zone, the final play after a long drive. Then Hayes scored a safety, making the score 6-2 going into halftime. We came back with another TD in the third quarter giving us a ten-point lead, but that was cut to four points when they scored another TD early in the fourth quarter after recovering a fumble. The game ended when our own Tom Kiley intercepted a desperation Hayes pass and almost ran it into the end zone for a score. A 12-8 victory and the 1961 CHSFL championship.

THE HOLY CROSS KNIGHTS. Now the talk began. Could Chaminade have its first Perfect Season – unbeaten and untied – in the school's 30+ year history? The first half was scoreless, but we finally broke through late in the third quarter when junior fullback Tom Higgins ran in for a score. We iced the victory in the fourth quarter on a long run by senior halfback Frank Biasi. A 16-0 victory. "The Perfect Season" was complete!!

SUMMING IT UP

Well there you have it – my recollections of the Perfect Season. A culmination for many but a beginning for me. After the season ended, both Bro. Carmine and Coach Thomas (also the JV basketball coach) asked if I'd be interested in being a manager for the team.

It seems that one of the managers had gotten into a little academic trouble and had to spend more time with second year Latin, first year Spanish and Geometry. After checking with my parents, I jumped at the chance. Actually, my grades improved significantly in the first half of my sophomore year (now a First Honors student) so this point was no longer an issue. I was joined by a fellow classmate, John Kiernan, as team manager and we continued managing both football and basketball for our two remaining high school years. In fact, John liked the job so much that he also was the baseball team manager for those years. I was also motivated to pursue an interest in journalism and became a regular contributor to the *TARMAC* sports page, reporting the results of varsity football and basketball games.

The Chaminade JV basketball team also had a championship season, winning the first city-wide CHSAA basketball title in the school's history. This added to the CHSAA Cross Country championship, and our football accomplishments led to the 1962 yearbook being titled "The Year of Champions." I went on to Manhattan College where I (what else?) managed the basketball team. During my four years there, we made two NIT appearances and played in several high-profile East Coast Christmas tournaments. By the way, I also continued my involvement in Marianist Sodality (now known as the Family of Mary) as an associate member in the Christian Life Community of Long Island and have kept in touch with Bro. Carmine for over 50 years as he continues to spread the gospel through education of young men in Zambia and Kenya.

Clearly the bonds that we began to forge nearly sixty years ago bind us tightly still. Certainly they have proved far more enduring than we could have imagined back in 1958.

— Tom Kiley

THE YEAR OF CHAMPIONS (1961-62)

By Edward J. Christie, Jr.

The history of your senior year has been recorded in these pages as "The Year of Champions." A fitting tribute, for as a class you have made excellent use of the opportunities offered to you – opportunities for physical, intellectual, social and spiritual growth. You have created history. You have achieved the exceptional. You have become Champions.

> — Albert J. Kozar, S.M.,
> Chaminade Principal,
> in the 1962 *Crimson and Gold* yearbook

At Chaminade Ed was a leader, a top student and an athlete, who excelled in basketball (co-captain) and baseball. Later he attended Stonehill College on a partial basketball scholarship and graduated with a degree in accounting. There he was elected to the Student Senate all four years and president of the student body as a senior; he also co-captained the basketball team.

After graduating, Ed became a CPA and worked primarily for non-profit organizations holding executive positions with United Way of America, USO World Headquarters and American Red Cross of Baltimore. Using principles learned at Chaminade and Stonehill, he also volunteered with the Knights of Columbus (elected Grand Knight and Knight of the Year for Council #12107). He was also a member of the Alliance Defending Freedom (ADF) board of directors, treasurer for six years and chairman of its foundation for three.

Ed and Mary Alice have been married for 53 years. Currently retired in Lakewood Ranch, Fl., they have three daughters, seven grandsons and one granddaughter.

We are grateful to him for the following outstanding contribution to this work. While he writes about other sports in addition to football, he concludes his fine essay "with a special yell out to the football team and their perfect season."

Many thanks, Ed.

Chaminade High School's "The Year of Champions" has many components to highlight. While this book focuses on the UNDEFEATED and UNTIED 1961 varsity football season, my perspective of the incredible year comes from several different areas. I hope you do not mind me going through several wonderful memories I had as a senior during the years 1961 and 1962 at Chaminade.

FOOTBALL

I was **not** a member of the varsity football team and their perfect season. Members of that team like Chuck Mansfield, John (Tiny) Reisert, Earl Kirmser, Tom Kiley, Al Groh, Frank Biasi, Bill Sellerberg, George Ackerson and many others were all too big, too strong, too skilled and too fast for me to compete with them. In a word I was a **chicken**!

I was part of the Year of Champions and Perfect Season, however, as a participant in the Intramural Football Season. My homeroom, the 4A Skyhawks, were the Intramural Football Champions for 1961, and **undefeated** for the fourth year in a row!!! Playing against our archrival homeroom 4D and one of my best friends Bob Kisch (a Marine officer who died in Vietnam) are memories that I reflect on often. (Sorry, Tom Kiley, I know you wanted 4D to win!)

The 1961 Flyers' all-male cheerleaders.

Since I was not a member of the varsity football team, I was not on the official field but I was close, as a member of the Flyers' cheerleading squad, who attempted to lead the Flyer fans in the stands to cheer as loud as they could for the football team. The squad was fun, close to each other and was 100% behind the team. All our members wore their straw hats, letter sweaters and smiling faces which was a sight to behold! It was a weekly thrill for me to be a part of that squad. Also, watching Vinny Testa and Tony Alfano put on a show at every game was epic. Performing the Chaminade cheer (the train) was entertaining to all, but I am not sure we ever got it correct! *F-L, F-L, F-L-Y-E, Y-E, Y-E, Y-E-R-S, F-L-Y-E, Y-E-R-S, F-L-Y-E, Y-E-R-S, FLYERS, FLYERS, YEA!*

From my perspective from the sidelines, the game I most remember from that championship year was the game with St. Francis. It was a home game early in the season. The Flyers won 6-0 with that game being the closest and most intense of the year. Both teams played their hearts out, with the Flyers scoring late in the game. After the game I witnessed the St. Francis team members going into their locker room. Many of the players seemed to have tears in their eyes! They gave it their all, but so did the Flyers! The Flyers' team really showed what they were made of during that game and set the winning tone for the rest of the season.

BASKETBALL

I did have the privilege to play basketball for Chaminade all four years; varsity level my junior and senior years. As a senior, I did share the co-captain designation with Fred Capshaw (God rest his soul). During the 1961-1962 season we did not go undefeated nor did we make the playoffs. Our record was seven wins and nine defeats. Our season started with a new coach and losses in the first four games. Our team was close, however, and we worked hard at practice to improve and never did get down on ourselves. Over time we did improve with each game. What I remember most about that season was the school supporting us at our last home game with our archrival, Archbishop Molloy. We won that game on our home court, and for that one game, we felt that we did belong to the Year of the Champions!!!

As a side note, during our junior year, Fred Capshaw, Bob Peterson (God rest his soul) and I were members of the 1960-1961 varsity team (we did not play very much). That team was led by Skip Orr and other very talented seniors. The team was just terrific to watch and went deep into the playoffs. I learned so much from those seniors that season playing against them at practice and seeing them perform during the games. It was so special for me to witness them as a team.

I remember one special playoff game at Fordham University my junior year. At half time, the team went into the locker room for a session with Coach Flynn. As soon as the team arrived in the locker room, Coach Flynn pointed to Fred, Bob and me and sent us out on the court to shoot around. It was very humbling for us for the rest of the team was in the locker room and we felt we were not part of the team that day. The Coach said, "You Rinky Dinks go and get some shooting practice in." After the last game of the season the three of us had a surprise, however. We were in the locker room cleaning out our lockers when Coach Flynn came to us and gave all three of us a varsity letter! We did not actually deserve that varsity letter, due to lack of playing time. Needless to say, today I do not focus on the

Rinky Dink comment but remember the varsity letter that I received from the coach. That season was Mr. Flynn's last as head varsity basketball coach.

BASEBALL

I also had the opportunity to play varsity baseball my junior and senior years. We had a great team in our senior year – led by very talented pitchers such as Phil Marzullo, Al Groh, as well as other skilled players such as Earl Kirmser, Carl LoGalbo, Tom Kiley and many others. The team went deep into the playoffs and would have gone further if I did a better job at bat in one of the playoff games. The game was in the seventh inning and we were tied. The first batter of that inning, Johnny Zimmermann, reached third base on a double and a ground out to the right side of the infield. While I was in the batter's box with one out, Coach McGuckin came to me and said he would put on the suicide squeeze bunt signal on the second pitch. As the second pitch was developing, Coach McGuckin gave his signal, Johnny on third gave his signal that he knew the bunt play was on and I signaled likewise. When the pitch was made, Johnny did his job running towards home plate. The pitch was high and I missed bunting the pitch. Johnny was coming towards home plate with the catcher holding the ball. He ran into the catcher, knocking him down, but the catcher held the ball and Johnny was tagged out! We lost the game by one run in the ninth inning! I am still sorry to this day that I missed that pitch.

There were many fun times with that baseball team, however. One event that I remember to this day happened after one of our games at Salisbury Park [now Eisenhower Park]. We won the game and the team was driving back to school in several cars. I was in the car with Al Groh driving. All of sudden Al and another Chaminade car driver (whom I do not remember) decided that they would drive at 20 MPH in tandem blocking both lanes on the highway. Needless to say, this stunt caused a long backlog of cars behind them. We could hear many car horns behind us but the drivers hung tough for several miles. I am sure there were several people who were late that evening for their family dinners and not in a very good mood!

SUMMARY

I was thrilled and very surprised that Chuck Mansfield asked me to provide some of my thoughts on "The Year of Champions" and the "Perfect Season." It is my thought that each member of the 1962 senior class did their best with the abilities that God gave them. This individual dedication created the atmosphere within the walls of Chaminade that helped create the "Year of the Champions" with a special yell out to the football team and their perfect season.

Chaminade Flyers forever!

In all humility, it is the team of '61 and the class of '62 that have been the paradigm for all of us who followed. As Hemingway said, "As you get older, it is harder to have heroes, but it is sort of necessary."

— Kevin Loughlin

A TROUBLING DREAM: CHAMINADE VS. HOLY CROSS 1961

By Tom Kiley

My troublous dreams this night doth make me sad.

— Gloucester
Henry VI, Part II

It is a very sad day for all of us, but for me, especially. We have just blown our undefeated season as I stand by helplessly.

For some reason I arrive at our big game very late, disorganized, unprepared as usual, confused and feeling unwell. I am having trouble figuring out on which field we are playing. I am in bad physical condition and carry my personal effects – glasses, wallet and keys – in my hands. After a while I realize our big game is being played in a deep ravine below. I watch from high above but see no way to get down to it. Adding to the general confusion – there are many other games going on, between different teams of different ages, making it hard for me to discern our game from all the others being played at the same time.

At some point I realize it is already very late in the fourth quarter. The score is 20-20. The next score will likely be decisive. I clearly hear the Holy Cross coach tell his players to continue to go unbalanced left. I know I could help if only I could get down there. I know just what defense to call but I've forgotten its name. All of a sudden Coach Thomas appears next to me and tugs at my sleeve. He is tanned and slim, just as he looked on the first day of practice in August. I ask if I can go into the game, but he shakes his head saying nothing. I beg him. He seems angry with me. Just then the Holy Cross halfback runs untouched around left end and goes forty or fifty yards for a touchdown. Our perfect season is in grave danger, but we still have time. If only I could figure out how to get to the bottom of the ravine. I think, "Had I been down there I would have blitzed on the short side, cut parallel to the line of scrimmage and cut the Holy Cross back off before he reached it."

Coach Thomas is very angry now and berates us for giving up so many points in such a big game. I plead with him to put me in but he points out that I am wearing sneakers. I am forlorn, confused and angry. It seems nearly certain that our undefeated season is about to go a-glimmering.

Right then I awaken, sweating, frustrated and in much distress, a 76-year-old man left to contemplate the meaning of what he has just dreamt. And, finally, after a while, I am much relieved.

I know just what defense to call but I've forgotten its name.

— Tom Kiley

CONGRATULATIONS TO BRUCE SALERNO!

By Chuck Mansfield

In that era, '61 was the most talented team that Chaminade ever fielded. This fact, coupled with our incredible training and coaching, enabled us to go into each game knowing that we were the best team on the field.

— Pete Eisenhauer

Bruce received High School All American honors after the 1962 season and was named by Newsday *to its first All-Long Island football team.*

Although Bruce was deservedly recognized as an All American and by Newsday *in 1962, one year after Chaminade's 1961 perfect season during which he was the Flyers' outstanding center, it is fitting to mention it here.*

Warmest congratulations, Bruce.

As a junior, Bruce started at center in our 1961 season, playing between Bill Sellerberg at left guard and me at right. A great snapper and a brutal blocker, he and Zimmy were an awesome combination who ignited our powerful offense and sparked myriad outstanding plays. As Zimmy has written, "I was blessed to have one center in my four years playing for the Flyers – Bruce Salerno. I'm probably wrong but I don't remember ever having a fumbled snap."

In his senior year, Bruce achieved first-team All-Long Island honors as an offensive guard.

TOM KILEY AND CHUCK MANSFIELD

*Gentlemen, it is better to have died a small
boy than to fumble this football.*

— John Heisman

CHAMINADE VARSITY FOOTBALL
BEST TEAM RECORDS

Year	Won	Lost	Tied	Championship	Comments
2012	11	1	0	Yes (AAA)	
1978	10	0	0	Yes	Undefeated and untied (3rd time)
2013	10	2	0	No	Played in AAA championship game
1998	9	2	0	Yes	Matthew Groh '99, Al's younger son, was the starting quarterback on this title team.
1961	**8**	**0**	**0**	**Yes**	**Undefeated and untied (1st time)**
1977	8	0	0	Yes	Undefeated and untied (2nd time)
1992	8	1	1	Yes	
1997	8	2	0	No	
1999	8	2	0	No	
1951	7	0	1	Yes	Undefeated but one scoreless tie with Cardinal Hayes
1953	7	1	0	Yes	
1957	7	1	0	No	
1958	7	1	0	Yes	
1962	**7**	**1**	**0**	**Yes**	**Only CHS team to win a 3rd consecutive League title**
1968	7	1	0	Yes	
1933	7	1	1	No	
1987	7	2	0	Yes	
1971	6	0	2	Yes	
1960	6	1	1	Yes	
1956	6	2	0	Yes	
Totals	**154**	**21**	**6**		**These 20 teams' winning percentage is .851.**

Chaminade teams were champions in 15 of the 20 years cited. The five Flyer teams that did *not* win the championship had a combined record of 40-8-1, a winning percentage of .816!

We were a confident team but never a complacent or comfortable team. Winning brought with it all the needed positive reinforcement, and the coaches made sure we stayed humble and hungry.

— Al Groh

CHAMINADE VARSITY FOOTBALL TEAM RECORDS BY DECADES (1931-2019)

Decade	Won	Lost	Tied	Head Coach(es)
1930s	36	31	7	Frank "Boiler" Burns, Ned Gagliano
1940s	32	40	6	Frank "Boiler" Burns, Edward J. Flynn, Joseph F. Thomas (1)
1950s	57	18	3	Joseph F. Thomas
1960s	56	19	4	Joseph F. Thomas
1970s	50	31	2	Robert Polo, Thomas P. Kiley, Jr. '62, George Toop (2)
1980s	42	43	0	George Toop, Michael Pienkos, William J. Basel '58 (3)
1990s	66	33	1	William J. Basel
2000s	21	22	0	William J. Basel, Stephen G. Boyd (4)
2010s	49	51	0	Stephen G. Boyd, Kevin J. Dolan '85 (5)
2020s				Kevin J. Dolan*

(1) Mr. Thomas, now deceased, served as head varsity football coach from 1948 to 1969 and compiled a record of 120-46-7, including an 8-0-0 perfect season in 1961, the first in Chaminade's history. His teams were League champions seven times and he was named "Coach of the Year" also seven times.

(2) Mr. Toop, also deceased, served as a football coach at Chaminade from 1958 to 1981. As head varsity coach he compiled a record of 137-42-4 and led Chaminade's second and third undefeated and untied varsity football teams to League championships in consecutive years, 1977 and 1978. His 1978 team became Metro Bowl I champions with a 10-0-0 record, so far unequaled in Catholic High School Football League play.

(3) Once a star Chaminade quarterback, Mr. Basel retired from coaching at the end of the 2008 season with a record of 125-88-1, including two League championships. He has also served as chief executive of the Chaminade Golf and Tennis Open for many years.

(4) A Boston College All American and two-time All Pro linebacker with the Detroit Lions, Mr. Boyd's record was 38-37, including one CHSFL AAA championship in 2012, ending a 13-year drought. The 2013 season marked the first time the Flyers played in back-to-back AAA championship games since 1975. The following year the team beat St. John the Baptist for the AA championship after not qualifying for the AAA playoffs.

(5) Mr. Dolan played both football and lacrosse in his four years as a Chaminade student and captained the varsity football team as a senior. His record is 17-20.

* As a consequence of the COVID-19 pandemic, according to www.silive.com, "The CHSFL is planning to implement flag football for its league when authorized football practices begin Sept. 21 [2020] with an eye toward having a traditional season sometime after the new year, according to a source.

"The flag football scenario, which, of course, will not include linemen, will provide participating schools an opportunity to prepare for the traditional tackle season over a six-week span this fall. Schools are not obligated to participate and must inform the league if they'll opt in once the plan is officially announced.

"The principals of the schools that participate in the CHSFL were forced to vote on what the league was going to do concerning the 2020 season after the NYSPHSAA** recently announced football for the 2020-21 school year wouldn't be played until the spring."

** *NYSPHSAA is the abbreviation for the New York State Public High School Athletic Association.*

*Our coaches were always positive but also
were always pushing us for more.*

— Al Groh

CHAMINADE VARSITY FOOTBALL
ALL-TIME SERIES RECORDS

Team	*Won*	*Lost*	*Tied*
Archbishop Stepinac	20	12	0
Cardinal Hayes	17	13	2
Cardinal Spellman	11	4	0
Freeport	7	11	0
Glen Cove	5	5	0
Hempstead	7	13	1
Holy Cross	28	13	0
Holy Family	8	6	1
Holy Trinity	19	13	1
Iona Prep	26	17	1
Monsignor Farrell	14	21	0
Mount Saint Michael	24	18	2
Saint Anthony	13	35	0
Saint Dominic	5	3	0
Saint Francis Prep	27	26	1
Saint John the Baptist	11	13	1
Saint John Prep	23	1	0
Sewanhaka	14	12	2
Totals	**279**	**236**	**12**

"BROTHER, YOU OWE ME!"

By Patricia Mansfield Phelan

*Sometimes on a fall weekend, I went with my
father to watch my brother play football.*

— Pat Phelan

*Pat, Chuck's sister, was a loyal Chaminade football fan and
attended several of our games. She submitted a similar reflection
on August 20, 2011, in anticipation of our team's 50-year reunion.
Thank you, Pat.*

In 1961, I was 12 years old. Sometimes on a fall weekend, I went
with my father to watch my brother play football. I remember a game
shortly after Halloween when toward the end of the fourth quarter
there was some great tension – was Chaminade losing or merely tied?
It's so long ago, I forget the circumstances. But back then, I knew
they were dire. I believed in those days that I could somehow change
the course of the universe by negotiating with God, so I vowed that if
God would let Chaminade win – and thus be undefeated and untied –
I would not eat my Halloween candy for a week. *Voilà*, Chaminade
immediately won the game, and the stands and players went a bit
mad with joy.

For the next seven days, I did not touch my stash of Halloween
goodies, which, with all that chocolate lying around, was my own
private hell. What can I say except, brother, you owe me!

*Authors' note: It was the St. Francis game and the score was tied
0-0 right up to the end of the fourth quarter when Zimmy threw that
incredible, unforgettable 52-yard pass completion to Bobby Bowman,*

*who took it to the St. Francis two-yard line. On the next play Zimmy
again hit Bobby, all alone in the end zone, and Chaminade won 6-0.*

*The Flyers' team really showed what they were made of during that
game and set the winning tone for the rest of the season.*

— Ed Christie

MY MOTHER MARY, NON-FOOTBALL FAN

By Chuck Mansfield

The womb [is] that space we are born out of, into this world, where the soft iambics of our mother's heart become the first sure verses of our being.

—Thomas Lynch
in *Bodies in Motion and at Rest:*
On Metaphor and Mortality

My mother was a leader in her own right and an exquisite role model. She was born on December 15, 1921, and passed away on October 10, 2007, at age 85. I still miss her.
May she rest in peace.

I played football since I was in the fourth grade and every year thereafter up to and including my freshman year in college. That's a total of ten consecutive seasons in all. And yet, through all those years of putting on shoulder, hip and thigh pads, my mother never attended any of my games, not one. I actually never wondered why, for I assumed that Mom remained at home of necessity because there were several younger children to be cared for while I was playing football, and her husband and eldest daughter, avid Chaminade fans, were at my games.

Pictured above in 1955 are Chuck Mansfield (left) and his St. Anne's School teammate, John Cronin, who later played for Chaminade rival Holy Cross and John Carroll University.

(Photograph courtesy of Chuck Mansfield and used with permission.)

Specifically, I played football for five seasons in grade school, four at Chaminade and one at Holy Cross. First, I played the line, usually right guard, and line/linebacker on defense, for St. Anne's School in Garden City, N.Y. In the eighth grade I was invited to try out for the Garden City Rams, a highly organized team for 12- and 13-year-olds also based in Garden City. I enjoyed a great 1957 near-championship season with the Rams and was named "Best Lineman." Next came my Chaminade career, followed by the College of the Holy Cross, where I played freshman football, made the varsity team as a sophomore but, with deep regret to this day, chose to give up the sport I loved most because academics demanded it. Still, football was in my blood and, at each Holy Cross game I later attended as a mere spectator, I would lament my decision to leave the team and imagined myself back on the field. It troubles me even now, more than fifty-seven years later.

Mary Elizabeth Charrot Mansfield was my natural mother, a mere biological fact, but she was so much more to me. Since she brought me into the world more than seventy-five years ago, she has been an inspiration to me, and to others, in more ways than she could have known. Together with my Dad she made me what I am, thanks to the marvelous family life she created, the way she reared me, and her unconditional love and support. Her encouragement was always unswerving. For instance, when I faced a test in grammar school and was nervous about it, she would say, "Just do your best. You'll do fine." And she was right.

Her life as a young woman growing up in Brooklyn was remarkable. Her multiple and manifest talents, leadership, scholarship, character and integrity were and are of the highest order. The values on which Mom built her life are desired by many but attained by few. She lived the Christian life to its fullest, and all who knew her were witnesses to this. For instance, in a note of condolences after her passing, one of her closest friends wrote that she "always wanted to be like Mary but never quite made it."

She was dynamic and energetic, even in her eighties. Still walking two miles every day, she put many younger folks to shame! I will always have images of her, even as the mother of six, doing cartwheels and standing on her head in her backyard. I have observed her staying youthful too, even as she aged. And she swam in the ocean, as she did all her life, as recently as two months before she passed away. Indeed, I believe I got what athleticism I enjoyed from her.

Mom's personal strength and resiliency were extraordinary. In the months following my Dad's passing, many people were justifiably concerned about her, and some suggested that she might succumb to a deep depression because of the loss of her husband of fifty-five years. Indeed, this has been true of many who have lost their spouses after a lifetime together. But she lived out her life as strong and resolute as ever.

In middle age I came to understand that my mother's values and personal attributes – deep faith, leadership, scholarship, character, integrity, dedication, positive attitude and hard work – were precisely the ones that Coaches Thomas and McGuckin stressed and sought to inculcate in their players. Accordingly, the linkage between my Mom's philosophy and training and my coaches' was strong and is surely a principal factor in why Chaminade fit me and my formation so well. And yet this tower of strength, my mother Mary, never attended even one of my football games! For heaven's sake, why not?

Perhaps twenty-five years after my college graduation (when she was nearly 70 and I, 46) Mom and I had a conversation about football, although I have no recollection of how or why the topic came up, for she never was a fan of the game. Moreover, I have no memory of how I came to inquire about or learn what she was going to tell me. Then, as we sat together chatting, I was floored when she took my hand and, with tears welling up in her eyes, informed me that she never attended my games because she couldn't bear to watch me play, to quote General MacArthur, "on the fields of friendly strife" for fear that I would be injured. What a revelation! I was astonished, tried to console her and lamely whispered, "Mom, I'm still here. Neither football nor Vietnam could take me from you." What love she gave me.

Requiescat in pace.

Men are what their mothers made them.

— Ralph Waldo Emerson

DO YOU REMEMBER?

By Chuck Mansfield

*Do you remember Coach Thomas's stated standard for the intensity
of our play on game day? It was "110% for forty-eight minutes."*

—Chuck Mansfield

*There are many things I remember about our team's '61 season
(and the three previous ones) that the late Chaminade history teacher
Mr. Joseph Fox would likely characterize as "little-known and less-
cared-about information." Still, I believe you may relate to some of
these, so please humor me.*
Thank you.

Do you remember

> ➢ Coach Thomas using the term "reckless abandon" or "R.A."
> to describe the aggressive nature of play he wanted us to
> demonstrate on the gridiron, especially when covering punts
> and kickoffs?
> ➢ Coach Thomas encouraging us to have a steak for breakfast
> on Sunday before our games but only if our family could
> afford it?
> ➢ Coach Thomas instructing us that 90% of success in both
> football and life was "a positive mental attitude"?
> ➢ Both coaches emphasizing to us the importance of staying
> in shape in the off-season by running, lifting weights, etc.?
> ➢ Coach Thomas warning us against the evils of smoking?
> ➢ Coach Thomas throwing a player off the team for smoking?
> ➢ Coach Thomas's stated standard for the intensity of our play
> on game day? It was "110% for forty-eight minutes."

➤ Speaking of intensity, the huge epic energy and vibrant visceral vector that Coach Thomas conveyed to us in his pre-game and halftime talks? As I have written elsewhere, they were "the most compelling motivators I have ever heard or seen. Significantly, it mattered not that we were winning or losing. (Make no mistake; clearly, he preferred the former.) What did matter, and mattered most in his mind, was that there was a game or another half to be played, and played as well as it could be, for the real name of the game called football, as he never failed to communicate to each of his players, is excellence."

➤ Coach Thomas exhorting us never to take "the line of least resistance"? Some of us came to call it the LLR.

➤ Coach Thomas, tongue-in-cheek, encouraging a player who had suffered a nasty foot sore from blister-causing friction to "Put a little Tuf-Skin on it"? (Tuf-Skin provides a consistent spray and mild adhesive coating to an area that is frequently taped or wrapped.)

➤ The power, excitement and electrifying atmosphere, the Chaminade Spirit, at pep rallies in the old Chaminade gymnasium on Friday afternoons of game weekends?

➤ Coach Jerry Rossi in '62's freshman season calling Earl Kirmser, Krimser?

➤ Coach Ed Flynn in '62's JV season calling Rhett Siegel, Ginsburg?

➤ Mike Reisert in '62's JV season, while returning on the team bus from a scrimmage, making this observation about Mr. Joseph Fox and Mr. Patrick Stafford, both of whom were history teachers and completely bald. "If Mr. Fox and Mr. Stafford were to put their heads together, they'd make a complete ass of themselves."

➤ Coach Thomas teaching us the rules referees must follow so that we could be smarter players?

➤ Monday afternoons during the season? With no practice, we would instead meet as a team, watch the preceding day's game film and secretly relish the thought that we didn't have to run wind sprints for another 24 hours.

➢ Coach Thomas saying, "Take it all to the field, and leave it all on the field."?

➢ Coach Thomas comparing the stages of life to a football game? From birth to age 20 is the first quarter; from 21 to 40, the second quarter; from 41 to 60, the third; and from 61 to 80, the fourth. After 80, he said, "You're in overtime and may have to face sudden death." Having lived into his 96th year, Coach made it well into overtime.

➢ These words of wisdom reportedly attributed to Messrs. Thomas and McGuckin?

"The size of your muscles helps, but it is the size of your heart that counts."

"The best player on the field is often the humblest."

"Getting a penalty is often stupid, costly or painful."

"Admire the player at the end of the bench and be proud of him when he gets the call."

"Getting up is tougher than going down."

"When you shake a hand, show that you mean it."

"Being on the back of the bus or the front of the bus doesn't matter as long as you feel in your heart that you have earned the right to be on the bus."

"Make your dad prouder by trying as hard as you can and your mom happier by getting better faster."

Ah, yes, I remember it well.

— Maurice Chevalier
in *Gigi*

DEFENDING AGAINST ORR, MANSFIELD INTERCEPTS STAUBACH AND SCORES!

By Chuck Mansfield

Roger was the starting quarterback and Skip his primary wide-receiver for the 1963 Navy team that went 9-2 and played Texas in the Cotton Bowl.

—Chuck Mansfield

Retired airline pilot, former real estate executive, 1960 Chaminade championship quarterback and once star Navy wide-receiver Edward A. "Skip" Orr, Jr., president of the Chaminade class of 1961, has written, "Having the opportunity to play football under legendary coach Joe Thomas at Chaminade ... was a truly memorable and life-altering experience.

"I was fortunate enough to have that experience in 1959 and 1960 and had my friend Chuck Mansfield as a teammate during the 1960 season when we won the Catholic High School Football League championship. The following season, Chuck and his teammates once again won the League championship and, in doing so, completed the first undefeated and untied season in Chaminade football history. A season such as that creates a strong and lasting bond among all the teammates." Thanks, Skip.

Although the following events took place nearly two or more years after the 1961 football season, they may be worthy of mention in the lore of Chaminade players' post-graduate years just for a good laugh.

Leaving aside that my modest football career was history, I hope you enjoy this story.

It was the summer of 1963 and several Chaminade alumni and a few others were working out at St. Paul's field in Garden City in preparation for the upcoming college football season. Among them were five members of Chaminade's 1961 first undefeated and untied varsity football team – Al Groh, Tom Kiley, Earl Kirmser, Carl LoGalbo and yours truly, all '62 alumni. Al played at the University of Virginia while Tom, Earl and I were at Holy Cross. Carl was a rugger at Fairfield. We were joined by Ed "Skip" Orr '61, who had brilliantly quarterbacked Chaminade's 1960 team to yet another CHSFL championship, and his Naval Academy classmate, close friend and teammate, Roger Staubach. Roger was spending some free summer days with Skip and his family before returning to Annapolis for the start of their third year at the Academy.

According to www.cottonbowl.com, "If Dallas only knew what the future held when Roger Staubach, Navy's junior quarterback, brought his Heisman Trophy to the 1964 Cotton Bowl Classic. In a dream matchup that pitted No. 1 Texas vs. No. 2 Navy, Staubach gave football fans something to get excited about. Despite Navy's loss to the Longhorns, he was brilliant in defeat. Staubach completed an astounding 21 passes for 228 yards. However, it was Staubach's nimble feet that got Navy into the end zone that day against Texas. Late in the fourth quarter, he ran two yards for the Midshipmen's lone touchdown. At the time, no one realized that 'Captain America' was about to find a home. His efforts for the Cotton Bowl didn't end on the playing field. As a Dallas civic leader and a former color analyst for CBS, Roger Staubach has established a lasting relationship with Dallas' New Year's Day Classic."

Roger was the starting quarterback and Skip his primary wide-receiver for the 1963 Navy team that went 9-2 and played Texas in the Cotton Bowl. (Skip had tried out for the QB job but...the rest is history.) However, Skip's versatility and athleticism – he lettered in football, basketball and baseball at Chaminade – virtually guaranteed him a starting position in Navy's offense.

Back to St. Paul's and our summer evening workout, after which we played touch-football sideline to sideline. Even here Roger and Skip were teammates, to which their opponents should have objected, and Roger chose to pass to Skip often. On one play, a down and out, I (all of 5'9") faced the daunting challenge of covering the quick, strong and much taller Orr. Almost miraculously, I managed to get in front of Skip and leap high enough to catch the ball. Not only did I intercept the future All Pro Staubach, I ran the ball back for a touchdown, the only one I ever scored!

Now there are two amusing footnotes to this story. First, on a fall Sunday afternoon in 1978 my sons, Chas and John, and I were watching our New York Giants play the Dallas Cowboys on television. I just happened to tell my boys, then ten and eight, respectively, the story of my interception of the great Staubach. Suddenly, John, my younger guy, stood up and, with hands aloft, loudly exclaimed, "Dad, you never told us you played pro football!"

Chuck Mansfield (right) presents Coach Thomas with a book of mementos written by players and other admirers at Chaminade's Joe Thomas Testimonial on September 11, 1988. The event honored Mr. Thomas on his retirement from Chaminade after forty years of service.

(Photograph courtesy of Chuck Mansfield and used with permission.)

Second, fast forward ten years to Ott Field,* renamed since we had long ago played our Chaminade home games there, and the Joe Thomas Testimonial, which honored Coach on the occasion of his retirement after forty years of dedicated service to *alma mater* and her students. At the invitation of the Chaminade Alumni Association I had the pleasure of serving as the master of ceremonies for the occasion, and I believe everyone enjoyed the afternoon immensely.

The tribute was attended by some 500 former players and other admirers of our great Coach. It was September 11, 1988, and Coach was there with his family, along with notables such as two-time Tony Award-winning actor Brian Dennehy '56, who played tackle for Coach Thomas in 1954 and '55, flew in from Australia for the event and, sadly, passed away on April 15, 2020; then-Senator Al D'Amato '55, who ran track for Mr. Thomas; U.S. Marine Corps Major General Matt Caulfield '54,** who played Flyer JV football in 1951 and presented Mr. Thomas with a signed citation from then-President Reagan; Matt's classmate, retired Navy captain and former Blue Angel Norm Gandia '54 and many others, including the great Skip Orr.

After the various speeches and presentations, refreshments and a magnificent outdoor buffet were served. At this time I found myself with several former teammates and other friends, Skip among them. For reasons I can no longer fathom, I chose to recount the then-25-year-old story of that ancient touch football game at St. Paul's and my improbable interception of a Roger Staubach pass and TD runback while defending against the always superb Skip Orr. Without missing a beat and with a smile on his face, Skip insisted in front of all those who had just heard my interception and runback story that I "PROVE IT!" Hysterical laughter followed and, of course, I was at a total loss to meet Skip's challenge.

Sic transit gloria!

* *What we called the Chaminade Bowl in days of yore was subsequently renamed Ott Field, after Chaminade's founder and first principal, Alexander Ott. Since then a new stadium has been built on the north*

side of the football field, replete with concession stands, rest rooms and other amenities. In 2014 the new facility was renamed Gold Star Stadium and dedicated as a permanent memorial to Chaminade's 56 Gold Star alumni who made the ultimate sacrifice in service to our nation. Alma mater*'s Gold Star Mass has been celebrated in their memory every year since 1945.*

** *A fine catcher, Matt caught Mr. Thomas's eye when Coach watched him practice throwing to second base. Immediately, Coach began grooming Matt to be his quarterback for the 1953 varsity football season because, as Matt has written, "He concluded that my throw was similar to the way a quarterback should throw. ... Then one fateful day a foul tip hit my clenched fist (and) I was out for the season."*

*Three things can happen when you throw
the ball, and two of them are bad.*

— Darrell Royal
University of Texas

CRITERIA FOR THE CHAMINADE MAN AWARD

By Chuck Mansfield

Chaminade has always been right for all the ages, and the age that we are now in is one that is going to decide our survival as a nation and the ideals we believe in. Now, more than ever, we need the Chaminade man making his mark.

> — Matthew P. Caulfield,
> Major General, USMC (Ret.),
> Chaminade class of 1954,
> addressing the Chaminade
> community just after 9/11

The Chaminade Man Award is presented each year to the graduating senior who is "outstanding in leadership, scholarship and character." Back in the day, it was called the American Legion Award, an attractive nine-inch-tall loving cup bearing the American Legion seal and mounted on a marble base. Today's award is more than two feet tall.

It occurred to me while reading The Chaminade Man values that all of them were stressed and inculcated in each of us players by Messrs. Thomas and McGuckin. Not all of us made the honor roll, but I can still recall Coach Thomas saying, "Show me a student's notebook and I'll tell you if he can make it on our team." In short, he wanted and needed smart players.

As for "significant participation," being "a pleasure to teach," having a "cooperative spirit," exercising "positive leadership" and demonstrating "religious and moral values," I am confident that all of our teammates excelled in those categories.

Coaches Thomas and McGuckin were truly extraordinary! May they rest in peace.

To be designated "The Chaminade Man," a student must have:

➢ Been on the honor roll for four years.
➢ A wide and significant participation in activities and/or athletics.
➢ Been considered a pleasure to teach.
➢ Demonstrated a cooperative spirit in his activity or athletic participation.
➢ Exercised positive leadership among his peers.
➢ Demonstrated the religious and moral values that Chaminade attempts to inculcate in its students.
➢ Exemplified the practice of "doing the right thing at the right time because it is the right thing to do, not just because someone is watching."

It's kind of hard to rally around a math class.

— Bear Bryant
Alabama

THE CHAMINADE FLYER FIGHT SONG

Typically accompanied by Chaminade's pep band, the song is sung with gusto following a touchdown, as well as on other occasions.

W e are the Flyers, strong and warriors bold,
So proud to wear the Crimson and the Gold.
We fight for right and victory,
And you'll soon know that we can show the world
We're men who'll fight the foe for dear ol' Chaminade.

The Flyer Fight Song

Lyrics by Bro. George MacKenzie   Music by Angelo Ferdinando

(Music score provided by Bro. Robert Lahey, S.M. '65 and used with permission.)

Football's values are priceless to any youngster who wants to play; its danger and pain are part of its value. Football teaches a boy to cope with the risks of physical danger and pain, risks often inseparable

from the act of living itself. The game also demonstrates the value of work, sacrifice, courage and perseverance. Football is only for the boy who is physically qualified to play it and for the high school that conducts it properly.

— *Look* Magazine
August 28, 1962

"LIFE TAKES US TO MANY PLACES, BUT LOVE ALWAYS BRINGS US HOME AGAIN."

By Tom Kiley

The fifties – well they just seemed to spill into 1962, the year we were graduated from Chaminade High School. Then came the deluge.

— Tom Kiley

Tom is a lifelong friend and fellow 1962 graduate of Chaminade, where he was the Most Outstanding Player on the school's first undefeated and untied varsity football team and graduated with honors, and a fellow 1966 alumnus of the College of the Holy Cross, where he also excelled on the gridiron and academically.

He delivered the following speech to his Chaminade classmates on the occasion of their 50-year reunion in 2012.

Thank you, Tom.

Good evening everyone. My name is Tom Kiley and I will be your host tonight. I have to be honest with you and tell you straightaway how very excited I am to stand before you. Some of you are the best friends I ever made in life and many others are the best guys in the world, some of whom I haven't seen in over fifty years. So emotions are running a little high right now.

Of course a night like this is all about visiting with old friends, some of them for the first time in a very long time. It is a night for bringing guys up to date about our lives and, above all, a night for reminiscing, for thinking about the old days once again, when we were young and our world was green and it seemed that anything was possible. Of course it was not, as we were soon to learn, but we must smile when we consider that we once thought so. And, of

283

course, many of us are here tonight with our sweethearts, some from long ago, some of more recent vintage. But our sweethearts they are and we love them very much and are happy they are at our side once again, as they have been for all of our most important moments.

So here we are together again, all of us pushing 70 now. The Bible, with the thumping certitude for which it is famous, says that the "days of our years are three score and ten." So, if we make it another year or two, we will be playing, as it were, with house money. Therefore, pretty soon, I guess, there will be no need to give up our red meat or nightly martini.

To be a member of the Class of 1962 means you were born not too long after Pearl Harbor and lived through a war that was already raging, as well as the Cold War that followed. Yes, we were born in the '40s and raised in the '50s. Our year of graduation may be 1962, but the '60s were not really the decade of our youth; the '50s were. The fifties – well they just seemed to spill into 1962, the year we were graduated from Chaminade High School. Then came the deluge.

Of course, we lived on through the '60s and '70s, perhaps the toughest times for many for us. We came to know assassination and riot. Like our parents, we came to know the horror of a war that took from us family members, classmates and friends, all lost in their youth and prime. We survived all that and the years that followed. Some of us embraced what came and some of us resisted with all our might. But come it did, and the one thing that can be said about all of us here tonight is that without exception – WE HAVE SURVIVED!

For some reason the Good Lord has given us the gift of long life. We did not ask for it and most of us do not know why we were granted it. Perhaps we will never know why. But here we are, together once again, to recall the laughter and the good times we shared way back in 1962, when we were still delicately balanced on the last edge of childhood.

I recently asked Chuck if he knew the origin of the word nostalgia. He looked up from the Latin to Greek translation of *NO KIDS, NO MONEY AND A CHEVY* that he is working on and opined that, in the original Greek, nostalgia means "the pain of an old wound." I thought – yes that's it! An old wound, a twinge in the heart, a delicate but powerful emotion that lets us travel back in time to a place where we know we are loved. And how lucky to be loved by the greatest parents in the world! How lucky to be born children of what has been acclaimed in book and song the greatest generation. What Moms and Dads they were. Their children were their top priority. Selfless, self-sacrificing, always willing to do whatever it took, whatever it cost to see that we were educated in the best possible way. Our parents worked hard. Most of them worked hard all their lives. Many of them truly sacrificed to send us to Chaminade. Whether blue collar guys or newly minted executives, they made it out of World War II alive and they wanted to ensure that their sons got every chance to better themselves, to do better than they had done. They were children of the Depression and had experienced the dread and drama and separation of World War II, and their lives were informed by both of those cataclysmic events. I remember overhearing my parents discuss quite seriously, when they thought I was out of earshot, how they could possibly pay Chaminade's thirty-five dollar monthly tuition. But Mom believed God would provide, and provide He did, even during our senior year when tuition was raised to an impossible thirty-seven dollars and 50 cents a month!

Our erstwhile teachers peer out at us tonight from the yellowing pages of our old yearbook, many of them young men then, too many of them gone now. We were most fortunate to be influenced by such a wonderful group of educators who wanted nothing but the best for us and knew that discipline was the necessary road to be traveled to get there. They also knew that discipline is an expression of love and high expectations are a form of faith. They all did their very best and some of them inspired us in ways that continue to influence us today.

The problem with expressing appropriate gratitude tonight is that it would take much too long. It is a heck of a lot easier to address a lifeguard who has just saved you from drowning. There were so many who figured so importantly in our educational and spiritual formation here at Chaminade as to make unfeasible singling out any one of them. Indeed, only one of them is in this room tonight,

Brother Peter Pontolillo, and I hope he knows how we feel about him and about all those who instructed us between 1958 and 1962. I also hope he knows that the anonymity in which they are shielded does not bespeak any shallowness in the depth of our appreciation.

So, in conclusion, I would just like to say that it is indescribably satisfying to spend my Class of 1962 50-year reunion in your company. As some of us begin an orderly retreat from the old tempos of life, we may do so with great satisfaction and great confidence, certain that we still have much to offer this world, still have much love to give to family and friends, still have much we can do to help those who are most in need of our help.

It is said that you can only grow up once, and I am sure everyone present tonight is glad that it happened here in Mineola, at Chaminade High School, fifty years ago.

Life takes us to many places, but Love always brings us home again.

Thank you very much.

Tom Kiley
Class of 1962

The only people who grow old were born old to begin with.

> — Cary Grant as The Angel
> in *The Bishop's Wife*

ODE TO CHAMINADE, CORNERSTONE AND CLASSIC

By Chuck Mansfield

In 2020 Chaminade High School turned ninety. I first wrote the following poem about alma mater *for her seventieth anniversary in 2000 but have updated it slightly in order to share it with my 1961 football teammates, other Chaminade family members and friends.*

Fully ninety years have already passed
Since where you stand now potatoes grew last.
Those boys you first welcomed way back then
Alas now are either gone or today's old men.

FORTES IN UNITATE your familiar seal doth proclaim.
'Tis so recognizable there's nary a need for your name.
Its three symbols – the Cross, the torch and the rule –
Convey a clear message that you're no ordinary school.

Fully faithful to your mission have you always been:
Spiritual, intellectual and moral maturity for young men.
You have become and will remain for many years hence
"A community of faith, a commitment to excellence."

Your students are strong, enthusiastic, vibrant and bright.
The Chaminade Man, they will learn, will do what is right,
Always for the right reason, no matter who looks on.
His moral code endures when ephemeral culture is gone.

Catholic is your tradition (elsewhere confusion abounds),
Thanks to your brothers and priests whose influence redounds.
Consistency, rigor and excellence underpin your lore,
Evinced in academics, athletics and *esprit de corps.*

Your young men while students may not always get it,
As they wonder sometimes, 'How does Chaminade fit?'
Yet they, when alumni, with warm affection return,
Drawn by true depth of feeling, for which they still yearn.

You teach and develop in context and environment
Character, principles, self-discipline, sound judgment.
Faith, service and values you integrate in daily life
To create happiness from within, never mind joy or strife.

Your rubric for the Chaminade Man is about being whole;
One alumnus has called it the 'awakening of his soul.'
Another lauds your diligence, once beyond his ken,
In shaping highly disciplined and morally grounded young men.

Your sons today number twenty-two thousand some,
And year after year many back to you come.
The Marianists you shelter once showed them the way
With a template for life that thrives to this day.

Down through the decades to your beliefs did you hold;
After all, that's the significance of your crimson and gold.
You have created the Chaminade Family; yes, it is real,
For you still forge a bond that all its members can feel.

Faith, morals, friendship, ethics, leadership, integrity;
Lo, these are your lasting life-lessons and legacy.
Young men do you challenge, test their mettle you can,
For a boy enters your doors and emerges a man.

Godspeed, Chaminade, as the Lord's work you continue
With all the goodness and grace and spirit within you.
Be courageous and steadfast in Mary's great love,
And long may you serve blest by God above!

Beyond this wonderful book, someone should write a screenplay. In an era when we are seeing values eroding, Chaminade and its 1961 undefeated team remind us of what is "the best in us" and it should serve as a blueprint for leaders in business, law, education and medicine.

— Kevin Loughlin

IN MEMORIAM

I am the master of my fate,
I am the captain of my soul.

— William Ernest Henley
in his poem *Invictus*

Here are the names of those from our perfect season who have gone home to the Lord.

Francis X. Biasi, Jr. '62
Robert W. Bowman '63
Edward J. Flynn, *Athletic Director*
Robert Gabriele '63
Raymond E. Hess '62, *Manager*
John A. Kernaghan '62
Donald J. McDonough, Jr. '63
Charles G. McGuckin '50, *Assistant Varsity Head Coach*
D. Barry O'Connor '62
Robert E. Pacifico '62, *Manager*
Paul Swanson '64
Robert G. Swanson '64
Joseph F. Thomas, *Varsity Head Coach*

Requiescant in pace.

At this writing, our three team moderators are octogenarians all. Bro. Carmine Annunziata, S.M. is active in East Africa. Bro. Raymond Gohring, S.M. lives at a Marianist residence in San Antonio for retired and infirm brothers, as does Bro. Peter A. Pontolillo, S.M. '56.

*Football players, like other mortals, die though
they were once young and brave.*

— Tom Kiley

"WE PLAYED AS ONE."

By Tom Kiley

Despite their outward differences and various backgrounds, players quickly learn that what they do have in common actually makes them the "same guy;" thus a strong connection is made among the players.

— Al Groh

'We could play ball," says contributor Tiny Reisert. Of that there is little doubt, but at our best during that long ago '61 season, we also achieved a kind of poetry in motion, as our defensive game rose to near perfection at certain times during the year. As defensive quarterback and signal caller for the Flyer eleven, I stood, rather uniquely, between our coaches, who devised our defensive game plan each week, and our players who executed the plan. Usually they would give us the defensive scheme on Tuesday afternoon and we would do our best to carry it out to a T on Saturday or Sunday. Sometimes in the heat of battle, when I was really feeling it, the game became a slow motion ballet, even as four or five of us tried to take the shortest route to the ball carrier and arrive in the worst humor possible. It was a beautiful feeling for me to glide behind our nearly unblockable front seven.

In 1961 much of Long Island had only recently been claimed from the farmland it originally stood on. For many of us the game was not second nature the way basketball was, especially for those who came from the cracked asphalt of Brooklyn or Queens or the Bronx, where basketball was loved best. But we sensed something big was happening in Mineola and we wanted to be part of it, so we took a chance on a new game. Some of us did so at first without even the proper football shoes necessary to play. The game itself was just coming into its own nationally, and coincidentally linebacking was becoming one of the most prominent positions on the field. Not thirty years before Art Rooney had purchased the Pittsburgh Steelers for $2500, his winnings from a good day at the race track.

A couple of years before, Giants linebacker Sam Huff had appeared on the cover of *Time* magazine, the first NFL player to do so. Then came the documentary, "The Violent World of Sam Huff," so it was propitious that at that very moment Charlie McGuckin converted me to linebacker, which gave me a chance for a degree of self-expression and exposure I would never have had as an undersized tackle.

During our undefeated and untied season we proved just how tough our brand of ball was. Within a rather strict framework, we were permitted to express our individuality and let it fly so to speak, especially during big games. There was no better feeling than seeing 11 defensive guys blend their talents on Saturday or Sunday. What we did for eight weeks was special by any standard and the result of long and arduous practice sessions. After a while though, we played instinctively and at times we approached the ideal of how the game of football should be played. We hustled, we pursued quarterbacks and gang-tackled running backs relentlessly. At our best we played as one. Ultimately, we achieved football harmony, a place where, at the snap of the ball, we were in perfect rhythm, always trying to cover for one another, always trying to help each other out. We were not competing for any consolation prize. It was a beautiful thing to be a part of.

It was the sheer joy of playing the game that we achieved eight times out of eight tries on eight successive weekends in the splendid autumn of 1961. No matter what the score was in any of those games, we continued to work at it like it was a close game. Ultimately, we achieved an unusual football cohesiveness and a rare level of teamwork, playing the game the right way. This joy radiated outwards to our family and friends and, especially, our loyal fans who attended our games week in and week out in their thousands. It was a beautiful time to play football for the Crimson and Gold.

Today the allure of the high school game has faded due to fear of injury, among other things, and is limited to those who play the game and their parents and relatives and not too many others. After all, the "others" now play soccer or lacrosse or swim or bowl or participate in the many other activities offered by Chaminade. Football is no longer King as it once was. Frankly, it is just another sport, one of many. The day of the 30-bus road trip to an away game is long gone.

But, if in the unlikeliest of cases, our inessential houses melt away and return Long Island to the farmland from whence it came, and even if nothing else remains the same, then this book, *The Perfect Season*, will prove that we left behind a story that will be remembered long after the final gun has sounded.

Tom Kiley
Defensive Quarterback and Signal Caller
1961

These memories—and there are many—are still with me but among the most vivid certainly are those moments of inspiration and exhilaration that always came on autumn Sunday afternoons. It is these memories that were provided, actually created, by Coach Thomas, for his energy and spirit were palpable.

— Chuck Mansfield

EPILOGUE

By Tom Kiley

Rejoice, we are victorious.

— Pheidippides

And so it was that after a quiet prayer of thanksgiving before Our Lady and the echoes of the last cheers had faded away, the seniors removed the Crimson and Gold for the final time after the Holy Cross game. We graduated soon after and went off to college. Most of us did not play college ball. Perhaps we were not big enough or fast enough or good enough. Perhaps we simply lacked the desire. The few who did came to understand even more acutely than those who did not just how unique the Chaminade football experience had been. The juniors on our squad were the lucky ones. They got the chance to do it again and they did, winning a third straight title the following year, completing a never to be duplicated "threepeat" for Chaminade. Whatever hopes we had of a fourth straight title went a-glimmering in the failing light of a November afternoon in 1963, when a Holy Cross field goal found its way past a darkening sky and through the uprights at the end of the last game of the season. The Chaminade Bowl fell starkly silent then like a church after Mass. Without anyone realizing it, the golden age of Chaminade football was abruptly brought to an end, although there were still more titles up ahead and even two more undefeated and untied seasons to be celebrated. But for those of us who were a part of it, this era of Chaminade football remains a magical time.

Fifty years is a long time to recall the events of eight short weeks during a long forgotten football season. Sixty is nearly a lifetime. And yet we do remember that long-vanished time in our lives, as the foregoing recollections amply demonstrate. The '61 season has given us a lifetime of differing memories, forged as they were from the grime and toil and sweat of the back field, the sun's anvil, during those 90-degree double-session days. But in the end it produced a terrible beauty, a Perfect Season.

These memories still echo down the corridors of time or at least the corridors of our septuagenarian minds. Now they too are coming to an end. Indeed, we have already buried too many of our teammates. Our coaches too are gone, although the fullness of time permits us to see the living, imperfect, honorable men they were. We will not forget any of them. And so it is right and fitting altogether that we have had this time together to reminisce one more time, maybe for the last time. After all, in 1961 none of us thought to wave goodbye.

And He led me towards the hills and the
breaking of day in the lone East.

— Minnie Louise Haskins
in her poem
The Gate of the Year

ABOUT THE AUTHORS

Thomas Patrick Kiley, Jr. was born in Brooklyn and raised in Elmont, N.Y. He graduated from Chaminade High School in 1962 where he played football and baseball. He also played football at the College of the Holy Cross where he received his bachelor's degree in Political Science in 1966. After graduation he coached high school football and basketball on Long Island and then football at the United States Merchant Marine Academy. Thereafter, he became a firm administrator for Rosenman & Colin, a large New York City law firm, from which he retired in 2013. He and his wife Barbara have three children and seven grandchildren and live in Levittown, N.Y.

Another Brooklyn boy, Chuck Mansfield is a '62 Chaminade alumnus too. He also graduated with Tom from Holy Cross but with an A.B. (Sociology) and was commissioned an officer in the U.S. Marine Corps Reserve. Deployed to Vietnam in 1968, he served as a platoon commander. Later, he received an M.B.A. (Finance) from New York University. A former director/trustee of the funds of Federated Hermes, Inc., a $619-billion Pittsburgh-based complex listed on the New York Stock Exchange, he served in that capacity from 1999 through 2020, chaired the board's audit committee for four years and currently serves as a director *emeritus*. He and his wife Mary Ann have three children and four grandchildren and reside in Stuart, Fla., and Westhampton Beach, N.Y.

It is finished.

— John 19:30

Printed in the United States
by Baker & Taylor Publisher Services